4.4.11

56051   61.13
         YBP

EDISON COMMUNITY COLLEGE
LIBRARY.
1973 EDISON DR.
PIQUA, OH. 45356
937-778-8600

Becoming Bicultural

Becoming Bicultural

Risk, Resilience, and Latino Youth

Paul R. Smokowski and
Martica Bacallao

NEW YORK UNIVERSITY PRESS

New York and London

NEW YORK UNIVERSITY PRESS
New York and London
www.nyupress.org

© 2011 by New York University
All rights reserved

References to Internet Websites (URLs) were accurate at the time
of writing. Neither the author nor New York University Press is
responsible for URLs that may have expired or changed since
the manuscript was prepared.

Library of Congress Cataloging-in-Publication Data
Smokowski, Paul R. (Paul Richard)
Becoming bicultural : risk, resilience, and Latino youth / Paul R.
Smokowski and Martica Bacallao.
p.   cm.
Includes bibliographical references and index.
ISBN 978-0-8147-4089-7 (cl : alk. paper) — ISBN 978-0-8147-4090-3
(pb : alk. paper) — ISBN 978-0-8147-8359-7 (e-book)
1. Biculturalism—United States. 2. Minority youth—United States.
3. Hispanic Americans. 4. Assimilation—United States.   I. Bacallao,
Martica. II. Title.
E184.A1S6655 2010
305.800973—dc22   2010033818

New York University Press books are printed on acid-free paper,
and their binding materials are chosen for strength and durability.
We strive to use environmentally responsible suppliers and materials
to the greatest extent possible in publishing our books.

Manufactured in the United States of America

c 10 9 8 7 6 5 4 3 2 1
p 10 9 8 7 6 5 4 3 2 1

To our sons, José and César Smokowski,
con todo nuestro amor.

Contents

Figures

Tables

Acknowledgments

The authors wish to thank Flavio Marsiglia, Ph.D., Distinguished Foundation Professor of Cultural Diversity and Health, and Monica Parsai, Ph.D., both of Arizona State University, for their work coordinating data collection in Arizona. Melissa Chalot, M.P.H., and Rachel Dudenhausen, M.S.W., provided project management. Special thanks go to the Latino families who participated in the Parent-Teen Biculturalism Project and the Latino Acculturation and Health Project. These studies were supported by grants from the United States Centers for Disease Control and Prevention's National Center for Injury Prevention and Control (R49/CCR42172-02) and from the Centers for Disease Control's Office of the Director (1K01 CE000496-01).

1

From Melting Pot to Simmering Stew

Acculturation, Enculturation, Assimilation, and Biculturalism in American Racial Dynamics

On January 20, 2009, Barack Obama was sworn in as the forty-fourth president of the United States. Although he was heralded as the first African American to serve in the highest and most powerful position in the nation (and perhaps in the world), President Obama's cultural heritage was more subtle and complex. He was born in Honolulu, Hawaii, to an American mother, Stanley Ann Dunham, whose family (in Wichita, Kansas) was primarily of English descent, and Barack Obama Sr., a Luo from Nyang'oma Kogelo, Nyanza Province, Kenya. His father and mother married in 1961 and divorced in 1964, after which his father returned to Kenya.

After her divorce, Dunham married Indonesian student Lolo Soetoro. In 1967 they moved the family to Indonesia, where Barack attended schools in Jakarta from ages six to ten. He finished his schooling (grades five to twelve) in Honolulu while living with his maternal grandparents. Thus, not only was Obama of mixed race, but he also grew up in a state where more than 25 percent of the population reports a heritage of two or more races. The multicultural environment in Hawaii influenced his cultural perspective. Obama wrote,

> That my father looked nothing like the people around me—that he was black as pitch, my mother white as milk—barely registered in my mind. . . . The opportunity that Hawaii offered—to experience a variety of cultures in a climate of mutual respect—became an integral part of my world view, and a basis for the values that I hold most dear. (Obama 1995)

This mixed-race heritage and multicultural childhood provided the foundation for Obama to become the first biracial and bicultural president. His campaign appealed to young voters and minorities. Overall, 68 percent of voters between the ages of eighteen and twenty-nine years cast their ballots for Obama, versus 30 percent of that age group who supported John McCain (Hebel 2008). Fifty-two percent of the 30- to 44-year-olds supported Obama. Final exit-poll tallies indicated that Obama won the Asian American vote 62 percent to 35 percent, the Latino vote 67 percent to 31 percent, and the African American vote 90 percent to 10 percent (Chen 2009). Certainly, Obama's biracial heritage and multicultural skills catalyzed a trend among younger generations and allowed him to connect with diverse groups of voters. He is widely praised for his ability to listen to many perspectives and seek common ground in making decisions.

Further raising the visibility of biculturalism in the United States, Sonia Sotomayor was confirmed by the United States Senate on August 6, 2009, as the first Latina Supreme Court justice. Sotomayor was born in the Bronx, a borough of New York City, to Juan Sotomayor, who was from the area of Santurce, San Juan, Puerto Rico, and Celina Báez from Santa Rosa in Lajas, a rural area on Puerto Rico's southwest coast. Spanish was her first language and her family regularly visited Puerto Rico to see relatives during the summers. Sotomayor became fluent in English later in childhood, and was inspired to pursue a legal career through reading Nancy Drew novels and watching Perry Mason on television.

The life stories of Obama and Sotomayor encapsulate many of the themes in bicultural development. Both of these individuals grew up in racially diverse environments with meager resources and single parents who were determined to get their children ahead through education and hard work. Obama and Sotomayor both struggled through a process of cultural identity development, but eventually were able to navigate within and across complex institutional settings, engaging disparate groups of people with their sophisticated communication skills and insight into complicated social issues. Having succeeded in meeting the many challenges inherent in the acculturation process (e.g., learning new languages, coping with discrimination, adopting norms and behaviors to meet the needs of different cultural situations), Obama and Sotomayor serve as examples of the twenty-first-century bicultural American Dream that is characterized by maintaining one's cultural roots while successfully meeting the demands of the larger sociocultural system.

Although Barack Obama and Sonia Sotomayor are currently two of the most famous biracial, bicultural people in the United States, they represent millions of other bicultural people. U.S. Census data from 2000 show that 1.9 percent of whites; 0.6 percent of African Americans, American Indian/Alaskan Natives, and Asians; 0.2 percent of Native Hawaiian/Pacific Islanders; and 1.1 percent of people reporting other racial heritages claim a heritage of more than one racial group (U.S. Census Bureau 2007). These percentages sum to 14,168,760 people in the United States who claim a mixed racial heritage (5,470,349 combination with white; 1,761,244 combination with African American; 1,643,345 combination with American Indian/Alaskan Native; 1,655,830 combination with Asian; 475,579 combination with Native Hawaiian/Pacific Islander; and 3,162,413 combination with some other race). Moreover, these numbers include only those individuals who report biracial heritage. Many people may be bicultural but not biracial. These people are likely to affiliate with one racial or ethnic group but adopt perspectives from both their minority cultural group and the larger host culture within the United States. Given that nineteen million immigrants obtained legal resident status from 1990 to 2008 and approximately twelve million undocumented immigrants are trying to adjust to life within the U.S. cultural system (Department of Homeland Security 2008), it is clear that becoming bicultural is a common theme for many people throughout the United States.

Demographic Change in the United States

> The racial and ethnic makeup of the U.S. has changed more rapidly since 1965 than during any other period in history. The reform in immigration policy of 1965, the increase in self-identification by ethnic minorities, and the slowing of the country's birth rates, especially among non-Hispanic White Americans, have all led to an increasing, and increasingly diverse, racial and ethnic minority population in the United States. (U.S. Department of Health and Human Services 2001, 56)

As the surgeon general's report *Mental Health: Culture, Race, and Ethnicity* cited above indicates, the United States is currently experiencing the largest growth of racial and ethnic minority populations in its history (see also Suarez-Orozco and Suarez-Orozco 2001). As shown in figure 1.1, during the eighteen years between 1990 and 2008, nearly nineteen million immigrants obtained legal resident status in the United States. The only other decade that approaches the highest immigration rates from 1990–2000 (9,775,398) or 2000–2008 (9,168,612) was at the turn of the twentieth century, when 8,202,388 immigrants obtained legal resident status from 1900 to 1910.

National statistics illustrate dramatic demographic changes. In July 2006, the U.S. minority population reached 100.7 million, which equates to one in three residents of the nation having minority status (U.S. Census Bureau 2007a). The nation's overall minority population on July 1, 2008, was 104.6

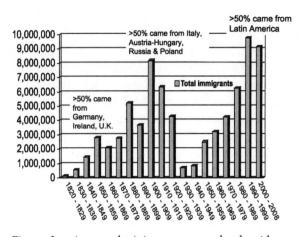

Fig. 1.1. Immigrants obtaining permanent legal resident status, 1820–2008 (U.S. Department of Homeland Security 2008)

million or 34 percent of the total population (U.S. Census Bureau 2009). Hispanics or Latinos are the largest and fastest-growing minority group, which reached 46.9 million in 2008, an increase of 3.2 percent from 2007. In 2008, nearly one in six U.S. residents was Hispanic. Asians were the second fastest-growing minority group from 2007 to 2008, increasing by 2.7 percent to 15.5 million persons in 2008. Following the Asian population in growth were Native Hawaiians and other Pacific Islanders (increasing 2.4 percent to 1.1 million), American Indians and Alaska Natives (increasing 1.7 percent to 4.9 million) and blacks or African Americans (increasing 1.3 percent to 41.1 million). In 2008, 5.2 million people were recorded as being biracial or multiracial, which was a 3.4 percent increase from 2007. The population of non-Hispanic whites who indicated no other race showed the smallest growth, increasing by 0.2 percent to 199.5 million. Table 1.1 highlights United States demographic shifts from 2000 to 2008 by race and ethnicity (U.S. Census Bureau 2009).

Dynamic demographic changes are occurring across the nation, specifically in the majority-minority balance. A population is defined as having majority-minority status when more than half the population is a group other than single-race, non-Hispanic whites. The most recent report on the shift in the majority-minority status of counties, issued by the U.S. Census Bureau in 2009, showed that as of July 1, 2008, nearly 10 percent (309) of the nation's 3,142 counties were majority-minority status; of that total, 56 have become majority-minority status since April 1, 2000. Taking a wider perspective, four states had majority-minority status in 2008: Hawaii (75 percent), New Mexico (58 percent), California (58 percent), and Texas (53 percent). The District of Columbia was 67 percent minority. No other state had more than a 43 percent minority population.

The Pew Research Center estimates that by 2050, Latinos will make up nearly one-third of the U.S. population and that non-Latino whites will become a minority constituting 47 percent of the U.S. population. African Americans will continue to make up 13 percent of the population, and the percentage of Asian/Pacific Islanders will increase from 5 percent in 2005 to 9 percent in 2050. Foreign-born immigrants will rise from 12 percent of the U.S. population in 2005 to 19 percent in 2050. According to the Pew Research Center projections, immigrants who arrive after 2005, and their U.S.-born descendants, may account for up to 82 percent of the increase in the national population during the 2005–2050 period (Passel and Cohn 2008).

TABLE 1.1

Cumulative Estimates of the Components of Resident Population Change by Race and Hispanic Origin for the United States: April 1, 2000, to July 1, 2008 (Census Data)

Race and Hispanic Origin	Total Population Change[a]	Natural Increase	Vital Events		Net International Migration[b]
			Births	*Deaths*	
TOTAL POPULATION	22,635,122	14,124,166	34,126,003	20,001,837	8,114,516
One Race	21,365,815	12,959,248	32,834,262	19,875,014	8,016,720
White	14,532,742	8,723,471	25,740,280	17,016,809	5,491,911
Black or African American	3,353,963	2,701,399	5,120,493	2,419,094	602,751
American Indian and Alaska Native	419,583	352,629	449,702	97,073	62,943
Asian	2,959,942	1,112,783	1,444,513	331,730	1,829,069
Native Hawaiian and Other Pacific Islander	99,585	68,966	79,274	10,308	30,046
Two or more races	1,269,307	1,164,918	1,291,741	126,823	97,796
Race alone or in combination					
White	15,676,516	9,789,154	26,911,834	17,122,680	5,564,235
Black or African American	4,021,799	3,332,564	5,786,367	2,453,803	636,244
American Indian and Alaska Native	636,842	549,936	718,034	168,098	80,785
Asian	3,473,602	1,563,097	1,933,511	370,414	1,890,111
Native Hawaiian and Other Pacific Islander	205,500	159,214	184,568	25,354	45,136
HISPANIC	11,637,235	7,257,703	8,159,060	901,357	4,318,003
WHITE ALONE, NOT HISPANIC	3,914,462	2,248,702	18,421,528	16,172,826	1,405,021

Note: Hispanic origin is considered an ethnicity, not a race. Hispanics may be of any race. The original race data from Census 2000 are modified to eliminate the "some other race" category. For more information, see http://www.census.gov/popest/archives/files/MRSF-01-US1.html

[a] The sum of the components of change may not equal total population change due to reconciliation of quarterly and monthly data in the processing. See National Terms and Definitions at http://www.census.gov/popest/topics/terms/national.html.

[b] Net international migration includes the international migration of both native and foreign-born populations. Specifically, it includes: (a) the net international migration of the foreign born, (b) the net migration between the United States and Puerto Rico, (c) the net migration of natives to and from the United States, and (d) the net movement of the Armed Forces population between the United States and overseas.

While approximately 44 percent of Latinos live in the western United States (Current Population Survey 2002), the impact of Latin American immigration is becoming widespread. From 1990 to 2000, the Latino population in seven states increased by 200 percent or more. At least twenty-five additional states had increases between 60 percent and 199 percent. Although Texas, California, and New York saw increases below the national average of 60 percent, these states already had large Latino populations. Some of the states, such as Georgia and North Carolina, where the growth of the Latino population was largest between 1990 and 2000, are not traditional areas for this type of immigration. North Carolina is one example of the seven states where the Latino population burgeoned during the past decade, increasing nearly 400 percent from 76,726 individuals in 1990 to 378,963 individuals in 2000. In contrast, during the same time, North Carolina's overall rate of population growth was only 15 percent (U.S. Census Bureau 2001a). In 2000, Latinos constituted 4.7 percent of North Carolina's total population (U.S. Census Bureau 2009). With an increase of 655 percent, Mexican immigrants are the largest subgroup driving this trend in North Carolina. The remarkable growth of the Latino population, and the movement of this population into diverse geographic areas of the United States, is illustrated by the fact that between 2000 and 2007, the number of Latinos grew in all but 150 of the 3,141 U.S. counties. That is, 2,991 U.S. counties reported an increase in the Latino population between 2000 and 2007.

These trends are even more pronounced for children. Children and adolescents represent significant proportions of the growing racial and ethnic minority populations (U.S. Census Bureau 2007a). Currently, one-fourth of the U.S. population is younger than eighteen years old. In contrast, youth younger than eighteen years comprise a third of the Latino population, nearly a third of the Asian/Pacific Islander population, and slightly more than a fourth of the American Indian/Alaskan Native population. Foreshadowing anticipated results for the 2010 Census, the Census Bureau (2009) has estimated that nearly half (47 percent) of the nation's children younger than five years were a minority in 2008, with 25 percent being Hispanic/Latino. For all children under eighteen years, 44 percent had minority status and 22 percent were Hispanic/Latino. Latinos are not only driving U.S. population growth, but they are the only demographic group producing families large enough to sustain the population (the population is sustained when two parents have two or more children). Recent Census Bureau figures report the average number of children for Asian couples as 1.7 children, 1.8 for non-Latino whites, 2.0 for African Americans, and 2.3 for Latinos (U.S. Census Bureau 2009). Societies that have an average of less than two children per family become dependent on immigration to maintain social stability and the labor force.

The Hispanic/Latino population is much younger than the population as a whole, with a median age of 27.7 years in 2008, compared with 36.8 years for the total U.S. population. Thirty-four percent of the Hispanic/Latino population was younger than eighteen years and 6 percent age sixty-five or older, as compared to 24 percent and 13 percent, respectively, for the total population (U.S. Census Bureau 2009). The combination of rapid growth and young age of the Hispanic/Latino population suggests that this group will have a profound impact on the future of the United States. As the aging non-Hispanic white workforce retires, they are likely to be replaced by young Latino workers. Considering the rapid growth and relative youth of the minority population, it is critical that we focus attention on promoting the health, well-being, and academic achievement of minority children, particularly Latino youth, given their substantial role in the future of the United States.

The rise in the U.S. Latino population is the result of immigration of youth and families born in other countries as well as high birth rates among Latino families. In 2004, approximately a quarter of the U.S. Latino population reported non-U.S. nativity, with the largest percentage coming from Mexico, followed by Puerto Rico and other Central American countries (U.S. Census Bureau 2007b). A majority of Latino immigrants have come to the United States since 1990, clearly demonstrating that a large segment of the Latino population is still adjusting to life in this country. Of the nearly three-quarters of the Latino population who are U.S. citizens, approximately 61 percent are U.S. born and are associated with the significantly higher birth rate among Latino women relative to non-Hispanic white women (U.S. Census Bureau 2007c). Given the number of these young Latino workers who are also recent immigrants, these statistics also underscore that a substantial group of adolescents is likely to be wrestling with acculturation-related issues during formative stages in their development.

From 1986 to 2006, Mexico had been the country-of-origin for the most foreign-born immigrants admitted to the United States for legal permanent residence, with more than double the number of immigrants compared to the next country-of-origin on the list (U.S. Department of Homeland Security 2008). During 2008, the top countries-of-origin for immigrants obtaining permanent legal residence were Mexico (188,015); Caribbean nations such as Cuba, the Dominican Republic, Haiti, and Jamaica (134,744); all of Europe (121,146); all of Africa (100,881); all of South America (96,178); China (75,410); India (59,728); the Philippines (52,391); and Russia (45,092).

In addition to these authorized immigrants, the Department of Homeland Security's Office of Immigration Statistics estimates that there were about 11.5 million unauthorized migrants in 2006, of which 6.6 million, or 57 percent, were Mexican born.

The remarkable growth of the Asian/Pacific Islander population is also fueled by both recent immigration of Asian individuals and greater-than-average birth rates of both Asian and Pacific Islander families (U.S. Census Bureau 2007d). For instance, approximately 33 percent of the current Asian population came to the United States during the 1990s, and an additional 17 percent immigrated since 2000. A majority of these immigrants originated in either China or Japan, and became residents in Hawaii. In contrast, 78 percent of Pacific Islanders are native. In addition, Asian/Pacific Islander women are significantly more likely to have children than their non-Hispanic white counterparts (U.S. Census Bureau 2007e).

Although Latinos and Asians dominate the foreign-born U.S. population, these are not the only minority groups showing significant growth. Currently, there are more than 550 federally recognized American Indian tribes and Alaskan Native groups (U.S. Department of the Interior 2007). In 2004, approximately 2.2 million persons identified themselves as American Indian/Alaskan Native and an additional 1.9 million self-identified as being mixed heritage of American Indian/Alaskan Native and another race (U.S. Census Bureau, 2007f). Further, the American Indian/Alaskan Native population continues to grow at a relatively higher rate than the general population, as evidenced by the 65 percent increase that was experienced from 1990 to 2007 (Indian Health Service 2007). In part, this rate of growth is a result of American Indian/Alaskan Native women having relatively higher birth rates than non-Hispanic white women. In addition, American Indian adolescent mothers aged fifteen to nineteen years have the second highest birth rate (67.8 per 1,000) compared with African American (63.1 per thousand) and Hispanic (82.6 per thousand) adolescent mothers (Martin et al. 2006).

The minority population in the United States is important not only because it is growing rapidly but also because of the risk factors this heterogeneous group faces. Compared to non-Latino whites, Latinos are more likely to be younger than eighteen years, unemployed, residing in large family households, and living in poverty (U.S. Census Bureau 2001b; Ramirez and de la Cruz 2003). In addition, Latinos have a lower median age (twenty-five years compared to twenty-seven years for African Americans and thirty-one years for non-Latino whites), lower educational attainment, and lower income levels than non-Latino whites. In 2000, the median income for Latino men was $19,833, compared to $21,662 for African American men and

$31,213 for non-Latino white men (U.S. Census Bureau 2001a). Similarly, Latino women had the lowest median incomes ($12,255) in 2000, compared to $16,081 for African American women and $16,805 for non-Latino white women (U.S. Census Bureau 2001a). Considering that the 2000 federal poverty threshold for a family of four was $17,463, many Latino families are coping with socioeconomic disadvantage. Official estimates report the Latino poverty rate at 22 percent, which is identical to the rate for African Americans, but nearly three times the non-Latino white rate of 7.8 percent (U.S. Census Bureau 2001a). In 2007, the poverty rates were 21.5 percent for Latinos, 24.5 for African Americans, 10.2 percent for Asians, and 8.2 percent for non-Hispanic whites (U.S. Census Bureau 2009). With many minority families experiencing socioeconomic disadvantages and challenges associated with recent immigration, it is important to turn our attention to the ways in which these demographic changes are fueling cultural changes throughout the United States.

Demographic Change Prompts Cultural Change

Although the United States has always been a nation of immigrants, the recent demographic shifts resulting in burgeoning and youthful Latino and Asian populations have literally changed the face of the nation. The current wave of massive immigration has led to the country's struggle with the necessity of becoming bicultural. Becoming bicultural, both for immigrant families and for the larger host society, is a difficult and sometimes painful process, requiring the integration of multiple, often conflicting messages concerning stability and change from different people and social systems. Consequently, there are abundant signs indicating that the ethnic mosaic of the U.S. population is both rapidly growing and becoming more diverse. Today, a sign on the Montgomery County library door in Silver Spring, Maryland, welcomes patrons in ten different languages because the library's consumer base is so diverse. The Charlotte-Mecklenburg school district in North Carolina's largest city serves 133,664 students who come from 161 different countries with 140 native languages. On a smaller scale, a trip to nearly any grocery store makes it obvious that an increasing amount of space and prominence is devoted to Mexican and Asian foods. It is commonplace to see product labels and instruction manuals written in Spanish and English. Now, when calling a customer service line, it is more the rule than the exception to hear "*Para proceder en Espanol, pulse el numero dos.*" These small examples show that daily life in the United States is slowly becoming bicultural. Despite the scramble for interpreters and cultural-competence training in businesses, schools, social services, and health care agencies, an even more intense process is occurring for immigrant individuals and families who are trying to fit into the host society as welcome or unwelcome guests.

This book examines the process of becoming bicultural. We explore the individual psychology and family dynamics behind bicultural development and delineate what factors lead to positive or to negative consequences for immigrant youth. This book was written for developmental psychologists, psychiatrists, social workers, human and family development scholars, and other social scientists, students, and practitioners who study or work with immigrant families experiencing cultural changes. It has been fashioned to meet the needs of readers interested in risk and resilience within the acculturation process. We combine reviews of quantitative research studies on the different dimensions of biculturalism with discussion of qualitative findings on cultural experiences.

Importantly, many of our examples are drawn from the Parent-Teen Biculturalism Project and the Latino Acculturation and Health Project. We conducted these research projects from 2001 through 2008, collecting surveys and interviews from more than four hundred Latino adolescents and their parents in North Carolina and Arizona. North Carolina and Arizona were selected in order to further our understanding of cultural change within new immigrant communities with little cultural capital or influence, such as those in North Carolina, and established communities with large Latino populations that go back generations in Arizona. We conducted extensive qualitative interviews and followed immigrant families for three years, measuring changes in acculturation and health indicators every six months. We also designed and tested a prevention program to help immigrant families cope with acculturation stress and develop bicultural skills. Reflecting national demographics for the Latino population, approximately two-thirds of the families in our studies were from Mexico. Twenty percent of adolescents were born in the United States and the rest immigrated from Mexico, Colombia, El Salvador, Brazil, Chile, and a number of other Caribbean, Central American, and South American countries. Cuban and Puerto Rican families were not represented in our studies because these groups are not well represented in North Carolina or Arizona. We note what other scholars have found when researching Cuban and Puerto Rican families.

It is important to remember that Latinos are a heterogeneous group with many different variations in language, customs, and culture. Although we try to be as specific as possible when discussing research findings, many studies do not have enough participants to evaluate differences between distinct Latino subgroups (for example, Mexicans versus El Salvadorians).

In this book, we have sought to identify common challenges and cultural assets across Latino subgroups. These common risk and resilience factors should be broken down by subgroup in future research. Further, although we believe that we have delineated widely applicable themes, much more research has been done with Latino families, particularly Mexicans, compared to Asian/Pacific Islander or Native American families. Although we highlight findings for other minority groups, Latino families are our primary focus. Latino families are the largest and fastest-growing demographic group in the United States and, in comparison to Asian/Pacific Islander or Native American/Alaskan Native families, we have a stronger research foundation upon which to draw conclusions about Latino families. Studies of Asian/Pacific Islander or Native American/Alaskan Native families are included in our discussions of research findings in chapters 5 and 6; however, our qualitative examples of immigrant family adaptation after immigration in chapters 2 through 4 are drawn from Latino families.

What Is Biculturalism?

Bicultural individuals may be immigrants, refugees fleeing war or oppression, sojourners (e.g., international students, expatriates), indigenous people, ethnic minorities, those in interethnic relationships, and mixed-ethnic individuals (Padilla 1994; Berry 2003). As illustrated above, many people considered bicultural fit into several of these categories. For many children and grandchildren of immigrants, affiliation and involvement in their ethnic cultures, as well as mainstream U.S. culture, is the norm (Phinney 1996). Consequently, biculturalism is hard to define and even harder to label. Biculturalism commonly has components from the psychological domain (e.g., identifying with values from multiple cultural groups), behavioral domain (e.g., speaking more than one language), and social domain (e.g., affiliating with peers from different cultural backgrounds). Loosely defined, bicultural identity is based on self-identification of group affiliation (e.g., "feeling Asian American"). However, researchers are often interested in a more strict definition that focuses on individuals who have internalized more than one cultural system (Benet-Martínez et al. 2002). Because this definition is less inclusive, students who have studied abroad for limited amounts of time or individuals in a mixed-race marriage who remain monolingual are not usually considered fully bicultural under this strict definition. Fully bicultural individuals have the ability to switch between cultural schemas, norms, and behaviors in response to cultural cues in any given situation (Hong et al. 2000).

Our discussion of biculturalism focuses on individuals who are developing this ability to navigate between ethnic cultures (not work or institutional cultures, geographic cultures, subcultures, or different cultures between generations or age groups). Perhaps most important for our purposes, bicultural individuals have been immersed in the acculturation process of adjusting to a new cultural system. The acculturation process has two critical dimensions, culture-of-origin involvement (also called "enculturation") and host cultural involvement (also called "assimilation"). Biculturalism is the integration of or navigation between these two dimensions. We provide important definitions and opposing theories of cultural change in the next section.

Cultural Adjustment: Acculturation, Enculturation, Assimilation, and Biculturalism

Acculturation: The Overarching Process of Cultural Contact

Acculturation was first defined as "phenomena which result when groups of individuals having different cultures come into continuous first hand contact with subsequent changes in the original culture patterns of either or both groups" (Redfield, Linton, and Herskovits 1936, 149). This original definition stressed continuous, long-term change and allowed the process to be bidirectional, wherein both of the interacting cultures could make accommodations.

A historical example may make this acculturation concept more transparent. The continuous process of bidirectional accommodation is illustrated in the early interactions of Massassoit's Wampanoag tribe with the early English settlers. The United States has been an immigrant nation from its inception. Every elementary school child in the United States learns that the Native Americans of Chief Massassoit's Wampanoag tribe taught the Plymouth pilgrims to grow corn, helping the pilgrims survive the harsh northeastern winter. The subsequent first Thanksgiving in 1621 was a celebration of a harvest that flowed directly from bicultural collaboration. Chief Massassoit's warriors could have easily wiped out the immigrant pilgrims the year before when half of the new settlers had died from disease, hunger, or exposure. Instead, a workable, though tenuous, alliance arose out of the cultural brokering of Massassoit and a young Pilgrim named Edward Winslow. Both Massassoit and Winslow grew to become moderately bicultural, learning parts of the other group's language, norms, and behaviors, and understanding how cooperation could promote the goals of both groups. Unfortunately, subsequent waves of British immigrants would trample such bicultural cooperation, and as the Anglo-Saxon immigrants increased in number and power, they adopted policies characterized by assimilation or elimination. The earliest stages of acculturation are focused on the contact between the two cultures. Pilgrims clearly benefited from learning Native American ways of planting while Wampanoag tribe members were pleased to receive European supplies, such as metal pots, knives, and steel drills that made their lives easier. Jill Lepore, a noted historian, described this early contact, saying,

> Those peoples [Native Americans and English settlers in the 1620s] become more and more dependent on one another, and exchange more and more goods, and ideas, and people—children, wives, families—have more and more contact with one another. In a sense, the two peoples come to share a great deal. The English come to be more like Indians in many ways. They dress more like Indians. They use Indian words. They're familiar with Indian ways. And the Indians come to be more like English. A lot of Indians speak English. They wear English clothes. They build houses that are English. There's a reciprocity of exchange that actually turns out—we might think, "Oh how lovely. What a nice multicultural fest that is." But actually it makes everyone very, very nervous. ("We Shall Remain" 2009, 9)

From Contact to Conflict

John Berry (1980) characterized the course of the acculturation process as flowing from *contact* between dominant and nondominant cultural groups to *conflict* or crises between those groups that eventually results in *adaptations* by one or both of the conflicting groups. These acculturation phases characterize not only large-scale sociological group dynamics over long periods but also cultural interactions between social groups during different eras as well as individual psychological and social processes that affect a person's adjustment to a new cultural situation. For example, this problematic flow of events from contact to conflict is readily seen in relations between the Native Americans and the English as the fragile mutuality seen initially in the 1620s was supplanted by questions concerning who controlled critical tangible resources (e.g., land rights) and who had the "true" religion or "civilized" way of behaving. Cultural conflict may develop gradually and extend continuously over generations, as it did for Native American people, or it may be quite abrupt and intense, such as the unsettling immersion experienced by a newly immigrated Latino or Asian child who speaks no English when he or she enters a U.S. school for the first

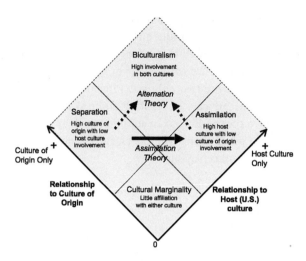

Fig. 1.2. Acculturation criteria and theoretical frameworks

time. Although acculturation phases describe a sociological phenomenon that occurs between groups, a parallel interpersonal process is thought to occur among immigrant individuals and families.

Two criteria determine the end point of acculturation adaptations: whether the acculturating individual or group retains cultural identity and whether a positive relationship to the dominant society is established (Berry 1998). Juxtaposing these two criteria makes it possible to pursue four different types of acculturation adaptations: separation/enculturation (e.g., remaining solely affiliated with one's ethnic culture), assimilation (e.g., affiliating with the national or host culture), integration or biculturalism (e.g., balancing between ethnic and national cultures), and marginalization (e.g., having no cultural affiliation). These two criteria and four adaptation styles are charted in figure 1.2. We discuss each of these adaptation styles below and examine how each fits into the acculturation phases throughout this book.

Enculturation: The Relationship to the Culture-of-Origin

There are several important underlying concepts within the overarching acculturation process. In contrast to acculturation, which occurs between cultural groups, *enculturation* is the adoption and maintenance of behaviors, norms, values, and customs from a person's culture-of-origin. Every culture indoctrinates children by exposing them to, or socializing them with, specific ideas, beliefs, routines, rituals, religious practices, languages, and ways of being in the world. The resulting cluster of beliefs and behaviors culminates in a person's ethnic identity. This sense of ethnic identity is a person's self-definition based on membership in a distinct group derived from a perceived shared heritage (Phinney and Ong 2007). The broad concept of enculturation encompasses the individual's level of involvement in his or her culture-of-origin, which is nurtured through early childhood exposure to cultural symbols and messages transmitted primarily through family interactions. By early adulthood, consistent exposure to these cultural beliefs and behaviors leads to an individual's working sense of ethnic identity (e.g., an affiliation with a cultural group and an understanding of how that cultural group expects its members to be in the world). The enculturation process both defines the characteristics of the group and secures its future by indoctrinating new members.

Retaining enculturation or culture-of-origin identity alone without establishing a positive relationship to the dominant culture would indicate *separation* and unwillingness to assimilate. The Separation quadrant in figure 1.2 represents strong enculturation and low assimilation into the dominant or host society. Separation is the adaptation style that characterizes most immigrant parents who cling strongly to their culture-of-origin identity and who find the acculturation process particularly stressful. Individuals and families using this Separation coping style may structure their lives to live within ethnic communities with little contact with the larger or dominant culture. For example, if Asian immigrants conduct their business in San Francisco's Chinatown and do not venture out, it is quite possible to remain highly involved in Chinese culture without adopting, or adapting to, what we would consider mainstream U.S. culture. The same dynamic holds for Little Havana, which is widely known as a center of social, cultural, and political activity for Cuban immigrants in Miami, Florida.

Enculturation is an important factor in the three phases of acculturation given above. During intercultural contact, differences in enculturation between the two groups become apparent. For instance, Native Americans believed that land was a gift from the Creator, and no individual owned this gift. In contrast, the pilgrims, indoctrinated in the European currency economy and believing that they were God's chosen people, saw no difficulty in buying, trading for, or taking land for personal ownership. Differences between worldviews like this example make groups wary of outsiders, triggering an urge to close ranks and defend the way of life the group understands. It is easy to see how conflict may arise. With the future at stake, enculturation prompts individuals to choose *us* versus *them*—our beliefs and ways of doing things or theirs. Although this is a simplistic introduction to enculturation and ethnic identity, these concepts are discussed in depth in chapter 2.

Assimilation: Involvement in the Dominant or Host Culture

The central issue after contact becomes who has power and control, and how the dominant group will use that power. Usually, the nondominant group is strongly influenced to take on norms, values, and behaviors espoused by the dominant group. The intensity and negativity associated with this process are largely contingent upon the receptivity of the dominant group in welcoming, respecting, or stigmatizing the nondominant group (Berry 1998). Further, the attitudes held by the dominant group influence the adoption of policies for relating to the nondominant group. For example, dominant group attitudes towards immigrants that influence policy are reflected in the debate in the United States regarding whether English should be declared the country's official language, in the question of whether school districts support English immersion or bilingual education programs, and in restrictions requiring certain forms of identification that are difficult for some immigrants to obtain in order for them to receive a driver's license.

During the conflict and adaptation phases of acculturation, antagonistic attitudes from the dominant group towards immigrants often prompt calls for assimilation or elimination. The term *acculturation,* which denotes the bidirectional process of cultural contact and change, is often erroneously used interchangeably with the term *assimilation,* which captures unidirectional adaptations made by minority individuals to conform to the dominant group.

During the decades since acculturation was first defined, a number of alternative definitions have been offered that stress unidirectional, rather than bidirectional, change. For example, Emily Smith and Nancy Guerra (2006) refer to acculturation as "the differences and changes in values and behaviors that individuals make as they gradually adopt the cultural values of the dominant society" (283). These unidirectional assimilation trends suggest that cultural change results from interactions between dominant and nondominant groups, and such change is commonly characterized by nondominant groups taking on the language, laws, religions, norms, and behaviors of the dominant group (Castro et al. 1996; Berry 1998). Consequently, the original Redfield (1936) definition captures the bidirectional notion of acculturation whereas the description offered by Smith and Guerra (2006) denotes the unidirectional assimilation approach. These

competing unidirectional and bidirectional approaches dominate acculturation research, influencing conceptualization, measurement, analytic
strategies, and results of empirical studies in this area (Cabassa 2003). We
explore these issues further in chapters 5 and 6.

The common notion of assimilation entails persons losing their culture-
of-origin identity so as to identify with the dominant cultural group. That
is, a movement in figure 1.2 from separation to assimilation, which a person
completes by swapping the positive relationship with his or her culture-of-
origin for a positive affiliation with the dominant culture. The assimilation
model assumes that an individual sheds her or his culture-of-origin in an
attempt to take on the values, beliefs, behaviors, and perceptions of the target culture (Chun, Organista, and Marin 2003). The individual perceives
the dominant culture as more desirable whereas the culture-of-origin is
seen as inferior. In this model, change is "directional, unilinear, nonreversible, and continuous" (Suarez-Orozco and Suarez-Orozco 2001, 8).

The experience of European immigrants appeared to fit the unidirectional assimilation framework that has been the dominant way of conceptualizing acculturation change (de Anda 1984; Feliciano 2001; Padilla and
Perez 2003). In the earliest days of the United States, colonists saw the new
republic as the beginning of a utopian society where immigrants from different nationalities, cultures, and races blended into an idealized American
"new man."

[W]hence came all these people? They are a mixture of English, Scotch,
Irish, French, Dutch, Germans, and Swedes. . . . What, then, is the American, this new man? He is neither a European nor the descendant of a European; hence that strange mixture of blood, which you will find in no
other country. I could point out to you a family whose grandfather was an
Englishman, whose wife was Dutch, whose son married a French woman,
and whose present four sons have now four wives of different nations. He
is an American, who, leaving behind him all his ancient prejudices and
manners, receives new ones from the new mode of life he has embraced,
the new government he obeys, and the new rank he holds. . . . The Americans were once scattered all over Europe; here they are incorporated into
one of the finest systems of population which has ever appeared. (J. Hector
St. John de Crevecoeur, *Letters from an American Farmer*, 1782)

The concept of the great American *melting pot* was popularized in the
era spanning 1890 to 1910, which was the height of a large wave of European immigrants that flooded into the United States. After the premiere
of the play *The Melting Pot* by Israel Zangwill in 1908, the term "melting

pot" came into general use. In the play, Zangwill's immigrant protagonist declares, "Understand that America is God's Crucible, the great Melting-Pot where all the races of Europe are melting and reforming! A fig for your feuds and vendettas! Germans and Frenchmen, Irishmen and Englishmen, Jews and Russians—into the Crucible with you all! God is making the American."

The melting-pot theory of ethnic relations focused on American identity created by the assimilation and intermarriage of white immigrant groups. In the play, the Jewish Russian protagonist falls in love with a Christian Russian woman. The couple is able to overcome their differences and celebrate assimilation to new identities within their adopted homeland. The play captured a common drama during this historical period. During the late nineteenth and early twentieth centuries, large numbers of non-Protestant, Southern European, and Eastern European immigrants were immigrating to the United States, causing concern over how these new groups of Irish, Polish, Italian, and Jewish settlers would mix with the Northern European, often Anglo-Saxon, Protestant majority who no longer thought of themselves as newcomers. These new white settlers were eligible for naturalization under the racially restrictive Naturalization Act of 1790 and had to be integrated in some way. Non-Protestant European immigrant groups such as the Catholic Irish, Italians, and Jews suffered from forms of discrimination but were gradually accepted as "white" American citizens, enjoyed political freedom, and eventually assimilated through intermarriage into the white majority.

There has always been unequal access to the great American melting pot for non-White ethnic and racial minorities. These minorities, both immigrants and natives, have been barred from full participation in U.S. society as citizens, banned from immigrating, and subjected to oppressive assimilation policies and practices. Assimilation fervor has a long history, dating back to the earliest days of contact between the English settlers and Native Americans. In 1651, John Eliot, a Puritan minister, started the first "praying town" in Natick, Massachusetts, to convert American Indians to Christianity. "Praying towns" were settlements where American Indians moved to relinquish their native heritage and take on a Puritan way of life. Those who agreed to forsake their native religion, beliefs, and traditional ways of being in the world to live by Puritan moral codes were promised both eternal life and physical safety. The conversion experiences of Native Americans were chronicled in a publication called *Tears of Repentance*.

Praying Indian #1: I heard that Word, that it is a shame for a man to wear long hair, and that there was no such custom in the Churches; at first I thought I loved not long hair, but I did, and found it very hard to cut it off; and then I prayed to God to pardon that sin also.

Praying Indian #2: When they said the devil was my God, I was angry, because I was proud. I loved to pray to many Gods. Then going to your house, I more desired to hear of God . . . then I was angry with myself and loathed myself and thought God will not forgive my sins.

Praying Indian #3: I see God is still angry with me for all my sins and He hath afflicted me by the death of three of my children, and I fear God is still angry, because great are my sins, and I fear lest my children be not gone to Heaven. ("We Shall Remain" 2009, 9)

By 1671, there were only a thousand members of the Wampanoag tribe remaining when Chief Massassoit's son Phillip began to fight back against English assimilation pressure; nearly half were dispersed across fourteen different praying towns. However, assimilation adaptations and painful conversion experiences were often not enough to allow these cultural groups to peacefully coexist. During the subsequent Indian uprising led by King Phillip, Native Americans who were living a Christian life in praying towns were banished, taken to Deer Island in Boston Harbor, and left in the middle of winter without blankets or food.

Assimilation sentiments have underpinned cultural relations and prompted public policy throughout American history. During his presidency in 1801, Thomas Jefferson wrote,

The American settlements will gradually circumscribe and approach the Indians, who will in time either incorporate with us as citizens of the United States, or remove beyond the Mississippi. Some tribes are advancing, and on these English seductions will have no effect. But the backward will yield, and be thrown further back into barbarism and misery . . . and we shall be obliged to drive them with the beasts of the forest into the stony mountains. ("We Shall Remain," chap. 2, 4)

Native Americans were enrolled in tribes and because they did not have U.S. citizenship until the Indian Citizenship Act of 1924, they were subjected to government policies of enforced cultural assimilation, also termed "Americanization." Native American children were taken from their families and placed in boarding schools to teach them how to interact in civilized society. African Americans were also excluded for not being white. Slave owners deliberately broke up families of African slaves so that they would be easier to control. Even after the Emancipation Proclamation banished slavery and made African Americans citizens, intermarriage between whites and African Americans was illegal in many U.S. states under antimiscegenation laws, which continued from 1883 until 1967. Asian immigrants such as Chinese, Japanese, Koreans, and Filipinos were ruled to be nonwhite and banned from marrying whites in several states where existing antimiscegenation laws were expanded to include them. After a number of conflicting rulings in American courts, Punjabi people and others from British India were also deemed to be nonwhites. In the late nineteenth and early twentieth centuries, laws such as the Chinese Exclusion Act severely limited or banned immigration by Asians. The Immigration Act of 1924 severely restricted immigration from areas outside Northern and Western Europe.

Assimilation fervor peaks during times of national distress. There was a backlash against German immigrants during World War I. Many Japanese American adults who were imprisoned during World War II tried to discard their ethnic identity and assimilate after the end of the war, attempting to avoid any association, shame, or embarrassment that came from being imprisoned. Attitudes towards nonwhite immigrants and natives gradually improved after World War II in the second half of the twentieth century. Since the successes of the American civil rights movement and the enactment of the Immigration and Nationality Act of 1965, which allowed for a large increase in immigration from Latin America and Asia, intermarriage between white and nonwhite Americans has been increasing. However, after the terrorist attacks on the World Trade Center on September 11, 2001, assimilationist rhetoric enjoyed a resurgence and remains central to the immigrants' drama of adjusting to life in the United States.

Assimilation theory has been applied in a range of policies and practice situations. For example, English as a Second Language (ESL) programs in which instructors speak only English and policy proposals that declare English to be the state's or country's "official" language have deep roots in assimilationist ideology. In 1998, California voters passed Proposition 227, which requires that all public school instruction be conducted in English, by a wide margin (61 percent vs. 39 percent; now EC 300-340 of the California Education Code). Similarly, in 2000, Arizona's voters passed Proposition 203, which mandates that school instruction must be in English and severely limits opportunity for bilingual instruction. Both propositions are examples of the assimilationist Structured English Immersion approach to educating immigrants who are not proficient in English. We examine assimilation in greater detail in chapters 3 and 5.

Integration or Biculturalism: Navigating between
Two Cultures

While assimilation theory continues to be popular, a growing body of
research has begun to question whether it is indeed adaptive for a person
to give up his or her cultural identity to fit into the dominant culture (de
Anda 1984; Feliciano 2001; Padilla and Perez 2003; Suarez-Orozco and
Suarez-Orozco 2001). Critics of the assimilation model usually support the
further development of alternation theory, a framework that rejects linear conceptualizations of acculturation and revisits the Redfield definition
of acculturation that allowed for dynamic bidirectional change (Trimble
2003). Following figure 1.2, integration, or biculturalism, would ensue from
both retaining ethnic cultural identity and establishing a positive relationship with the dominant culture. In contrast to the unidirectional approach
of assimilation, the bidirectional approach considers enculturation (i.e.,
adoption and maintenance of behaviors, norms, values, and customs from
a person's culture-of-origin), ethnic identity (i.e., a person's self-definition
based on membership in a distinct group derived from a perceived shared
heritage), and biculturalism (i.e., ability to integrate attributes of two cultures and competently navigate between cultural systems [Gonzales et al.
2002; LaFromboise, Coleman, and Gerton 1993]) as important aspects of
the acculturation process.

Alternation theorists believe that individuals can both retain cultural
identity and establish a positive relationship with the dominant culture.
Proponents of the alternation theory of cultural acquisition assert that
there is great value in the individual maintaining her or his culture-of-
origin while acquiring the second culture (Feliciano 2001). These theorists
believe that the unidirectional change approach espoused by assimilation-
ists may have fit prior groups of white European immigrants but does not
adequately characterize adaptations made by subsequent waves of immigrants from Latin America or Asia (de Anda 1984; Padilla and Perez 2003).
Prior groups of white European immigrants assimilated into the dominant
Anglo majority through education and intermarriage, but new waves of
immigrants from Latin America or Asia arguably have more obstacles in
their path to integration because they will always remain racial minorities.
Intermarriage no longer brings assimilation, but now creates a new generation of biracial youth.

In this alternation theory perspective, biculturalism, or having the ability to competently navigate within and between two different cultures, is
the optimal end point for the process of cultural acquisition (LaFromboise,
Coleman, and Gerton 1993). For the immigrant individual and her or his

family, alternation theory supports the *integration* of cognition, attitudes, and behaviors from both the culture-of-origin and the culture of acquisition. This integration may result in bilingualism, cognitive code switching, and the development of multiple identities (e.g., immigrant adolescents behaving "American" at school and "Latino" at home) to meet disparate environmental demands (Dolby 2000; Suarez-Orozco and Suarez-Orozco 2001; Trueba 2002).

Of course, the influence of the dominant or host culture plays an important role in the acculturation process. Just as assimilation ideology pushes immigrants to accept host culture norms and behaviors, environmental contexts that actively support and value multiculturalism can also prompt individuals and families toward integration or biculturalism (Berry 2001; de Anda 1984). The concept of cultural pluralism first emerged in the early decades of the twentieth century among intellectuals debating United States immigration and national identity (Kallen 1915; Bourne 1916). For example, Randolph Bourne (1916, 86) wrote in Trans-National America, "No reverberatory effect of the great war has caused American public opinion more solicitude than the failure of the 'melting-pot.' The discovery of diverse nationalistic feelings among our great alien population has come to most people as an intense shock."

Beginning in the 1960s, multiculturalism gained traction, prompting melting pot metaphors to be replaced with references to a cultural salad bowl or cultural mosaic. In this newer multicultural approach, each "ingredient" retains its integrity and flavor while contributing to a successful final product. However, considering the backdrop of heated stress and tension, these ethnic relations are better characterized as a simmering stew than a salad bowl. In recent years, this multicultural approach has been officially promoted in traditional melting-pot societies such as Australia, Canada, and Britain, with the intent of encouraging more tolerance of immigrant diversity. Meanwhile, the United States continues to vacillate between assimilation and alternation (or multicultural) approaches to immigration and ethnic relations.

Alternation theory has been used in practice, but few macro policies have been based on this framework. English as a Second Language (ESL) and Two-Way Immersion programs that teach content in both English and Spanish are underpinned by alternation theory. Bicultural skills training programs are another reflection of the way alternation theory has been applied to practice (e.g., see Szapocznik et al. 1984; 1986; 1989; Bacallao and Smokowski 2005). Bicultural development and the integrative adaptation style are discussed in detail in chapters 4 and 6.

Deculturation

Finally, losing cultural identity without establishing a positive relationship to the dominant culture would be the hallmark of *deculturation,* or cultural marginality (Berry 1980; LaFromboise, Coleman, and Gerton 1993). Less common than the other three adaptation styles, deculturation may be a stressful stage experienced by many immigrants as they construct a new or integrated cultural identity. Some authors refer to deculturation as "cultural homelessness," a state in which individuals do not feel an affiliation with any cultural group (Vivero and Jenkins 1999).

Conclusions

The size and political, economic, and social influence exerted by minority families, especially Latinos, in the United States is growing rapidly because of both immigration trends and the comparatively higher birth rates of these minority groups. One critical difference between the subgroups of Latino, American Indian/Alaskan Native, and Asian/Pacific Islander adolescents and many of their peers from other minority and majority racial groups is that the adolescents in these subgroups have to cope with the complexities inherent in the acculturation process in addition to the stress of adolescence as a developmental stage. Considering that a quarter of the U.S. Latino population is foreign born and that a majority of these Latino immigrants have come to the United States since 1990, a large segment of the Latino population is still adjusting to life in this country. The same dynamic holds for the Asian population in the United States. Consequently, it is important to examine the roles that cultural factors, especially acculturation processes, play in promoting or inhibiting the social, educational, psychological, and physical well-being of minority adolescents.

Acculturation is the overall process of cultural involvement. Assimilation is generally associated with high levels of host culture involvement. A moderate-to-high level of involvement in both cultures marks integration or biculturalism. Separation or maintaining ethnic identity alone (enculturation) is associated with high levels of involvement in the culture-of-origin, whereas having no affiliation with either culture is the hallmark of deculturation or marginalization. These four cultural adaptation styles and two major theories of cultural change (assimilation and alternation theories) are depicted in figure 1.2. Revisiting Berry's (1998) criteria, assimilation theory posits that a positive relationship to the dominant society is established without retention of ethnic identity (see the right-hand quadrant), whereas in alternation theory, a moderate-to-strong positive relationship to the dominant society is established and a moderate-to-strong positive relationship to ethnic identity or culture-of-origin is retained (upper-middle quadrant). Neither theory has much to say about cultural marginality, which occurs when a positive relationship is not formed with either the new culture or the culture-of-origin (lower-middle quadrant). Cultural marginality can result in apathy, lack of interest in culture, or the formation of a negative relationship with both cultures.

William Flannery, Steven Reise, and Jiajuan Yu (2001) conducted the earliest direct comparison of the assimilation and alternation models. In a sample of 291 Asian Americans, they reported that both models had adequate predictive validity for use in acculturation research. They recommended using the unidirectional assimilationist model as an economical proxy measure of acculturation, and using the bidirectional alternation model for "full theoretical investigations of acculturation" (Flannery Reise, and Yu 2001, 1035).

Turning our attention back to the conceptualizations of acculturation, alternation theory is aligned with the original Redfield definition that allows for dynamic bidirectional adaptations to occur in either or both cultures. Assimilation theory is aligned with the modified definition of acculturation that assumes unidirectional change from the dominant to the nondominant group. Assimilation and alternation theories, and the various cultural adaptation styles introduced above, are fascinating sociological constructs; however, these ideas become ever more critical when linked to health and mental health. Throughout this book, we examine quantitative and qualitative research that tests the relationships between acculturation constructs and health behaviors in minority and immigrant youth and adults.

A Dynamic Model for Becoming Bicultural

Although acculturation is inherently a process that unfolds over time, few investigations have had sufficient longitudinal data to consider acculturation as a developmental process. It is more common for research studies either to examine differences between immigrants who have been in the United States for disparate amounts of time, or to compare differences between generations, and, in both cases, to ascribe discrepancies to temporal changes. Acculturation researchers have directed more attention to group differences (foreign born versus U.S. born; first generation versus subsequent generations) than to individual differences over time, with

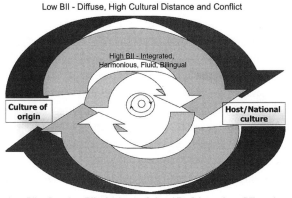

Fig. 1.3. The acculturation cycle and bicultural identity integration (BII)

a few exceptions (e.g., Smokowski, Bacallao, and Rose 2010; Smokowski, Rose, and Bacallao 2009).

It would be ideal to have a dynamic model of cultural adaptation after immigration. A dynamic model would help immigrants immersed in acculturation to grasp the turbulence and change inherent in the adjustment process. Such a model would also serve as a guide for social services providers and health care practitioners in targeting prevention, intervention, and public policy initiatives. Despite the significant attention the four cultural adaptation styles have received from the research community, these styles often become static categories when analyzed by researchers, failing to capture the chaos and complexity that characterizes cultural contact, conflict, and adaptation.

In order to move towards a dynamic, temporal model for becoming bicultural, we suggest that acculturation should be modeled as a circle, with culture-of-origin on one side and host culture on the other (see figure 1.3). The circle denotes a movement between ethnic and mainstream cultural contexts without assuming the linear, unidirectional flow of assimilation from culture-of-origin to the host culture. In our circle model of acculturation, movement is fluid and bidirectional depending upon the cultural situation. However, individual and family stress commonly occurs as immigrant adolescents move from the culture-of-origin context to the host- or dominant-culture context.

Shortly after immigration, the distance between the culture-of-origin and the host culture seems quite large, complex, and fraught with conflicts. This outer trajectory is characteristic of new immigrants who tend to perceive the acculturation process as difficult. As reviewed in the discussions in chapters 4 and 6, these individuals are particularly sensitive to the differences between the cultures, typically report that navigating between the two cultures is difficult and takes effort, and may lack proficiency in bicultural and bilingual skills. This diffuse stage of cultural adaptation has been associated with poor psychological and sociological adjustment (Berry et al. 2006). In addition, this diffuse stage may be a result, at least in part, of the brain's sparsely connected, distant neural networks that lack sophistication in processing diverse cultural, cognitive, and linguistic information.

As environmental demands dictate increased movement from one cultural context to the other, the circle often becomes tighter, more coherent, spiraling in on itself, with each revolution traversed more and more quickly. Navigating this circular process with increasing speed and skill signifies increasing levels of bicultural identity integration. The two cultural systems are increasingly viewed as integrated rather than distant and conflicted. Bilingualism is heightened and navigation of cultural contexts is fluid. This integrated cultural adaptation style is associated with healthy psychological and sociological adaptation and may very well be the result of closely interconnected neural networks that have been formed in the brain for processing cultural, socio-cognitive, and linguistic information.

Using research evidence from extant studies, we have developed a model of the stages of bicultural identity development. Shown in figure 1.4, this model incorporates our knowledge of cultural adaptation styles (Berry et al. 2006), bicultural identity integration (Benet-Martínez and Haritatos 2005; Nguyen and Benet-Martinez 2007), and ethnic identity development (Phinney 1989). After immigration, young individuals who have already developed an ethnic identity within their culture-of-origin experience a crisis because of assimilation stress and perceived discrimination. Their cultural worlds are suddenly threatened by a two-pronged cultural context in which their ethnic cultural ties are placed in sharp contrast to the norms of the host or dominant cultural system. Regardless of their prior level of ethnic identity development, this acculturation dynamic places new immigrants in a state of diffused and bifurcated bicultural identity formation. For many, this experience is the first time that their cultural context has been divided into culture-of-origin and host-cultural contexts, requiring a shifting of cultural behaviors between home and school or work. Low levels of bicultural identity integration, which commonly make these intercultural transactions difficult and conflicted, characterize the diffused stage of cultural development experienced by new immigrants.

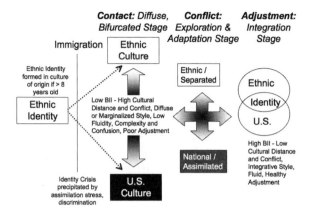

Fig. 1.4. Developmental model of bicultural identity integration (BII)

Over time, most immigrants move into an exploration and adaptation stage of cultural development; however, some youth and adults remain mired in a diffused or marginalized cultural adaptation style. These individuals may be older and more rigid, or may be isolated and lack access to ethnically mixed social networks (Berry et al. 2006). Other youth and adults choose to affiliate exclusively with their ethnic culture (e.g., separation), enjoying cultural protective factors and positive psychological adjustment. A third group of youth and adults assimilate to the host or national culture and report relatively poor adjustment and health behaviors (see chapter 5). Finally, what appears to be the largest group of immigrants passes through the exploration stage to the integration stage, in which they achieve a high level of bicultural identity integration. This bicultural group has been found to have the best profile of psychological and sociological adjustment (Berry et al. 2006; see chapter 6).

This book is structured into chapters that are devoted to major parts of these dynamic models of bicultural development shown in figures 1.3 and 1.4. In chapter 2, we focus on enculturation or culture-of-origin involvement, specifically examining how immigrant families maintain their ethnic identities. We discuss major changes in immigrant family systems that occur during the diffused, bifurcated stage of bicultural development. In chapter 3, we examine the relationship to the dominant or host culture as the second dimension of biculturalism. The relationship to the host culture is marked by a consistent undercurrent pushing adolescents toward assimilation. This assimilation pressure prompts adolescents and parents to explore and adapt to the host cultural system. Chapter 4 moves from the outside edges of the model in figure 1.3 to the center as we consider qualitative data on how adolescents and parents view the integration stage of bicultural development. Next, in chapter 5, we shift the tone of our discussion to present research on how these two dimensions—enculturation and assimilation—are connected to mental health, health, and adjustment in immigrant adolescents and adults. This exploration of enculturation and assimilation research is followed by a review of biculturalism research in chapter 6. Finally, in chapter 7, we consider how psychologists, social workers, and social service providers can help intervene in this acculturation process and provide information on the *Entre Dos Mundos/Between Two Worlds* bicultural skills training model.

2

Enculturation after Immigration

*How Latino Family Systems Change and
How They Stay the Same during the Diffuse,
Bifurcated Stage of Acculturation Contact*

*Mexico, lindo y querido, si muero lejos de ti, por siempre te extrañaré,
para siempre.*

[Mexico, beautiful and beloved, if I die far away from you, know
that I will always miss you. Always.]

—Yariela, Mexican female adolescent, twelve years old,
living in United States for one year

Elena is a Mexican female adolescent, age sixteen, who has resided in the United States for three years. She provided the following explanation for her drawing, shown in figure 2.1.

*Here is the United States [top country], and Mexico [bottom country]. The
United States . . . I represent it with many dollars, but the people are sad
[see blue figure composed of squares in the United States—it is a building where sad people live]. You have everything, but you don't have your
family. That's what the people in the middle represent, the sad people. I also
tried to draw a routine [see dotted lines underneath the two people in the
United States]; everything's the same . . . the same . . . the same. Your parents
go to work and come back. And you go to school and come back. And that is
your day. It's not like in Mexico where you visit with your grandparents and
your other relatives. In Mexico, you don't have money but you're much better because you're with your family. I know that my parents do this for our
well-being, so we're here. In Mexico, we celebrate with fireworks, lots of colors
exploding [see fireworks in bottom half]. All the people in Mexico are happy
because they are with their family. This [pointed to the red heart] is the district I am from. The feelings I have when I'm at the parties and festivals [in*

Mexico] *gives me a feeling, a feeling I can't really explain. You see, here in the U.S., it is mostly sadness. I feel like crying instead of feeling good. That's what I'm trying to draw. We used to always be with my family, and that's who I miss.*

Most of the research on Latino immigration, acculturation, and adjustment has been conducted with adults, leaving us with scant information on adolescents and even less on family relationships (García Coll and Magnuson 2001). Little attention has been given to the so-called Generation 1.5, that is, children and adolescents who were born and socialized in a foreign country and then immigrated to the United States (Hirschman 1994; Portes and Rumbaut 2001). Arguably, these Gen 1.5 children experience the most

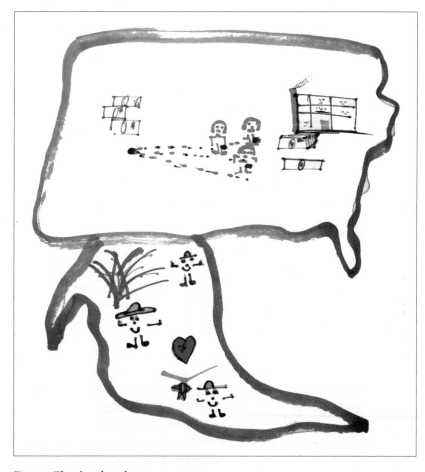

Fig. 2.1. Elena's cultural map

upheaval of the family system, and thus are most likely to either become bicultural or get caught between cultural systems (Hirschman 1994; García Coll and Magnuson 2001).

This chapter focuses on enculturation—specifically, on understanding the dynamics of the Latino family system and the changes that parents and adolescents experience following immigration to the United States. We explore three fundamental questions: How do Latino family systems change after immigration? How do these changes affect family members' levels of enculturation (or ethnic identity) and family relationships? What factors best explain postimmigration family system adjustment?

Both positive and negative immigration experiences contribute stressors that can undermine enculturation, leading to both acculturation stress and familial stress. Depending upon the reasons for their relocation—as well as the social environment the family left and the environment they entered—immigrant families often experience significant upheaval during migration. This upheaval includes shifts in socioeconomic status, loss of social networks, new or drastically restructured family roles, and disorienting cultural changes in the new land (Hernandez and McGoldrick 1999).

We present a combination of qualitative and quantitative data from a study that we conducted as part of the Latino Acculturation and Health Project; these data delineate how the challenges of immigration influence the functioning of Latino family systems and family relationships. As part of the Latino Acculturation and Health Project, more than three hundred Latino families living in either North Carolina or Arizona completed quantitative measures on a variety of psychosocial constructs. In addition, we conducted intense qualitative interviews with parents and adolescents from one hundred of those families (at least one parent and one adolescent); each of these interviews lasted between three and four hours.

Figure 2.2 shows the conceptual model generated from our analyses of qualitative data on Latino family system changes and enculturation after immigration, which used grounded theory methods (Bacallao and Smokowski 2007). The bold titles within each box are abstract concepts underpinned by the indicators shown by the bullet points in the lists. For all the families that were interviewed, these concepts and indicators were salient for both the adolescent and parent data. All of the concept-and-indicators clusters were associated with overall adjustment in the Latino families. This conceptual model of postimmigration Latino family adjustment guides our presentation of findings. Each element in the model is illustrated by examples from the interviews with adolescents and parents; to protect the identity of study participants, we have used pseudonyms for attribution of the quotations.

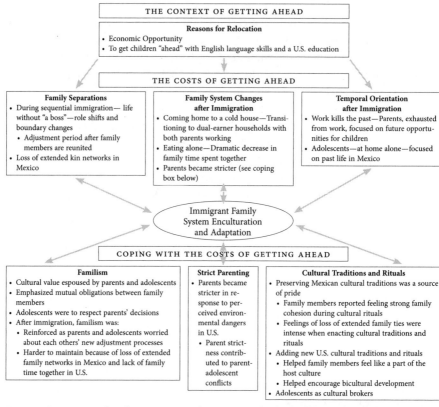

Fig. 2.2. Immigrant family system enculturation and adjustment after immigration (M. L. Bacallao and P. R. Smokowski, "The Costs of Getting Ahead: Mexican Family Systems after Immigration," *Family Relation* 56 [2007]: 52–66)

The Context of Getting Ahead

Relocation as a Means to "Get Ahead"

The Latino families interviewed for the Latino Acculturation and Health Project immigrated to the United States for two primary reasons. First, all of the families thought better job opportunities existed in the United States. Better jobs were important as a way to support not only the family that immigrated but also extended family in the country-of-origin. A number of the families thought of their immigration as a temporary status; they planned to save enough so they could return to their homelands and start businesses. All of the Mexican families discussed immigration as a means of escaping chronic poverty, and considered the most basic living conditions in the United States a marked improvement. One mother said,

Here, life is better for us than in Mexico. We have a plate of food at our table every night. We have this good, little house. We didn't have a house this good in Mexico. We earn a little money, and we eat well. Every night, we have food. It's good. (Sulema, mother)

The second reason the families gave for relocation was their desire to secure a better future for their children, referred to as "get our children ahead," which meant their children getting a U.S. education and learning English to increase their opportunities. "Getting ahead" was an organizing theme for all of the parents, which made immigration-related difficulties worthwhile and provided the parents with the inspiration to endure stressful times.

I have come to the conclusion that in this country, we, the parents, have to sacrifice so much to get our children ahead, to educate them. But at the same time, the children are a tremendous force for us [parents] to keep going. That's why I say, for me, the children come first. They are why we are here. (Guillermo, father)

Guillermo's response was typical of the parents' comments. One mother offered a metaphor:

I did not come here [to the United States] to become rich. I didn't even come here to be happy, no. We work like burros here. This is not a happier life. I came here to get my children ahead. I tell my children that we came here for them, and to become better persons. (Diocelina, mother)

Although the adolescents we interviewed understood that their parents brought them to the United States to give them a better future, the adolescents were not included in the decision to immigrate. Because of the strong hierarchical structure of the Latino family, the decision to relocate was made by the parents. Therefore, parents and adolescents had dramatically different orientations in the postimmigration adjustment process. Parents focused on the future and the enhanced opportunities their children would have with bilingual skills and a U.S. education. In contrast, the adolescents mourned their past life, focusing on the lifestyle, family, and friends they had left in their home countries. The following quotation captures one adolescent's ambivalence about living in the United States:

I understand it [immigration] was to give us a better future, for us kids, because my parents didn't want us to be in the same situation as them, they wanted us to do better than they did. Sometimes, I feel sad because I had to leave a place that I loved very much for something that's better, better in that we'd have better opportunities and that if we were to go back [to Mexico], I'd have more opportunities because I'd know another language, and maybe we'd be able to get better jobs. But, I miss my family, my cousins [in Mexico]. (Juana, female adolescent)

A Salvadorian male, Arturo, age eighteen, who had lived in the United States for three years, drew the cultural map presented in figure 2.3. He explained his enculturation feelings to the interviewer.

Arturo: *I was born in Mexico* [father is Mexican, mother is Salvadorian]. *I was a baby when we left. I was raised in San Salvador. My roots are there.* [paused] *My heart is there. I am Salvadorian. And we are here in the United States for our education.*
Interviewer: What holds those roots in the earth of San Salvador?
Arturo: *My family* [only nuclear family is in the United States], *my customs, the foods I love, my language, my friends, and my customs. I feel proud to be Salvadorian. My heart is there.*

Although parents and adolescents alike acknowledged the reasons for relocation—economic improvement and future opportunities for children—they went through different processes in their postimmigration adjustment to life in the United States. The possibility of getting ahead also entailed substantial costs to the family structure and dynamics. Immigration brought serious family system changes along with economic opportunities and enhanced prospects for children's futures. We discuss how these costs of getting ahead influenced the adolescents' and families' enculturation process in the sections that follow.

The Costs of Getting Ahead Undermine Enculturation

Family Separations

LIFE WITHOUT "A BOSS": SEQUENTIAL IMMIGRATION AND SHIFTING FAMILY ROLES

For many of the families, immigration occurred sequentially, with family members immigrating at different times over a period of a few months to many years. This type of immigration experience was common among the families, and disrupted family functioning long before the entire family

Fig. 2.3. Arturo's cultural map

immigrated. Fathers often relocated first to find work and lay the ground-work for bringing other family members to the United States. While trying to get settled in the United States, the fathers still contributed as much as they could to the well-being of the family by sending money home. At the same time, the father's absence influenced family equilibrium by causing a shift in members' roles and patterns of functioning.

The severity of separation problems appeared to depend upon the length of the separation. When the separation was short, six months to a year, families said they were able to cope with the stress. During the father's absence, mothers and children typically lived with and received support from extended family. Although families originally believed the separation from the father would last no more than a year, for a majority of families we interviewed the separation lasted considerably longer (three years or more). During these lengthy separations, the fathers who were undocumented immigrants were prevented from visiting their families because of their precarious legal status and the inherent risk and the high cost of being smuggled across the border (reported to be four thousand dollars or more for one undocumented person). Family members said that long separations brought significant changes in family roles and patterns of functioning, which contributed to family stress pre- and postimmigration.

The father's absence necessitated that the family restructure itself and establish new patterns of functioning. In several of the families we interviewed, both the father and the mother had immigrated, leaving their children in the care of grandparents, aunts, or uncles.

> *In Mexico, when my mother would get home from work, we would run and hug her, and then, when I came here, I didn't feel like running and hugging her. When they came here, they left me with my grandparents. I didn't see them* [parents] *anymore. There were other children living with them* [the grandparents], *and she* [the grandmother] *had to take care of them. And I did not see my mother or father. My mother wasn't there to take care of us. I knew that I would see her, because my mother told me when she came here* [to the United States] *that she would come for us, and I was only waiting for her to come for us. I waited eight months.* (Jorge, male adolescent)

The adolescents' loss of key relationships with their parent(s) undermined enculturation and family cohesion (familism). In the absence of these key relationships, adolescents, especially young males, sometimes drifted into high-risk situations such as getting involved with antisocial peers or engaging in illegal activities.

Adolescents said immigration caused the family to reconfigure itself around the parent who remained or the surrogate parents. Although this dynamic helped families cope with separation, it often created difficulties once the family was reunited. Manuel reported that during his father's absence he became strongly attached to his resilient mother. Manuel described his mother as the greatest influence in his life. After the family was reunited, Manuel and his father were unable to reinstate the quality of their previous relationship:

> *My mom probably influenced me the most. I got really close to her when my dad wasn't with me. She was like the head of the family, and somehow, even though my dad's with us now, that's never been restored. She's still the head of this family. Nothing against him, it's just the way she is as a figurehead. We grew up with her for six years while Dad was here* [in the United States]. *She takes charge.* (Manuel, male adolescent)

Another adolescent male also discussed intense bonding with his mother after his parents divorced following their immigration to the United States. The father returned to Mexico to take custody of his son when he heard that the boy had stopped going to school and was associating with delinquent peers. For the first time in eight years, the father and the son (and the father's second wife) began to live together. The son explained the difficulties he experienced in living with his father and stepmother:

> *We were separated seven or eight years. When I was . . . six, he* [father] *left* [for the United States]. *And he returned to get me when I was thirteen. I had little memory of him when he came back. Even though it's been three years that I'm here with him, it's still difficult for me to adapt to him, his way of being. Now I finally know how to control things better. Back there* [in Mexico], *there was no boss. My older brother was here. My stepfather was living in Chicago. There was no boss. It was difficult adjusting to a boss in this house. He told me when I got here that he was the boss. He didn't talk. But he would tell me to talk to my brother. Call my mother* [in Chicago]. *Talk to my sister. With my mother, I had a lot of trust. My father was more closed. I couldn't talk with him like I do with my mother. Well, he would tell me one thing: Use condoms. . . . That would be the only thing he'd tell me. My mother would explain everything to me. . . . I haven't developed that sense of trust with anyone else. . . . I'm still getting to know my father.* (Jaime, male adolescent)

Families described a postreunion adjustment period of family structural changes that involved reconfiguring roles, boundaries, and communication processes. For many families, the postimmigration reunion was a stormy period in which the father displayed aggressive behavior that had not been typical before immigration. Family members, especially mothers, said that it took at least one year to readjust to living with one another, and some continued to struggle with readjustment to family changes for several years.

THE LOSS OF EXTENDED KIN WHO DID NOT EMIGRATE

In addition to the stress of sequential immigration, those who immigrated also experienced separation from extended kin who remained in their country-of-origin. Given the importance many Latinos place on family cohesion, both adolescents and parents said it was difficult to bear the loss of close relationships with extended family (e.g., grandparents, aunts, uncles, cousins). Parents missed the companionship, support, and help provided by their extended family, and worried about aging relatives in their country-of-origin. Although one father said that he felt closer to his daughter after immigration because they had only their nuclear family in this country, this positive interpretation was an uncommon, contrasting view. All other parents and adolescents we interviewed said they missed the extensive family support that characterized their lives before immigration.

Indeed, adolescents reported missing extended family members as much as or more than they had missed their parents during sequential immigration separations. For adolescents, the family members who remained in their homelands were strongly linked to comforting childhood memories, especially if the relatives had served as surrogate parents during family separations. During the difficulties of adjusting to life in the United States, most adolescents thought of happy times with family members in their homelands. This focus on the past made adolescents report feeling ambivalent about their new lives in America.

> *It's going to be five years* [living in the United States]. *Sometimes it gets easier because you start thinking, well, in a little while I'll be going back* [to Mexico], *but sometimes it gets harder because you wonder, how are things back home? It's been five years that you're thinking about these things to yourself. Are they fat? Skinny? Big? Strong? How is everyone? How is it living over there now? Five years, and I haven't visited. My parents sometimes think about visiting, but in reality, I don't know if we'll actually do it. In my cultural map, I drew Mexico, where I'm happy, where I feel good because I know I'm from there. And that's where my family is, so that's where I feel good. And here* [in the United States], *I feel confused. I'm confused about whether I'm happy here, or if it would be better over there* [in Mexico] *where my family is. One always needs family. Usually when I start thinking about these things, my family over there, I try to think about other things. I miss one of my sisters. I love her, and we lived together, so she's like one of my sisters. We grew up together. But she's really my cousin. I was thinking to draw me missing her* [on the U.S. side of the paper]. (Juana, female adolescent)

A major piece of Latino family enculturation emphasizes *familism*, which is an overarching belief that family comes first and is at the center of one's world. Understandably, nostalgic memories were particularly enticing when adolescents felt lonely, isolated, and friendless, making most yearn to return to their homelands. Although a source of sadness, these memories and attachments also served to sustain one adolescent from Colombia during her difficult adjustment to life in America when she was depressed and suicidal. When the interviewer asked if she was thinking of hurting herself, the adolescent responded saying,

Sometimes—I've felt that way when I feel shut in, when there are prob-lems, when I've just had a fight with my mom or dad, things like that. The only thing I do is I get into my room and I make myself think. I just try to let it pass. I used to be a happy person. So, I just try to let this thing pass. [She started to cry.] *I think about my grandparents, my uncles, my friends* [back in Colombia]. *I haven't seen my uncles and grandparents for so long that I feel like I hardly know them. But I think about them and how they would suffer if this happened to me* [if she hurt herself attempting suicide]. *So, no, I can't let them down. They would suffer so much.* (Teresa, female adolescent)

Memories of her family in Colombia fueled this adolescent's sense of family loyalty and prevented her from hurting herself. However, for other adoles-cents, memories of extended family and associated feelings of loss and grief contributed to depression. This young girl's experience of shifting from be-ing "a happy person" to being depressed provides a bridge to broaden our discussion of family separations to postimmigration family system stress.

Family System Changes after Immigration

COMING HOME TO A COLD HOUSE: THE TRANSFORMATION INTO DUAL-EARNER HOUSEHOLDS

In most Latin American countries, fathers typically played the role of family provider, maintaining low-paying employment and shouldering fi-nancial responsibilities for the family. Mothers often managed the home and took primary responsibility for raising children. Parents and adoles-cents described traditional gender roles reinforced by the cultural norms (enculturation) from their country-of-origin.

After immigrating, the families often have to restructure into dual-earner households. Financial stress and the higher cost of living in the United States propelled many mothers to enter the labor force for the first time, which presented another difficult adjustment for families. Latino men who were invested in traditional gender roles said they found having a working wife particularly distressing because it publicly displayed that the father, as head of the household, could not solely provide for his fam-ily. Women found jobs in factories, cafeterias, restaurants, or hotel house-keeping services. According to both parents and adolescents, the amount of time the family had to spend together decreased dramatically. All fami-lies reported that this change took a toll on both the marital relationship and parent-child relationships. In addition, with both parents working outside of the home, adolescents were left unsupervised for long periods. This new dynamic conflicted with the cultural value that family should spend as much time as possible together. One father described his difficulty with the changes.

> *In Mexico, I would come home with my little briefcase, and my kids would come greet me when I came home. They'd say, "Dad! Dad! What do you bring?" I have this or I have that. . . . Now, no, I come home to an empty and cold house. Empty and cold, because there's no one here. We only share our time together for a little while. We miss out on some conversation, something we may need to say to one another. In Mexico, I had my worries from work, but as soon as I go home, my bad mood would be gone. The aggravations from work would go away because people are waiting for you. My wife would tell me, "Look, I just made you your favorite dish," or simply, "I made you your cup of coffee how you like it." In the U.S., we both come home from work with the same bad mood.* (Carmelo, father)

HOW WORK KILLS THE PAST: PARENTS' STRESS FROM
DEMANDING JOBS

Dual-earner families described being overloaded and having little flexibility to absorb additional stressors. In the example below, a mother described the conflict she felt about having to work while she worried about not having enough time to give to her adolescent children as well as her ailing mother who lived nearby.

> *I would like my daughter to talk to someone. She doesn't have papers, but she needs to talk to someone . . . like a psychologist. I'm not home to be with her. I had to work. The jobs here are tiring, very tiring. But we must keep our eyes on our children, and get them ahead. My husband and I have three teenagers, and one married daughter. . . . We have to sacrifice so many things to get the family ahead. There are so many more worries about our children here. I just want to sit here and cry, but my children, they lift me.* (Alicia, mother)

Family stress seemed to be aggravated by the nature of the parents' work, especially work that was physically exhausting and emotionally stressful. The parents' overall fatigue may be one reason why parents did not seem to mourn separations with extended kin to the same extent as adolescents. Exhausted parents had little time to reminisce; their focus was on daily life and the ongoing struggle to support their families in their homelands and in the United States. One parent described what it was like to be consumed by work.

Work kills all your concentration on what used to be. By working, you don't realize anything but what is in front of you, the job ahead of you. I concentrate so much on myself and on my job. That's how I adapted. You learn about the ways here at your job. (Miguel, father)

In addition to the demanding physical labor, parents found their skills did not translate to work settings in America, which required quick acquisition of new skills, often without the benefit of adequate communication with supervisors. The language barrier made this occupational adjustment particularly difficult. Men described having to learn complicated skills, such as using new machinery or furniture assembly, after watching a task performed only once or twice. Most fathers and some of the working mothers described their frustration about being unable to advance at work because of their limited English language skills. This frustration was compounded by daily experiences of discrimination such as being told, "Go back where you came from!" However, parents did not measure their success by their work, but rather thought of work and the stress inherent in their jobs as sacrifices they were willing to make to provide for their families. For the parents, success meant helping their children get ahead.

EATING ALONE: FAMILY RELATIONSHIPS AND THE DECREASE IN
SHARED FAMILY TIME

In dual-earner households, parents' stress related to work influenced parent-adolescent relationships, family dynamics, enculturation, and communication processes. Many parents worked twelve-hour days, six days per week, and most worked jobs with hourly pay, with the more hours worked meaning greater financial gain for the family. In addition, some adolescents took part-time jobs at fast food restaurants to help with family finances. These work schedules substantially reduced the amount of shared family time. Moreover, conflicting work and school schedules meant that some parents would not see their adolescents for one to three days. Because the Latino family is the crucible for maintaining enculturation, some adolescents said decreased family time undermined their culture-of-origin involvement. A female adolescent commented on the impact of work on family life.

My relationship with my parents has changed because, in El Salvador, Mom was always at home while we were at school. She would do the housework

... ironing. When I came home from school, everything was ready, the food would be prepared, the clothes were washed and ironed and all that, you know? I would sit down with Mom and Dad to eat. And in the U.S., sometimes I don't see my dad for three days. Living in the same house, you know? For example, I go to school, then I go to work and sometimes, I get home late at night, and he's already sleeping when I come home. And the next day, it's the same thing. I don't get to see him until the third day. That's changed our relationship when you don't eat with each other every day. (Marisa, female adolescent)

Less family time also translates into adolescents having to handle problems on their own. Some adolescents in our sample described feeling isolated, lonely, and depressed even when in their family home. Such feelings of sadness seemed to stem from grieving the loss of time and sense of intimacy with their parents and family that the teens had known prior to immigration; this experience was reflected in the words of a female adolescent:

I just stay in my room. I like to draw. . . . Sometimes, I'll sleep. There's no one in the house. I don't go out of my bedroom for anything except to brush my teeth and wash myself. My mother is always working or going to church. My mother and sister are gone, so, here is where I pass the time. Alone. Always alone. (Reyna, female adolescent)

Increased unsupervised time also allowed adolescents the opportunity to get into trouble. One father described how his son, who remained in Mexico, began habitually skipping school after the father immigrated. The father responded by bringing the adolescent to the United States; however, the teen continued to take advantage of his father's absence during long work days. On one occasion, the police escorted the boy home when he was found in an abandoned house, partying with friends who were involved with a Mexican gang. After the father exerted a great deal of effort and imposed structure on the teen's life, this adolescent began to attend school regularly. The father commented:

He's changed 100 percent. When he lived in Mexico, he did not go to school. I decided I had to go to Mexico and bring him here. He is relatively intelligent, and I had to get him out of that situation in Mexico. . . . Since he's been here, he has been told that he has to go to school, and if he doesn't go to school, he will get me in trouble. And if he doesn't obey me, he will get both of us in trouble, in trouble with the law. His behavior can either protect us, or can get us into problems.

Also, he doesn't have his mother near him since he left Mexico. That has been difficult for him. He's had to adapt to being more on his own in the house. When I come home from work, I have to pay more attention to where he's going, what he did that day, if the homework is done. It's difficult because I work all day, and then, this at home. (Victor, father)

The changes in family structure and the stressors related to these new family systems had different psychological impacts on parents and adolescents. The most difficult challenge for many of the immigrant families was dealing with the postimmigration acculturation gap that emerged between parents and adolescents when they adjusted to the new culture at different rates.

Parent-Adolescent Acculturation Gaps

A substantial body of research has suggested that following immigration, two occurrences substantially affect the family system: (a) acculturation differences (i.e., gaps) between parents and adolescents precipitate family stress (Szapocznik and Kurtines 1980; Hernandez and McGoldrick 1999) and (b) the strong sense of family cohesion (i.e., familism) that is inherent in many Latino immigrant families erodes over time (Rogler and Cooney 1984; Cortes 1995). These two major changes to family dynamics stand out among the costs of getting ahead in the United States.

Normative parent-adolescents conflicts can be exacerbated by acculturation stress, creating intercultural as well as intergenerational difficulties (Coatsworth, Pantin, and Szapocznik 2002). Children typically acculturate faster than adults, creating an acculturation gap between generations, which, in turn, can bring about additional family stress (Szapocznik and Kurtines 1980; Hernandez and McGoldrick 1999). Because of the potential for conflicting cultural ideas to disrupt family equilibrium, Latino parents fear their adolescents' adoption of the new culture, and respond by trying to preserve their culture-of-origin beliefs and norms within the family by making the family boundaries rigid (Hernandez and McGoldrick 1999). The resulting cultural conflict between new ideologies and preserving established cultural beliefs is likely to fuel adolescent rebellion, alienate adolescents from parents, and contribute to the development of adolescent behavioral problems (Szapocznik et al. 1986; Coatsworth, Pantin, and Szapocznik 2002).

The idea that differences in cultural adaptation between parents and their adolescent children cause stress and dysfunction in immigrant families is called *acculturation discrepancy theory*. This theory suggests that adolescents assimilate faster than their parents, and that males assimilate faster than females, leaving cultural gaps between both family generations and genders (Szapocznik and Kurtines 1980). The largest gaps, between mothers and sons, are often thought to arise because daughters (relative to sons) are given less freedom to be away from the family. The parent-adolescent tensions that are normative during adolescent development are often exacerbated by the acculturation gaps between adolescents who are rapidly assimilating and parents who are holding onto their culture-of-origin.

As predicted by the acculturation discrepancy theory, children of immigrants tend to acquire English, adopt new values and lifestyle preferences, and form cross-racial relationships more readily than their parents (Lau et al. 2005). Research indicates that intergenerational differences in social values become more pronounced the longer families are in the United States (Phinney, Ong, and Madden 2000). Moreover, research has provided evidence that adolescent U.S.-culture involvement (assimilation) is associated with family dynamics (e.g., parent-adolescent conflict, family cohesion, family adaptability, and familism). For example, Khanh Dinh and her colleagues (2002) reported that parental involvement in their adolescent's life mediated the influence of assimilation on teens' proneness toward problem behavior. Further, researchers who examined a large sample of 732 Mexican American adolescents reported that teens' assimilation significantly predicted family conflict (McQueen, Getz, and Bray 2003). In addition, other researchers found that adolescent assimilation was positively associated with changes in family dynamics such as family conflict, inconsistent discipline, and decreased parental monitoring (Samaniego and Gonzales 1999). Similarly, Nancy Gonzales and colleagues (2006) reported that family conflict was an important mediator that linked family linguistic acculturation to increased externalizing symptoms (e.g., aggressive behavior) among youth. Our work with the Latino Acculturation and Health Project showed that characteristics of family dynamics, such as familism and parent-adolescent conflict, mediated the effects of acculturation conflicts on adolescent aggression (Smokowski and Bacallao 2006).

Acculturation discrepancy theorists explain the deleterious relationship between adolescents' U.S.-culture involvement and family conflict not only as a sign that adolescents are turning away from their culture-of-origin as they integrate into the host culture but also as a sign that their parents are resisting their adolescent child's cultural change. In the early diffusion-bifurcation stage of bicultural development, it appears that adolescents expend disproportionate amounts of time and effort becoming involved in the U.S. culture; however, their involvement may appear disproportionate only because they are inundated with new information that they must integrate if they are to survive in their new cultural surroundings.

Qualitative studies have suggested that adolescents with high levels of integration into the host culture contribute to family resilience by both serving as language translators for their parents and serving as cultural brokers for their families (Suarez-Orozco and Suarez-Orozco 2001; Parra-Cordona et al. 2006). This new level of family responsibility often prompts adolescents to mature. However, some adolescents have abused the power inherent in their new roles and taken advantage of the complex changes in the family system that occur after immigration (Bacallao and Smokowski 2007).

Despite their valued new roles as cultural brokers, younger family members who are rapidly acculturating may adopt norms and values of the host society that conflict with those held by older, less acculturated family members (Szapocznik and Williams 2000; Coatsworth, Pantin, and Szapocznik 2002). For example, the U.S. system favors individualism, and Latino adolescents' increased autonomy within that system often clashes with their parents' adherence to traditional values that emphasize familism and parental control (Lau et al. 2005). Latino parents are often ambivalent about their adolescent child's acculturation, both seeing the advantages of educational opportunities opening in the new culture and worrying about opportunities for adolescent risk taking (Bacallao and Smokowski 2007). Latino parents may become protective, directive, or even authoritarian to preserve the cultural roles and patterns of their culture-of-origin (Hernandez and McGoldrick 1999).

Although the hypothesis that acculturation gaps lead to parent-adolescent conflict and family stress has been discussed since the 1980s, few researchers have attempted to go beyond clinical anecdotes and test the hypothesis empirically (Gonzales et al. 2002; Vega et al. 1995). However, Andres Gil, William Vega, and Juanita Dimas (1994) found that Hispanic youths' perceptions of intergenerational acculturation gaps were associated with increased conflicts with their parents, but these conflicts were not related to the youths' self-esteem. Similarly, William Vega and his colleagues (1995) found that neither parental acculturation nor youth reports of acculturation conflicts were related to parents' or teachers' ratings of youth behavior problems.

A few researchers have tried to measure acculturation gaps using psychosocial scales that gauge participants' involvement in both their culture-of-origin and the U.S. culture. For example, the Bicultural Involvement Questionnaire (BIQ) is a self-report questionnaire with forty items that comprise two subscales: involvement in Latino culture and involvement in non-Latino U.S. culture. Both BIQ subscales have twenty questions that use a five-point Likert scale to measure preferences related to language, food, recreation, and media. The scale anchors are labeled not at all to very much. Examples of questions for the U.S. cultural involvement subscale include, "How comfortable do you feel speaking English (1) at home, (2) with friends, (3) in general" and "How much do you enjoy (non-Latino) U.S. . . . (1) music, (2) television programs, (3) books and magazines?" Parallel questions are asked for Latino cultural involvement: "How comfortable do you feel speaking Spanish (1) at home, (2) with friends, (3) in general" and "How much do you enjoy (1) music, (2) television programs, (3) books and magazines from your culture-of-origin?" A quantitative measure of the acculturation gap is derived by collecting scales like these from adolescents and their parents. For each subscale, the adolescent's scores are subtracted from the parents' scores, resulting in a gap score.

Charles Martinez Jr. (2006) found that the adolescent-parent acculturation gap (as measured by BIQ "Americanism" scores) had a significant, inverse relationship with effective parenting practices. Similarly, Crane and colleagues (2005) examined a sample of forty-one immigrant Chinese families and found a significant relationship between parent-adolescent BIQ difference scores and adolescent depression and delinquency. However, when Lauri Pasch and her colleagues (2006) operationalized acculturation gaps using parent and adolescent reports on the language subscale of the Marin Acculturation Scale, they did not find a significant relationship between parent-adolescent acculturation gaps and parent-adolescent conflict or adolescent adjustment problems. In a fourth study, Anna Lau and her colleagues (2005) examined parent-adolescent acculturation discrepancy scores on both culture-of-origin and U.S.- culture involvement scales in a sample of 260 high-risk, predominantly U.S.-born Mexican American families. Acculturation discrepancy scores were not associated with parent-youth conflict or youth conduct problems.

In our research using the Latino Acculturation and Health Project sample of 402 Latino families living in North Carolina or Arizona, we found that parent-adolescent acculturation gaps measured by the BIQ subscales were related to family dynamics. Families with parents who were highly involved in their culture-of-origin and adolescents who had low levels of U.S.-culture involvement (i.e., families with small cultural gaps) tended to report high levels of family cohesion, adaptability, and familism. However, these acculturation gaps were not associated with parent-adolescent conflict as suggested by the acculturation discrepancy theory.

These studies have provided mixed evidence regarding the influence of an acculturation gap on adolescent behavior. However, the presence of an acculturation gap within a family appears to adversely affect family dynamics, especially familism. As a result, decreased family cohesion enhances the chances of parent-adolescent conflict occurring. The resulting conflict has been found to be a strong risk factor related to adolescent aggressive behavior (Smokowski, Rose, and Bacallao 2009), internalizing symptoms such as anxiety and depression (Smokowski, Rose, and Bacallao 2009) and substance use (Buchanan and Smokowski 2009)

Delineating the costs of getting ahead (e.g., family separations, decreased family time, stresses of dual-earner households, acculturation gaps, reduced family cohesion, and increased parent-adolescent conflict) provides a helpful bridge to shift our focus to the ways in which parents and adolescents cope with these challenges after immigration.

Coping with the Costs of Getting Ahead

Parental Strictness as a Means to Counter Americanization

Parents and adolescents who participated in our Latino Acculturation and Health Project (LAHP) interviews reported that parents tended to become stricter after immigrating to the United States. This change was both an important factor in parent-adolescent dynamics and a strategy for coping with new family stressors. Parents had little time to spend with their children and were worried about perceived dangers in the new environment (e.g., drug use, having too much freedom). In this new context for parenting and without a support network, parents did not allow their adolescents many opportunities to explore their new environment. In addition, parents reported feeling vulnerable to the effects of their adolescents' behavior, such as misbehavior that would bring involvement of authorities. Families in the United States without legal papers were especially worried about being involved with the police, which may be one of the reasons parents restricted their adolescents' freedom outside the home. These restrictions applied to organized activities as well, and adolescents' participation in school-affiliated activities was uncommon. Parents and adolescents acknowledged that the rules were stricter for daughters than for sons. Daughters were given little latitude to socialize outside of the home, and although sons generally had more freedom than daughters, sons were cautioned more frequently to obey the law and avoid legal trouble. A female adolescent commented on her understanding of the strict parenting:

I think for us Latinos there are more restrictions at home because our parents do not exactly know how it is out there, and how other [American] *people are. . . . They feel better if we stay home. Maybe because they do not want us to behave like [Americans] that we are [Mexicans]. In other words, that we don't become so liberal but rather that we remain like we were before we left our home country. So we do not change our way of being. When you are too liberal many things can happen to you. One of them is using drugs, or having trouble with your studies. Those are things the parents fear that will happen here. They do not want that to happen, so they do not want you to go out.* (Eva, female adolescent)

Adolescents said that parental strictness caused the most parent-child conflict. Among the families interviewed for the LAHP study, 70 percent of adolescents disagreed with their parents' decisions regarding restrictions, although they acquiesced to those decisions. It was difficult for adolescents to question their parents' decisions because these immigrant family systems strongly valued familism and respect for parents (*respeto*). This conflict left the adolescents quietly simmering against parents who set the restrictive rules. Several parents reported that having their children question their decisions brought home to them the extent to which the adolescents were becoming "Americanized." For example, when one father complained that his wife and daughter did not do any housework while he was working, the daughter contradicted him. Her mother advised her to show respect to her father by not disagreeing with him. She thought her daughter had learned this unacceptable behavior by watching American teens talk back to their fathers.

One mother commented on her daughter's Americanized attitude:

Eva will say to me . . . "Well, why is that not good?" And I'll repeat, "Why is that not good?" At her age, I wouldn't dare question my parents. I wouldn't even think of it. She's questioning her parent [facial expression widened with disbelief]. I say these kids are Americanized in those ways. But I will tell her "I don't have to answer that question because I am your mother. You don't ask me to explain 'why.'" I think that correction is needed because our customs are this way. (Zunilda, mother)

It was clear from our interviews that the acculturation gap itself did not prove to be particularly problematic in most families. This finding contradicts existing acculturation discrepancy theory about acculturation gaps. Perhaps the lack of conflict can be explained by the fact that at the same time that they picked up host culture ways, most of the adolescents maintained high levels of involvement with their culture-of-origin norms, values, and traditions. Although Miguel Hernandez and Monica McGoldrick's

(1999) report that parent-adolescent conflict arose from the acculturation gap, we found that parent-adolescent conflict revolved around the parents' fears of the dangers they perceived in the U.S. environment. In the families we interviewed for the LAHP, parent-adolescent conflict arose most often when adolescents requested—and were denied—permission to recreate outside the home. Indeed, the acculturation gaps may actually serve an adaptive purpose in allowing adolescents to become cultural brokers for their families, which is a role that encourages maturity and responsibility.

Thus, family discrepancies in cultural beliefs may not inevitably lead to family dysfunction and youth behavioral disorder. Rapid behavioral acculturation in immigrant youth, along with concomitant maintenance of culture-of-origin beliefs, may be associated with gains in functioning (Lau et al. 2005). Immigrant children tend to adopt roles of responsibility (e.g., cultural brokers, translators, caregivers for younger siblings), and these ecological demands may enhance rather than compromise their functioning. Language brokering has been associated with positive social and academic outcomes among Latino adolescents (Buriel, Calzada, and Vasquez 1982). Andrew Fuligni and his colleagues (Fuligni 1998, Fuligni, Yip, and Tseng 2002) have described how immigrant youth artfully balance their cultural obligations to their families with the demands of being a U.S. adolescent, with few psychological costs and notable benefits to the adolescents' emotional and academic functioning.

> They [parents] *need us because there's a barrier here for them. We've gotten over the barrier so we can help them. It's like, they know when they're going to hit the barrier, and before they hit it, we help them, so they don't have to hit it. It's easier that way for them. My parents didn't really* [emphasized the word "really"] *have to adapt because of us* [the children]. *We are there as their mediator between the two cultures, and when they need something, they'll say, "Can you help us out?" . . . We don't tell them that we need this or that. We go to the bank, the doctor, the store. We* [the children] *help them. Like at the bank, they'll say, "Say this for us." So they really didn't need to adapt too much. They live their way here, and when they want something from the outside, they come to us, and that's just how it is. We help them out.* (Manuel, male adolescent)

Along with this new power comes responsibility: the responsibility inherent in using new cultural knowledge and language skills to assist their parents. Just as any parent would worry about his or her young children venturing outside the safety of the home, immigrant adolescents experienced a role reversal in worrying about their parents being vulnerable in the new cultural system, without the language skills and ability to navigate in complex systems.

To summarize, we found that parent-adolescent relationships underwent poignant changes in the postimmigration adjustment period. Parents had less time to spend with their children because of demanding new jobs and the financial necessity that propelled mothers to enter the workforce. This decreased family time may not only increase adolescents' feelings of loneliness and isolation but can also lead to increases in adolescent risk-taking behavior. In response to perceived environmental threats, immigrant parents commonly adopted a more authoritarian parenting strategy, which often precipitated parent-adolescent conflict. However, these conflicts did not appear to be driven by acculturation gaps. On the contrary, acculturation gaps seemed to serve protective functions when acculturating adolescents take on new roles and responsibilities within the family by helping their parents navigate the new cultural system.

Cultural Assets and Family Strengths after Immigration

FAMILISM

Immediate family members relied on a strong sense of familism (i.e., family cohesion, trust, loyalty, and mutual support) to cope with stressors in the new cultural system (Parra-Cardona et al. 2006). Familism has been argued to be "the most important factor influencing the lives of Latinos" (Coohey 2001, 130). This strong sense of family orientation, obligation, and cohesion has noteworthy protective effects (Vega et al. 1995). For example, Carol Coohey (2001) found that familism was an important deterrent to child maltreatment in both Latino and non-Latino families. Andres Gil, Eric Wagner, and William Vega (2000) reported that familism had a highly significant, negative association with acculturation stress. Equally important, they found that this relationship was stronger for immigrant Latino adolescents than for U.S.-born Latino adolescents (−.43 immigrant, −.33 for U.S. born). For both groups, familism had an indirect protective effect on youths' use of alcohol by decreasing their disposition toward socially deviant behavior. In our LAHP study, we consistently found that familism was a cultural asset that was positively related to adolescents' self-esteem and inversely related to parent-adolescent conflict, adolescent aggressive behavior, and internalizing symptoms such as anxiety and depression (Smokowski, Bacallao, and Rose 2010; Smokowski, Rose, and Bacallao 2009). One adolescent captured the concept of familism when he expressed his devotion to his family.

I think it's being close to my family. That's always a really big part of the Hispanic population, being close to the family, and the family being a priority all the time. My friends, they've always got time for school sports, being at school after school. For me, it's my family. And it's not strange. I have people say, "Why do you want to go to a party where your family's at? Don't you want to get away from them?" You know, I don't really get tired of them. I've always been really close to them. That connection to my parents, that trust that you can talk to them, that makes me Mexican. (Juan, male adolescent)

Familism was an important cultural asset for the Latino adolescents who said they could relax physically and emotionally with family members unlike with anyone else. Among these adolescents, there was a pervasive sense that their families supported them emotionally, especially in difficult times. At the same time, the adolescents had important obligations, such as the respect and obedience that parents said they expected from their children. However, families had a shared sense of success and failure. Although parents believed their success and accomplishments were for their children, they also reported they would feel it a personal failure if their children did not succeed. Adolescents were aware of this obligation to succeed, and said that their own failure becomes their parents' failure.

Parents and adolescents alike said that familism, in the form of helping the family, was the force motivating some family members to become bilingual and bicultural. Adolescents were proud to take on the role of cultural broker or translator for their parents; parents were proud of their adolescents' new cultural skills, and regarded those skills as a sign that their children were getting ahead. Despite that pride, parents worried about how their adolescent's biculturalism would affect the family's future. Parents were highly invested in keeping their family together, and worried that the family might ultimately end up separated between two countries. One mother remarked,

Now, if the children want to stay here, and the parents have finished educating their children and want to return to their land, that is difficult because the family doesn't stay together after all this. . . . [W]e come here to grab . . . economic security for our children, and then the family separates in two countries? . . . That is worrisome. And it happens at the end, when the obstacles have been overcome. (Adriana, mother)

Although all parents and adolescents described familism as a core Latino family value both pre- and postimmigration, familism evolved into a complex concept after immigration that reflected a dialectic. Familism appeared to be strengthened after immigration because a new language and new systems fostered greater dependence upon family members. At the same time, family ties were often more difficult to maintain post-immigration because of new circumstances such as both parents working multiple jobs, distance from family left in the country-of-origin, and uncertainty over the family's future after adolescents had grown accustomed to life in the United States.

Unfortunately, familism is also thought to decrease as acculturation progresses. Lloyd Rogler and Rosemary Cooney (1984) found that, as adults, second-generation children had lower levels of familism than their first-generation immigrant parents. This deterioration of familism may go far in explaining why researchers have found significant differences between immigrant and U.S.-born generations. Moreover, the loss of family cohesion may open avenues for adolescents to engage in a greater number of risky health behaviors. However, few studies have taken a longitudinal perspective. It is possible that second-generation children may emphasize individualism during adolescence and young adulthood only to rediscover familism when they start raising their own children. If that is the case, these individuals would most likely strive to maintain a bicultural perspective (Zayas and Palleja 1988; Sanchez-Flores 2003).

CULTURAL TRADITIONS AND RITUALS

Maintaining cultural rituals and traditions was one way in which families described staying close to their culture-of-origin. For adolescents, practicing these traditions and rituals helped them to create a sense of cultural identity and ethnic pride even as they experienced outside pressure to assimilate to U.S. culture. Adolescents interviewed in the LAHP study said that they felt Mexican or Colombian because of the traditions their family observed. Parents said that they would never abandon the traditions and rituals that helped to build family identity and unity. Although some religious holidays (e.g., Christmas) were common to the country-of-origin and the United States, other celebrations and rituals differed substantially. Families mentioned maintaining observances of traditional Latin American holidays that are not typically celebrated in the United States, such as Dia de los Muertos (Day of the Dead), which honors deceased ancestors, and Posadas, which is celebrated from December 16 to December 24 to commemorate Mary and Joseph's arduous journey to Bethlehem. However, the family members reported that those holiday observances did not feel the same without their family members who remained in their homelands. One mother shared her insights about the importance of family traditions:

Customs and traditions have changed, yes, in the sense that I don't have my whole family here. We do celebrate Christmas, but it is not the same. Still, I wouldn't let go of my Mexican traditions. Now I must think of my family as my husband and my children. When there is a celebration where traditional foods are made, we really enjoy ourselves. There is much happiness. The traditions that I've brought from Mexico, how we celebrate holidays is very different. There is no Christmas here like there was in my town. We would begin Christmas festivities the 16th of December and continue them until January. (Graciela, mother)

In the diffused stage of postimmigration adjustment, cultural rituals and traditions may actually increase the bifurcation adolescents feel between their cultural worlds. Just as parents strongly supported the continuity of culture-of-origin identity at home, so the host culture dominated their school and work experiences. Adolescents commonly perceived a chasm between these two cultural worlds, which took time to reconcile.

ADOPTING AND ADAPTING NEW CUSTOMS

The postimmigration adjustment process also prompted families to adopt new traditions and rituals. Adopting and adapting U.S. cultural traditions and rituals helped the immigrant families take part in the host culture. One adolescent explained how learning celebrations and traditions was a key aspect of feeling part of the host culture and a sign of growing bicultural competencies.

I like to learn about the things that the [U.S.] culture likes to celebrate, its traditions. Halloween, St. Patrick's Day, Mother's Day, all of those. These holidays are different and that is why you learn and feel a part of them, even if you are not too much a part, but you feel a part of this culture. You learn your culture and you learn other cultures, and you mix the cultures, and you can make something new out of one and the other, or you can pick the way that you like how things are done. (Eva, female adolescent)

A mother from another family expressed a similar sentiment, explaining how her family adapts new cultural customs to participate in the host culture.

My daughter is learning a little more English, and we can start grabbing some of their [American] customs. Like here, the first year we heard, "No work tomorrow. It's Thanksgiving." And we say among ourselves, "What's Thanksgiving?" Then the second year, we started knowing a little more of

what Thanksgiving is. Little by little, we learn the customs. We know that we
give thanks to God on Thanksgiving. We said, "We can do that here at home."
We start grabbing a little of their customs because we live here. I think we
must learn their [American] *customs, and celebrate what we can of them.*
(Adriana, mother)

ETHNIC CULTURE-OF-ORIGIN IDENTITY

The combined power of familism and maintaining culture-of-origin tradition and rituals produced a high degree of ethnic identity in the immigrant adolescents we interviewed. Culture-of-origin identity was the foundation for Latino influence. Adolescents who were born outside the United
States had important memories of customs, lifestyles, places, and people
they had left behind when they immigrated. Parents often described this
sense of identity as "being in their blood." For example, when asked what it
was about Mexico he would never let go of, one adolescent responded, "My
blood, Mexican blood, my country's flag, and my color [pointed to arm]
—all this makes me proud to be Mexican."

Researchers have consistently found a positive relationship between
an individual's culture-of-origin involvement and his or her self-esteem
(Gonzales et al. 2002; Martinez and Dukes 1997; Phinney, Cantu, and Kurtz
1997; Phinney and Chavira 1995). After examining a sample of 669 Latino,
African American, and white U.S.-born high school students, Jean Phinney
and her colleagues (1997) reported that culture-of-origin involvement, in
the form of ethnic identity, predicted higher self-esteem in all three ethnic
groups. In contrast, assimilation, in the form of U.S.-culture involvement,
predicted self-esteem for only the white adolescents. This association has
been further confirmed in a meta-analysis that showed culture-of-origin
involvement to have a moderately strong, positive relationship with self-esteem across ethnicities, gender, and age groups (Bat-Chava and Steen 2000
as cited in Gonzales et al. 2002).

In the LAHP study, we found that culture-of-origin involvement and
biculturalism were cultural assets with a positive relationship to family
cohesion and adaptability (Smokowski, Rose, and Bacallao 2008). Our
initial findings showed that adolescents' levels of both culture-of-origin
involvement and familism were inversely associated with adolescent aggression (Smokowski and Bacallao 2007). Similarly, Taylor and colleagues'
(1997) findings showed that adolescent culture-of-origin involvement and
familism were inversely associated with adolescent aggression.

In our longitudinal analyses from LAHP, Latino culture-of-origin involvement influenced internalizing symptoms and self-esteem by decreasing feelings of humiliation and by promoting familism for immigrant and

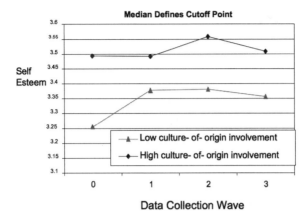

Fig. 2.4. Adolescent self-esteem by culture-of-origin involvement (LAHP: N = 323)

U.S.-born adolescents (Smokowski, Bacallao, and Buchanan forthcoming). Culture-of-origin involvement also leads to lower levels of adolescent aggression by increasing familism and self-esteem (Smokowski, Buchanan, and Bacallao forthcoming). The longitudinal association between culture-of-origin involvement and self-esteem for the 349 adolescents in the LAHP study is shown in figure 2.4 (Smokowski, Bacallao, and Rose 2010). Each of the four data collection waves was separated by a six-month interval; at all four waves, Latino adolescents with higher culture-of-origin involvement reported significantly higher levels of self-esteem.

Conclusions

This chapter explored three major questions: How do Latino families change after immigration? How do these changes affect family members, their interactions, and their sense of enculturation? What factors explain postimmigration family system adjustment? Using grounded theory methods, we created a conceptual model explaining Latino immigrant family adjustment (see figure 2.2). Past research on Latino immigrant families contends that the emergence of an acculturation gap in a family precipitates parent-adolescent relationship stress, and that familism decreases with time spent in the United States (Szapocznik and Kurtines 1980; Cortes 1995; Coatsworth, Pantin, and Szapocznik 2002). If these dynamics were indeed occurring, we wanted to illuminate why they were taking place and what underlying processes were fueling the changes in parent-adolescent relationships and the family system as a whole, using the conceptual model that emerged from the data.

The conceptual model shown in figure 2.2 delineated three major domains related to postimmigration adjustment of immigrant families: the context of "getting ahead," the costs of getting ahead, and coping with the costs of getting ahead. In the context for getting ahead, parents we interviewed said they had relocated to the United States for work opportunities and to get their children ahead by providing them with English language skills and a U.S. education. Families in this study also described a number of "costs" or challenges associated with getting ahead (e.g., family separations, becoming a dual-earner household, spending less time together, loss of relationships with extended family that remained in the country-of-origin).

Our conceptual model helps to explain why past researchers found that familism eroded over time spent in the United States (Rogler and Cooney 1984; Cortes 1995) and also posits new theoretical propositions for future research. Geographic separations disrupt the social support of immigrants, separating them from the extensive network of family relationships they enjoyed in their native lands. Immigrant parents reported that this truncated social network necessitated their redefining the notion of family to emphasize relationships with immediate, nuclear members.

From a theoretical perspective, our model suggests that family system changes (i.e., the "costs" of getting ahead) are more strongly connected to postimmigration changes in familism than to adoption of American cultural norms. Future research should examine this new proposition as an alternative to traditional assimilation hypotheses (Hirschman 1994).

Our conceptual model also proposes that parent-adolescent acculturation gaps are more complex than previously hypothesized. Hernandez and McGoldrick (1999) reported that parent-adolescent conflict arose from parents' insistence on maintaining culture-of-origin traditions in the face of their children's acculturation to the host culture—that is, conflict arose from the acculturation gap (see also Szapocznik and Kurtines 1980; Szapocznik et al. 1986). Coatsworth and his colleagues (2002) also asserted that parent-adolescent conflict resulted from acculturation gaps and contributed to Latino parents having low investment in their children. In contrast, we found parent-adolescent acculturation gaps were less problematic and found no evidence linking these gaps with low parental investment. The strong majority of the parents and adolescents in our study said they wanted to maintain their culture-of-origin traditions. Participants reported little conflict directly related to acculturation. Instead, parent-adolescent conflict seemed to revolve around the parents' perception of the U.S. environment as filled with dangers for their children's emotional and physical well-being. In these families, conflicts arose when adolescents requested—and were consistently denied—permission to recreate (i.e., socialize) with their Latino friends outside the home. These conflicts were especially complex from the adolescents' perspective because the youth wanted to socialize with Latino friends who shared similar cultural ways, but to do so in the U.S. environment. Adolescents were not necessarily rapidly adopting U.S. cultural behaviors, as shown by the 90 percent of participating adolescents who maintained high levels of involvement with their culture-of-origin norms, values, and traditions. This dynamic makes the acculturation gap between parents and adolescents more complex than if adolescents were eagerly assimilating to U.S. culture. Based on our conceptual model, we propose that postimmigration parent-adolescent conflict is related more to the increasingly restrictive parenting styles adopted in response to perceived dangers in the new environments than to acculturation gaps caused by the rapid assimilation of children.

Although the literature on parent-adolescent acculturation gaps has focused on how these gaps precipitate family stress, we found that acculturation gaps also serve an adaptive purpose. All of the parents we interviewed wanted their adolescents to become bicultural. Adolescents who learned English occupied a new, highly valued role in the family because they were able to act as cultural brokers for their families by helping their parents or younger siblings navigate the host culture. Theoretically, we posit that adolescent development of new bicultural skills in the host culture (e.g., becoming cultural brokers) is encouraged by the family as one way to foster family system adjustment and cope with the costs of getting ahead. Future research should examine the relative contributions of these competing explanations by investigating how acculturation gaps are connected to both stress and adaptation in immigrant families.

Implications for Clinical Practice with Immigrant Families

Our findings support the need for the development of prevention and intervention programs to decrease immigrant families' acculturation stress, help families cope with postimmigration changes, and promote cultural assets such as familism and ethnic traditions. Programs for Latino immigrant families have been developed and show promising results (see Bacallao and Smokowski 2005 for a review; see also Szapocznik et al. 1986; Coatsworth et al. 2002) but require dissemination and further testing. In particular, two family-focused programs, Familias Unidas (developed by Szapocznik and his colleagues as reported in Coatsworth et al. 2002) and our program, Entre Dos Mundos (Bacallao and Smokowski 2005), address parent-adolescent cultural conflicts and enhance coping skills for handling acculturation stressors. Based on the findings presented in this chapter, clinicians using these intervention programs should pay special attention to family members' experiences of accumulated loss and grief related to their separation from extended family in their countries-of-origin. Clinicians should help family members address relationship issues that develop during sequential immigration, and aid in creating adaptive new roles to meet postimmigration challenges.

Diffuse, Bifurcated Stage of Bicultural Development

The quantitative and qualitative data presented in this chapter makes a clear case that the home environments of Latino adolescents are rich in cultural traditions and ethnic pride. Even so, adolescents and parents must venture outside the protective family environment to interact with the dominant society. When they do, their cultural experiences diverge into two discrete spheres: a culture-of-origin system at home and a host culture sphere at school or work (see figure 1.3).

Having considered how immigrants strive to maintain cultural identity at home, and their struggle with postimmigration family system changes, we next examine what happens when adolescents and parents with strong culture-of-origin identities encounter acute assimilation pressures at school and work. In the next chapter, we explore how sustained contact with the host culture triggers the exploration and adaptation stage of bicultural development.

3

From Contact to Conflict

*How Assimilation Mechanisms Underpin
the Exploration and Adaptation Stage in
Bicultural Development*

This would be me living in the U.S. [see figure 3.1] *—people all around
me, and I feel out of place, most of the time. Uhm, I'm fine with it. I
don't get stressed about it, but I do feel out of place. It's not something
that gets me depressed or mad or anything. To me, I don't discrimi-
nate against others because they look different. I was raised where that
was never something that was instilled in me when I was growing up.
But here, coming over here, I was introduced to a lot of things. Racism
was one of them. I feel out of place most of the time. Sometimes, uhm,
I don't know, it's just hard sometimes. I can cope with it, but it does
bother me. I don't know, it would be easier living in Mexico right now;
I can imagine that it would be a normal life. There wouldn't be a race
issue. I come from a small town where there's barely tourism, well, it
isn't a big deal there. Same people. Same type of people, Mexicans.
Same type of ideas. So, it would be normal in that way to me.*

—Manuel, male adolescent

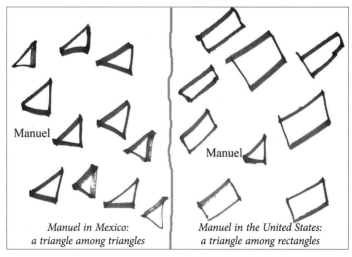

Fig. 3.1.
Manuel's
cultural
map

*Manuel in Mexico:
a triangle among triangles*

*Manuel in the United States:
a triangle among rectangles*

Few symbols capture the ambivalent nature of U.S. immigration policy better than the Statue of Liberty. The statue was conceived as a gift from the people of France to mark the centennial of the American Declaration of Independence. However, the unveiling in 1886 was ten years later than planned, largely due to lack of public financing. The statue of Lady Liberty is moving forward while trampling shackles underfoot, and she wears a crown with seven spikes that represent the seven continents while holding a torch that symbolizes enlightenment. She is facing the ocean, gazing towards Europe. Her tablet symbolizes knowledge and has the date of the American Declaration of Independence inscribed in Roman numerals. The interior of the pedestal contains a bronze plaque engraved with the poem "The New Colossus" by Emma Lazarus.

> Not like the brazen giant of Greek fame,
> With conquering limbs astride from land to land;
> Here at our sea-washed, sunset gates shall stand
> A mighty woman with a torch, whose flame
> Is the imprisoned lightning, and her name
> Mother of Exiles. From her beacon-hand
> Glows world-wide welcome; her mild eyes command
> The air-bridged harbor that twin cities frame.
> "Keep, ancient lands, your storied pomp!" cries she
> With silent lips. "Give me your tired, your poor,
> Your huddled masses yearning to breathe free,
> The wretched refuse of your teeming shore.
> Send these, the homeless, tempest-tossed to me,
> I lift my lamp beside the golden door!"

This poem has never been engraved on the exterior of the pedestal; rather, it is inconspicuously tucked inside. The bronze plaque in the pedestal contains a typographical error, leaving out the comma in "Keep, ancient lands" and causing that line to read " 'Keep ancient lands, your storied pomp!' cries she." This error changes the meaning in a way that would be particularly poignant for the Native Americans' perspective on the European immigrants' notion of Manifest Destiny. Although many immigrants from Europe took inspiration from the statue, especially during the large immigration wave from 1890 to 1910, "Mother of Exiles" never caught on as the statue's name. However, for many past and current immigrants, the statue remains a powerful symbol of freedom and the deeply ingrained idea that they are knocking on the "golden door" to enter a better life. Once inside that golden door, their immigration journeys end, and the story turns to the drama of assimilation. Manuel illustrated this aspect of culture shock in a cultural map he drew (figure 3.1) and for which he provided the explanation in the quotation that begins this chapter.

> Disproportionately, in an immigrant nation, the poor have always been the most recent immigrant group, which means they have always been "the other"—the strangers who dress differently, talk with strange accents, or follow strange customs. The stranger, the one who is different, has always caused fear. (Blank 1997, 47)

What roles do U.S. schools, workplaces, churches, and peers (Latino and non-Latino) play in the acculturation process of immigrant adolescents? In this chapter, we explore relationship to the host culture (see figure 1.2). The influences of the host culture and their impact on acculturation processes of Latino immigrant adolescents and their families are delineated. In the previous chapter, we illustrated how family systems and enculturation have to be restructured and reorganized to accommodate changes related to immigration. Of particular importance was the emphasis immigrant families placed on maintaining their culture-of-origin rituals, traditions, and values in their new homes. In contrast, this chapter illuminates the social processes immigrants experience when they venture outside of their homes to interact with members of the host culture and social systems in their communities such as schools, workplaces, and churches. The analysis was guided by assimilation theory, a conceptual framework that has dominated acculturation research for more than fifty years.

In the sections that follow, we discuss assimilation theory and two interpersonal and institutional mechanisms, monolingualism and discrimination, which drive assimilation in daily life. We then examine these mechanisms in specific transactions with others in schools, workplaces, and churches. Figure 3.2 summarizes the salient themes and juxtaposes them with findings from the previous chapter on family reorganization after immigration, and in so doing, builds an ecological model (Bronfenbrenner 1989) of risk and protective factors for Latino immigrant families. The sections below detail interactions with the exosystem, that is, settings and systems outside the immediate family.

Introduced in chapter 1, the assimilation model holds that an individual sheds her or his culture-of-origin to assume the values, beliefs, behaviors, and perceptions of the dominant culture (Chun, Organista, and Marin 2003). The dominant culture is perceived as more desirable while the culture-of-origin is perceived as being inferior for the individual. In this model, change is "directional, unilinear, nonreversible, and continuous"

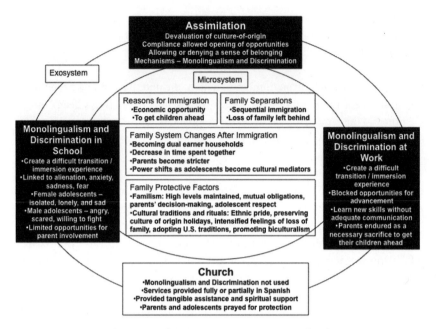

Fig. 3.2. How assimilation mechanisms impact immigrant families

(Suarez-Orozco and Suarez-Orozco 2001, 8). The experiences of European immigrants in the first half of the twentieth century appeared to fit this unidirectional framework, which has been the dominant way of conceptualizing acculturation change (de Anda 1984; Feliciano 2001). However, considerable controversy exists over how well this model describes the acculturation process for new waves of Latin American immigrants. Most notably, unlike their European counterparts, immigrants from the Caribbean and Central and South America are people of color and consequently experience racial/ethnic barriers, such as stigma, to fully integrating into U.S. society (Padilla and Perez 2003).

Assimilation theorists say that as acculturation progresses, individuals take on greater levels of "American" behaviors. The individual who is in the process of acculturating adopts "American" attitudes towards school, parents, teachers, peers, and customs, while devaluing his or her culture-of-origin attitudes. Of course, the United States population is not a homogenous group and people have diverse attitudes. Acculturating individuals appear to observe what is and is not supported and tolerated in the host society and change their behaviors accordingly. All of the Latino adolescents and parents we interviewed felt the pressure to assimilate.

One has to become like them [Americans]. *One has to talk like them, one has to act like them, one has to dress like them so that we can feel like them, and show them that we can belong here, too.* (Reyna, female adolescent)

It's not that I don't feel Mexican, but I have lost many things. I've stopped having, . . . well, at home we keep our country's customs and our family's customs. But since I don't spend a lot of time at home, I bring some new customs into our home. I don't know if they're American customs or what, but they're new things I've started doing. Like I make macaroni and cheese just for myself, and I wear more jeans than skirts. [See cultural map shown in figure 3.3.] And the way I talk [pointed to the phone] *to my friends, not criticizing what they did last night. So, I think that it's at these times that I stop feeling Mexican, just a little.* (Nohemi, female adolescent)

Fig. 3.3. Nohemi's cultural map

Assimilation to these adolescents meant Americanization. Belonging was paramount. Who can belong? How do you belong? Which physical characteristics do you have to have to belong? What do you have to do to belong?

When I was smaller and lived in Mexico [three years ago, when he was thirteen], *I wore boots all the time, and tight pants. And a belt. And a checkered shirt with long sleeves, that was tucked in. Como un vacero. Like a cowboy* [laughed softly in recollection of what he wore in Mexico]. *And with a hat. I was a cowboy. Aye* [Adolescent made a soft sound in his throat while looking at his drawing of himself in Mexico. See figure 3.4.], *I lived, I worked on my father's ranch. Well, here, you have to be with the fashions.* [started to laugh] *I came here. Went to school the next day after I got here. I went to school looking like a cowboy from Mexico. Aaagh. I went through that day and I wouldn't even take off my sombrero. Everybody was laughing at me. Then I started wearing shorts and "tennis"* [shoes] *to school. I used to never go to school dressed like this* [patting his pants legs—adolescent was wearing loose and wide-legged black jeans that sat low on his hips]. *And now, I started wearing these pants. And that's how it is. My friends in Mexico would laugh if they saw me now. You see, they live in a different place. A place of cowboys. Clothes have to change with where you live.* (Jaime, male adolescent)

For me, it means that the person has let go of their identity and has grabbed on to the customs of this country, and uses those customs in his life here. But these new customs aren't necessarily better [emphasized the word "better"] *customs. They are just other customs.* (Luis, father)

Environmental influences outside the family—especially workplace and school environments—spurred Americanization. It is important to note that parents supported parts of the acculturation process, such as learning English, but did not support assimilation. Although continuously reinforcing culture-of-origin values and traditions, most immigrant parents thought of Americanization as a gateway to future opportunities for their children, whether those opportunities were in their country-of-origin or in the United States.

We think it [Americanization] *is to assume attitudes and ideas* [from the United States]. *And yes, she does assume these. For instance, in our countries we never say, "What goals do you have?" I had never heard of a girl*

Jaime: a cowboy in Mexico

Jaime: a rock star in the United States

Fig. 3.4. Jaime's cultural map

having goals, but here, I've heard her express her goals. She's learned that here. (Adriana, mother)

She's said, "I'm going to be a lawyer, Dad. I want to be a lawyer." Then she'll change her mind and say, "I want to be an archeologist." And I ask her, "And what are you going to do with that? Do you even know what an archeologist does?" And then she starts telling me exactly what an archeologist does. They study ruins, the past, many things. They study mammoths and dinosaurs. Those are archeologists. (Carmelo, father)

The first goal [emphasized the word "goal"] *she has is to finish her high school. From there, she's in the phase of looking at her options. She's asking and informing herself, and this is the way that she's Americanizing because she's starting to look at these options from a young age.* (Guadelupe, mother)

For me, it [Americanization] *means like opening the door to a better future. That is how I see it. The Americanization of my children is like they will find better opportunities than in our country. That is how I see it. I think that in the language and in some ideas, she* [her daughter] *is becoming Americanized. I don't know if you saw that during the interview. But she is certain of what she wants. That puts my mind at ease as a mother, because I know she is firm in her principles.* (Zunilda, mother)

Well, it [Americanization] *means a lot* [emphasized "a lot"]. *An Americanized person has all the benefits of the Americans. That is, for me, the Americanized person can count on everything in this country. They* [the Americans] *are the privileged ones, us, no. She* [Yariela, his daughter] *is starting to take on customs from here. More than anything, it's the American customs she's taking. For example, the kids are telling her this is how it is, and this is how we do this or that. And the English, she's really using the language now. But she is not losing the customs that she has brought with her. Those customs, because she remembers them, she holds on to them. Had she been little when we brought her here* [to the United States], *her customs would be erased by these new customs. She knows the life she had in our homeland, and that has helped her maintain her customs. But she has taken on all the customs from here, while keeping her customs from there* [Mexico], *and it is like she's in between the two. She's in between the two customs, and that appears to be fine with her.* (Miguel, father)

This last quotation from Miguel, the father of a teenage daughter, underscores two of the main mechanisms through which assimilation functions: monolingualism and discrimination. Mentions of these two factors were pervasive throughout the interviews we conducted with the families. Both of these factors were common in ecological transactions at school, at work, with peers, and with coworkers. Becoming Americanized meant learning the English language. Adopting behaviors and customs from the host culture and speaking English were the primary ways in which an immigrant, adult or adolescent, could show he or she "belonged" in the United States. In contrast, "not belonging" meant enduring frequent and consistent discrimination. We discuss monolingualism and discrimination in detail in the following sections.

Monolingualism as a Mechanism for Assimilation

Monolingualism is the presence or emphasis of one language in spoken interactions or written materials. In the context of U.S. assimilation, of course that language is English. All fathers felt that they and their adolescents could not get ahead in the United States without understanding and speaking English. Monolingualism was a major barrier to advancement in the workplace and in school.

> *Well, the language. I have learned to say things with hand gestures and to understand, not well, but at least some words and gestures. That was a big obstacle. At the beginning, I was afraid. I did not know how to ask for what I needed at work, in a store. I think my biggest obstacle was the language. It is still the language.* (Adolfo, father)

> *The advice I would give* [to a cousin coming to the United States] *is to go to school to learn English after work, and go every day, and learn English, and then, you will get ahead faster. Without English, you cannot get ahead here.* (Ramon, father)

> *If you speak English well, you'll get a better job than we were able to get. Speaking English is very hard for us; because of our age, we can't learn it as well. But they* [adolescents] *can. They learn very fast. Very fast.* (Carmelo, father)

> *I have not triumphed because the obstacle that I find here is the language, and I have not learned it. They have invited me to English classes, but I have not been able to get permission from my husband. Almost all the classes are on the day when he is resting, and since we see each other just a few hours on the days when he is working, then the day he rests, he wants me to be close to him, waiting on him, and sharing things. And that is why he doesn't want me to go.* (Zunilda, mother)

Among adolescents, the language barrier was a significant barrier to making new, American friends.

> *For instance, when I first came here, I couldn't speak to anybody. I felt so alone. I would sit by myself because I couldn't talk. Well, not by myself, but I felt completely, completely alone. It was very difficult for me. And nobody talked to me. I remember how I tried to tell someone that my family and*

> *I went to the beach. But instead of saying beach, I said a bad word, and she started laughing at me. And I didn't know* (started laughing a little). *I said to her, "What did I say?" and she didn't say anything.* (Roberto, male adolescent)

Some adolescents thought that learning to speak English would help them feel more American. This perception might be a reflection of their buying into monolingualism to assimilate.

> *I still don't feel American or any part of me like an American. I think that I would if I knew the language. I'd feel a little American, but because I still struggle with English, I think that's why* [I don't feel American]. *I think it's mostly due to the language. If I spoke the language, I'm sure I'd feel a little more American.* (Nohemi, female adolescent)

Conversely, being unable to understand English made adolescents feel that they did not belong.

> *When I'm with my* [American] *friends and they say words, American words that I don't know, I don't feel American. And I won't understand what they're saying because I don't know the words. When I don't understand, I don't feel American. I say to myself, "I shouldn't be with them. I don't understand many of the words they're using." That's the only thing that doesn't make me feel American.* (Reyna, female adolescent)

Nohemi, who struggled with learning English, believed that becoming fluent in English is the gateway to a sense of belonging in the United States. Although Reyna speaks English well and has established friendships with American peers, she was still prone to relapse into feeling insecure about belonging with this peer group when she did not understand certain words or expressions. For adolescents and parents, learning English was a critical task for social, academic, and occupational development. Unfortunately, not only was achieving this task hampered by monolingualism, but Mexican adolescents and parents also had to contend with pervasive and frequent experiences of discrimination.

Discrimination as a Mechanism for Assimilation

Ethnic and racial discrimination play an important role in acculturation. The atmosphere upon arrival, that is, the extent to which the host culture supports or stigmatizes new immigrants, is a crucial element in determining how stressful postimmigration adjustment will be (de Anda 1984; Berry 1998; Padilla and Perez 2003). Diane de Anda (1984) pointed out that transactions between the individual and larger majority and minority cultural systems are important in promoting or inhibiting postimmigration adjustment. She hypothesized that six factors were largely responsible for the amount of stress in cultural adaptation. These factors were (1) the overlap between the two cultural systems; (2) the availability of cultural translators or models; (3) corrective feedback provided by members of each culture; (4) compatibility between the individual's cognitive style and those valued by the majority culture; (5) bilingualism; and (6) the degree of similarity in physical appearance between the minority individual and the majority culture. All of these factors contribute to the person-environment fit between the acculturating individual and the dominant host culture. A poor fit can inhibit postimmigration adjustment, causing stress and strain. In our interviews with Latino immigrant families, it was clear that their adjustment process was made more difficult by their meeting few cultural translators or models, experiencing corrective feedback in the form of discrimination, and having marked differences in physical appearance from other U.S. cultural group members.

Research has found that discrimination adversely affects Latino immigrants' health and well-being. In a study of 1,001 Mexican migrant farm workers (ages eighteen to fifty-nine years) living in California, Ethel Alderete and colleagues (1999) found that discrimination increased levels of acculturation stress experienced by the participants. In turn, this acculturation stress increased the odds of individuals experiencing clinical depression. Similar effects of discrimination were shown in a study conducted by William Vega and colleagues (1993) that examined acculturation and delinquent behavior in a sample of 1,843 Cuban boys and girls living in the United States. These researchers found that acculturation conflicts, such as language difficulties and discrimination experiences, were related to increased incidence of self-derogation among the youth. In addition, the researchers found that problems inherent in the acculturation process were also associated with lower self-esteem among the youth. Cuban adolescents who perceived higher levels of discrimination also reported having more peers who approved of drug use. As compared to adolescents without language difficulties, immigrant adolescents with frequent language difficulties reported increased incidence of self-derogation, more frequent belittling remarks made by their teachers, increased levels of peer drug use, and more frequent delinquent behavior.

In our Latino Acculturation and Health Project, we found that perceived discrimination had direct positive cross-sectional relationships with externalizing behaviors (Smokowski and Bacallao 2006) and internalizing symptoms such as anxiety and depression (Smokowski and Bacallao 2007) in both immigrant and U.S.-born adolescents. Further analyses looking at how an adolescents' perception of discrimination might influence mental health over time showed that experiencing discrimination is the beginning of a risk pathway that leads to higher adolescent aggression, heightened parent-adolescent conflict, higher levels of adolescent substance use, increased numbers of delinquent friends, lower levels of familism, and lower self-esteem. These pathways ultimately heighten the probability of aggressive behavior (Smokowski, Buchanan, and Bacallao forthcoming) internalizing problems (Smokowski, Bacallao, and Buchanan forthcoming) and adolescent substance use (Buchanan and Smokowski 2009) one year later.

Andres Gil, Eric Wagner, and William Vega (2000) suggested that immigrants may engage in negative health behaviors and delinquent behavior generally as a strategy for coping with acculturation stressors, such as language difficulties and discrimination. Maladaptive behavior is thought to derive from "increased perceptions of discrimination, internalization of minority status, and/or socialization into cultural attitudes and behaviors that have a disintegrative effect on family ties" (Gil, Vega, and Dimas 1994, 45). These acculturation stressors result in self-deprecation, ethnic self-hatred, and a weakened ego structure in the assimilated individual (Rogler, Cortes, and Malgady 1991).

We did not find any signs of ethnic self-hatred among the adolescents or parents we interviewed. However, comments from both adolescents and parents indicated a weakened ego structure and some self-derogation that were the results of consistent experiences of discrimination at schools and workplaces. The comments of participants clearly illustrated that these individuals were coping with multiple facets of discrimination. In turn, the ongoing experience of discrimination and oppression increased anxiety, fear, depression, and alienation.

I was on Porter Street with my friends, and this black man said something, I don't know what, and I kept walking, ignoring him. Next thing, he attacked me, started hitting me in the face. My two friends tried to pull him off. The police came. They're always around Porter [Street]. Told us to walk on different sides of the street. The black man went one way, and my friends and I went the other way. My face swelled where he'd hit me. At school, the blacks want to start fights with us. We just ignore them, keep walking, don't say anything. The blacks hate us. I don't know why. Maybe because of our color, coffee. They have a different color. They, too, came from a different country, from Africa, but as slaves. We come from Mexico, but not as slaves. Maybe that's why. We've come here, like them, but not as slaves. They've been here longer than we have. They speak English a little better than us. (Juan, male adolescent)

A few times I was physically threatened on the bus. It was close to becoming a fight several times. It never became a fight, but it got real close. It started with an argument. They'd threaten me pretty seriously. They'd say they were going to come after me if they saw me on the street, stuff like that. If they told me that now, I just know that these black guys talk and talk and they never do anything. Back then, I didn't know that, and I truly believed them, and I was scared to go anywhere. Every time I would have to go out [emphasized the phrase "have to go out"], *I'd take my brother. It would be just someone to be there, in case something happened. Everything like this, discrimination, racism, happened on the bus, mainly there. The bus driver would be on the bus, but I just felt scared because it was like he wasn't even on that bus. I was sitting in the middle. But I thought the bus driver was like the rest of them, so, he wasn't going to help me any. I just kept it to myself, and I didn't think the principal would do anything about it. So I just kept it to myself. I felt helpless.* (Manuel, male adolescent)

The two participant comments above illustrate serious problems in race relations between Mexicans and African Americans. According to the Latino adolescents we interviewed, African American adolescents initiated much of the overt interpersonal discrimination that occurred (e.g., name calling, fighting on school grounds or while playing sports). Discrimination from European Americans tended to be both more covert (e.g., casting a demeaning look, laughing at mispronunciations, purposely not being inclusive) and institutional in the form of oppressive policies (e.g., English-only immersion programs at school, policies that severely lower the probability of attending universities). In contrast to the overt physical assaults described above, immigrant adolescents also described a more subtle, covert discrimination that made them feel different and alienated.

I feel very different here with my Mexican culture because when I am at home, it is almost like being in Mexico for me, but when I leave my house, it is different. The people are different and they are not like me because here [in the United States], *there are Hispanics, but they are not the majority. So, when I go out, I see that the people are not like me, they speak a different language, they look different and all. When I am here at home, I can communicate with my parents, with my sisters, and when I'm not* [at home], *I am more alone.* (Maria Dolores, female adolescent)

I don't have certain rights that they [Americans] *have. Not going to college, that stings. I wish I could go. I would love to go, keep studying. I can't.* [Head and eyes dropped; looked defeated. This adolescent was an excellent student, but North Carolina laws require universities to charge immigrants out-of-state tuition, which made it impossible for his family to afford higher education. Immigrants are also ineligible for financial aid.] (Manuel, male adolescent)

I have noticed, sometimes Americans look at me like, I am just Hispanic, but they have not said anything. They just give you this look, and you feel the disdain. But, not any bad words. (Adolfo, father)

It feels ugly to me when you find yourself entering in a restaurant, and you see Americans on one side, and the Hispanos on another side. I don't sit with the Americans because I'm not American, but I also don't want to sit just with the Hispanos because we live in this country, too. When I see the division between people, I realize I'm living in two cultures. Two cultures, living together, but separate. Another thing, when we enter a restaurant, I see people staring at us. [Laughed] *I think they're staring because Guillermo's* [her husband's] *coloring is the color of coffee and I am white. We stand there together with the three children. People think I'm American and I'm with a Mexican. They watch to see which side we'll go to* [in the restaurant]. *Still, people are not accustomed to seeing us together. I really notice this in restaurants. I think people wonder, "How did this dark-skinned man get such a white woman?" So many people stare at us in restaurants that my youngest son even noticed. He asked me about it. I told him, "I don't know. Who knows why?" But, what can you say to your children? It's a recurring situation. It's difficult.* (Diocelina, mother)

Because Mexican society is fairly homogeneous, most of the Mexican immigrants, especially the adolescents, were not prepared to cope with discrimination and difficult race relations. Prior to immigration, these Mexican families had never experienced being members of a minority group.

Well, I am not from here. The people that are from here speak the language, go to school, universities, and they can do everything here, work anywhere, and have friends. And in case anything happens, they can defend themselves. But since I am not from here, I cannot really defend myself. There are many

places where you go that there are only people from here because this is their
country, and they can do whatever they want, and we can't do other things
that they can do because we are not from this country. Like, I feel like I can-
not obtain a career like a lawyer or doctor. It's a very different way of life in
the U.S., and with the language, my sister and I don't like going out much. In
Honduras, we always went out. (Maria Dolores, female adolescent)

Discrimination and monolingualism worked in tandem to promote assimilation. Parents and adolescents experienced these assimilation pressures in remarkably similar ways, even in different ecological settings. For
example, both parents and adolescents said that the language barrier made
them unable to defend themselves against discrimination.

Below, we describe how monolingualism and discrimination functioned in schools and at workplaces. While adolescents and parents were
separated at school and at work, they encountered the same assimilation
mechanisms, which left them feeling battered by the discrimination outside their homes. However, once the family was reunited in the home, they
rarely spoke of these critical experiences. This silence does not imply that
family members were unaware that their loved ones were experiencing
similar discrimination and oppressive processes. Rather, in not discussing
the negative experiences, the family members believed they were protecting each other. They wanted to use the little time they had as a family to
relax and enjoy each other's company.

In stark contrast to school and work, attending church was an event that
united parents and adolescents. Churches did not promote assimilation
through monolingualism and discrimination, but instead provided an important example of how social systems might approach the acculturation
process in a different way.

Monolingualism and Discrimination in School

Low educational attainment is a critical concern for Latinos. The estimated proportion of the U.S. Latino population age twenty-five years and
older with at least a bachelor's degree in 2001 ranged from 25 percent for
Cubans to 7 percent for Mexicans (Jamieson, Curry, and Martinez 2001).
This educational disparity becomes very serious given that 67 percent of
the Latino population in the United States is Mexican and only 7 percent
of this group is prepared for employment in skilled occupations. In 1999,
slightly more than 33 percent of Latino adolescents ages fifteen to seventeen years were working below grade level in school (Jamieson, Curry, and
Martinez 2001). According to the U.S. Census Current Populations Survey,

the annual high school dropout rate for Latinos in tenth to twelfth grades was 7.1 percent, higher than any other group. For the same survey period, non-Latino whites had an annual dropout rate (3.8 percent) that was nearly half the Latino rate. One-third of Latinos ages 18–24 years (i.e., 1,340,000 individuals) had dropped out of school as compared to 8 percent of non-Latino whites and 16 percent of African Americans in this age group (U.S. Census Bureau 2009).

The alarmingly high Latino dropout rate probably has strong ties to acculturation processes through the politics of pedagogy. Schools are one of the primary battlegrounds for assimilationist ideology. Assimilation-based policies favor programs such as Structured English Immersion [SEI], which is an approach that emphasizes teaching English to non-English speakers before teaching other content. SEI does not use a bilingual education approach. Examples of the SEI approach can be found in Proposition 227, passed in 1998 by California voters (61 percent vs. 39 percent; now EC 300-340 of the California Education Code), and Proposition 203, passed in 2000 by Arizona voters. These public SEI policies use a sequential approach. First, the school district provides intensive English instruction. Once English language skills are achieved, other curriculum content is provided. Skills in the child's first language (e.g., Spanish) are deemphasized or actively discouraged. The goal is for the child to become fully indoctrinated in the dominant second language and culture and leave her or his first language and culture behind. By offering a one-year intensive SEI program and discouraging any instruction in the student's native language, SEI proponents hold that Latino students will demonstrate faster academic achievement and performance comparable to that of native English speakers. Proposition 227 allows bilingual instruction when parents obtain a waiver from the school system. The SEI approach reduces school systems' need for highly trained bilingual teachers. However, even when bilingual teachers are available in the school system, they are not allowed to teach in both languages.

There are important drawbacks to the SEI approach. While being immersed in learning English, language minority students often fall behind their peers in other academic areas, increasing grade retention and the risk for dropout. In addition, the single focus on assimilation may distance Latino youth from their parents because of the implicit message to children that their culture-of-origin is inferior or less valued. Rapidly assimilating youth are likely to disengage from their less assimilated parents. Youth who are disengaged from family and school may turn to more high-risk, problematic behaviors.

Policies promoting the SEI approach stem primarily from fear of the growing Latino population rather than from research. Despite political statements, there is little evidence of long-term benefits from Proposition 227 policies (Gandara et al. 2000; Mora 2002). Even so, copycat initiatives and anti–bilingual education bills based on Proposition 227 have been proposed in several other states, including Colorado, Massachusetts, New York, Oregon, and Utah.

An alternative to the SEI approach is bilingual education. Also called Two-Way Immersion programs, bilingual education uses a simultaneous approach to teaching English and other academic content. The school district teaches both English and grade-level curriculum content through bilingual instruction using students' primary language. The child's primary language skills are maintained and the result is bilingualism and biculturalism. Two-way immersion programs are predominantly found in early elementary through upper elementary (first through fifth) grades, but are far less common in middle and high school (Christian, Howard, and Loeb 2000). Proponents argue that teaching and testing Latino students in their native language until they have acquired adequate English language skills will eliminate the achievement gap. Bilingual education scholars believe that bilingual and bicultural abilities are valuable for achieving self-sufficiency (Hakuta, Butler, and Witt 2000). These bilingual and bicultural abilities will also be crucial in twenty-first-century workplaces that are influenced by diversity and globalization. Proponents of bilingual education hold that this approach enables students to access resources and support from both cultural systems, which increases positive adjustment and intellectual and social capital for English language learners. If curriculum content were taught in the student's native language, language minority students would not fall behind their peers by taking time out from academics to focus only on learning English. Highly trained bilingual teachers tailor teaching strategies to the particular needs of language minority students. Important linguistic skills in the child's native language would not be discarded. In addition, two-way immersion programs provide language majority students with valuable bilingual skills. Even so, some critics object to the cost of providing highly trained bilingual teachers when schools are being forced to cut art, music, and other educational areas due to funding shortages. This is a legitimate concern; however, these bilingual skills ultimately provide a critical advantage in multicultural workplaces and for reaching diverse new markets. These skills are central to competing within a global economy. Further, considering the demographic shifts taking place throughout the country (see chapter 1), we need to equip young Latinos with adequate education because they are going to replace the aging work-force in the United States.

Learning in two languages may be a slower process than learning in one language. Second language acquisition may precipitate some loss in proficiency in the first language (Henning-Stout 1996). Other research-ers have not found this loss in proficiency to be the case (Winsler et al. 1999). Kenji Hakuta and colleagues (2000) estimated that it takes between four and seven years for non-English speakers to acquire academic Eng-lish at a level equivalent to native English speakers. This time frame for acquiring English skills dwarfs the one-year English immersion program expected to be adequate under Structured English Immersion programs. Hakuta and colleagues' study found no significant difference in the rate of English acquisition between students in bilingual programs and those in English immersion programs. Jill Mora (2002) also reported that "na-tive language literacy instruction is producing on-grade-level achievement for thousands of Spanish speaking students classified as limited in English proficiency" (40). In other words, if tested on the same reading content in Spanish rather than in English, limited-English proficiency (LEP) students in bilingual programs do not show an achievement gap. They simply need more time to learn the content in English as well as in Spanish.

Ester de Jong (2002) evaluated a two-way bilingual education program that provides initial first-language literacy development for all students, teaches half of the curriculum in Language 1 and half in Language 2 by third grade, and selectively integrates native and non-native speakers of the target language. Both native and non-native speakers of both languages met academic standards by fifth grade. Maria Robledo and Josie Cortez (2002) examined ten exemplary bilingual education programs and found that the best programs maintained students' primary languages and cul-tures, viewing diversity as an asset. Moreover, there is growing evidence and enthusiasm for "bilingualism for all," which is seen in programs that use two-way immersion to mix native Spanish and native English speak-ers (Christian, Howard, and Loeb 2000). All of this research underscores the lack of evidence to support intensive one-way immersion programs for second language acquisition (i.e., the SEI, Proposition 227 approach).

These politics of pedagogy take a toll on immigrant children and ad-olescents as they struggle to adapt within the U.S. educational system. Carola Suarez-Orozco and Marcelo Suarez-Orozco (2001) note that im-migrant children arrive in U.S. schools with positive attitudes. They found that 84 percent of Mexican immigrant students answered yes to the state-ment, "In life, school is the most important thing." In the Longitudinal Immigrant Student Adaptation study conducted by the same authors, 98 percent of the four hundred newly arrived immigrant adolescents participating in the study agreed with the statement, "School is important to get ahead." When asked to complete the sentence, "School is ____," 72 percent of immigrant children gave a positive answer (Suarez-Orozco and Suarez-Orozco 2001, 125).

In our interviews, parents and adolescents offered similar sentiments to those found by Suarez-Orozco and Suarez-Orozco (2001). Parents had immigrated to get their children ahead, and education was the means to that end. Adolescents knew that their parents were making great sacrifices to get them ahead and were invested in getting an education in the United States. Most adolescents and parents said that teachers they had interacted with were kind, caring, supportive, helpful, intelligent, good people.

There is a critical contradiction here. With such investment, effort, and positive attitudes from Latino immigrant adolescents, why do national statistics reflect that 33 percent of Latinos ages 18–24 years drop out of school (U.S. Census Bureau 2007a; 2007b)? What is driving these trends? To understand this process, we asked the immigrant families participating in our study interviews to describe their school experiences. Their responses clearly illustrated that the effects of monolingualism and discrimination experienced in school settings overshadowed their high investment and positive attitudes concerning education. Among the Latino immigrant parents and adolescents we interviewed, all agreed that the U.S. education was best, and through U.S. education children have a "future." At the same time, schools were experienced as strong agents of assimilation, making even the low-acculturated immigrant adolescents feel more American during school hours. This phenomenon is illustrated in an exchange between a male adolescent, Cesar, and the interviewer:

Cesar: *The school is pure American. The way they run the school. How things are done, like, like the classes. How the classes are. The teachers, how they teach, what they teach. The language everybody speaks. How the other* [American] *students are.*
Interviewer: Just to make sure I understand this, when you're at school, you feel more American?
Cesar: *Yes. Speaking in English, being with Americans. Yes.*

The Latino families said that the initial adjustment to school, which might last from the first three months to one year, was extremely difficult. The start of school was commonly a monolingual English-only immersion experience that was made difficult by the Latino youths' limited proficiency in English and the lack of supportive resources to ease the adjustment.

Fig. 3.5. Maria Dolores's cultural map

I cannot communicate with the children or the teachers at school. I cannot do my work. See? [pointed to figure 3.5, a picture she drew of herself at a desk on the U.S. side, crying; she is seated farther away from the teacher than where she was seated in her Mexican school]. *I am alone, and I'm crying because I can't read, and I can't talk to them, and I need to learn. In Mexico, I liked to do my* [school] *work. I liked to do all of it. I have a friend* [in the American school], *and she helps me and then, I don't have to ask the teacher as much. What I don't understand, I tell that teacher that I can't. Maybe as time goes by, I will learn more and more.* (Maria Dolores, female adolescent)

There was no one at the school that would help her at first. Very difficult. It was also difficult because the school was pure English, and I don't know any English so I couldn't go to the school and explain that she needed help. She would bring her homework and we would put it on this table. Both of us would look at it, and look at it, and try to figure out what she was supposed to do. We would do this all night, from the minute she arrived home until she went to bed. I couldn't read in English. It was pure English. And she didn't know either. So, she would look up words in the dictionary and I put these two hands together and prayed. I kept thinking, why doesn't the teacher put another [Spanish-speaking] *child to help her, to explain to her the home-work?* (Sulema, mother)

When I'm talking in English it does not make me feel my roots in El Salvador. Yeah. At school. At school, they make us speak in English. That makes me feel less, that language. I have to speak it at school, that language. I don't like speaking English to Mexicans in school because they speak Spanish, and I speak Spanish. Why can't we speak the language we best know with each other? (Jaime, male adolescent)

When they [adolescent children] *were newly arrived, they were happy. Later when they went to school they wanted to go back to Mexico. They were not adapting to the culture here. Once they started to feel comfortable at school, they began to adapt, to take on another culture. When you first come, you are timid and you do not adapt well to another culture. You think about it a lot, and you are not comfortable, except in your home. You feel alone and with no friends, and that makes it more difficult.* (Ramon, father)

Researchers have established that English immersion programs and policies are assimilation based, coercive, value laden, and lacking in empirical evidence (Gandara et al. 2000; Hakuta et al. 2000; Mora 2002). Whatever their intention, monolingual programs and policies are a form of institutional discrimination that is oppressive to struggling Latino youth. Popular support for these initiatives largely stems from assimilationist fervor and fear of immigrants who have different cultures, customs, and languages.

Evelyn Marino Weisman (2001) exposed the shortcomings of the assimilation model in a qualitative study in which she conducted in-depth interviews with four Latina bilingual elementary-school ESL (English as a Second Language) teachers to investigate whether the teachers conveyed a higher status to the English language than to the Spanish language. She found that Spanish was used as an instructional tool to learn English, and by the time the Latino students were in third grade and had developed bilingual skills, all Spanish was removed from the curriculum. Although the United States has no official language policy, the assimilation model clearly predominates. As Marino Weisman writes, "Although we permit languages other than English to protect constitutional rights, the right of subordinate language groups to develop and preserve their heritage language has frequently been denied" (4). This was evident in our interviews with immigrant adolescents who reported that they were discouraged from speaking Spanish in some schools. Once they were out of ESL classes, their school instruction was strictly in English.

Well, being the new kid didn't help, and being different from them only made it worse. I don't look like them. I don't talk like they did. The first year was the worst because I talked different than them. But now, I've caught on to their ways, and I've learned their language. And I've learned how to handle situations when they come up. (Juan, male adolescent)

Female adolescents described a system of mutual self-help in which they assist one another with language difficulties in the classroom. They formed small networks of informal cultural guides who usually shared the same country-of-origin. These cultural self-help networks were especially helpful for newcomers.

It was a little difficult because arriving here with no English, not knowing the schools. I couldn't do the homework. It was all very difficult. In the classroom, I could only ask a [female] friend. I would guess at the words the teacher was saying, and aaah, it was very difficult to adapt here. But God is good, and the other Mexican girls in my class helped me. When a new Mexican student comes, I explain to them what the teacher is saying. I try to help them because they [Mexican girls] helped me when I came. (Reyna, female adolescent)

The adolescents' assimilation stress intensified because they had to study, complete homework, and prepare for tests in English. Adolescents' families were already experiencing difficulty adjusting to many transitions, losses, and shifts in routines after immigrating. The expectation put upon the adolescents to learn English and assimilate in school as quickly as possible prompted some of them to long for the familiarity, family, and friends that they had left behind in their country-of-origin. At the same time, the adolescents were under intense pressure to keep up academically but were given few school support structures or resources. Although many Latino parents were supportive, they were unable to provide tangible assistance with schoolwork, which added to the parents' stress.

Latino parent support for academic achievement was a difficult area. All of the parents wanted their children to do well, especially in school. At the same time, there was an important chasm between the immigrant parent and the school system. The Latino parents did not understand the U.S. school system and were generally too intimidated to enter their child's school. The language barrier was a serious setback in this area. One Colombian adolescent was held back a year in school. The retention shocked her family members because they had thought she was progressing in her classes and nothing was wrong. She told this story.

Before, my dad didn't know anything about the [school] system, he didn't set any goals. He didn't really know. The [Latino] parents can't really help us.

If they did know about the school system, they'd set goals. Latino kids don't really care to study because their parents aren't there for them. They're not there telling them what to do, setting goals for them in school like the American parents. It's not that they [Latino parents] don't care. It's that they don't know. They don't know. Latino kids don't have parents to push them, help them, and they achieve less. It's pretty sad. (Olivia, female adolescent)

Olivia's father agreed with her assessment.

I didn't know how the school [system] functions here. It's very different in Colombia. And nobody, nobody at the school explained it to us, the parents. If one doesn't speak English, one knows very little [about the school system], which is my case. So, that has changed. I am getting to understand what the school tries to do, and not do. But before Ling [bicultural Korean-American wife of 1.5 years] was with us, I felt lost trying to understand the school. And I would ask Olivia, but she didn't really understand. I would ask her what the teachers say, and they were telling her she was doing well, but in reality, she was not. They'd tell her not to worry, that she would pass high school, but with the grades she was getting, she would not be able to continue her studies in the university. We were worried. But they would tell her not to worry. I felt confused. But all that has changed, thanks to Ling. (Jorge, Olivia's father)

Latino immigrant parents had a difficult time understanding the American school system and the ways in which it differed from the system in their country-of-origin. The language barrier was a serious impediment to parent involvement in school. Latino parents instructed their children to listen to their teachers because the parents' ability to help was limited. This dependency on teachers, rather than parents, became problematic when tension occurred between adolescents and teachers. Below is an example that illustrates this problem as related by a bicultural Colombian adolescent.

My ESL teacher last year, she wouldn't let me get out of ESL. She would say, "You need my help. You can't get out of ESL because you need my help, and if you get out, I won't help you anymore. You need to stay in ESL." I think that's really discriminating against me. Being in her class didn't let me know things or people at school really well. For example, there's a problem with many of my teachers, whether they're ESL or not. Just because I'm a Latina, they think I need a special thing, like if I say, "Oh, I didn't finish this homework" they say [in an exaggerated slower, louder voice], *"Oh, that's okay. You can do this whenever you want." It's like because I'm from Colombia, I need more time to do things. I get this extra favor. For example, if some American person said that to a teacher, the teacher would say* [in a stern voice], *"You had a lot of time to do that. Get it done by the end of the day." I think teachers have to be fair with all the people.* [Pause] *They feel pity!* [appeared to have made an insightful discovery] *They feel sorry for us and they, like, try to give us extra time to do things, or not even do them. And I don't like that. We are not stupid. And for example, they have really low expectations of us* [tone of voice expressed anger]. *Like if I'm making a C, and I go to the teacher, the teacher says, "Oh, Anna Marie! Your grade is really good." I say, "What's my grade?" And she says a "C." I think, "What? A 'C'? That's not really a good grade. A 'B' is a good grade." But the teacher says, "You are doing just fine." And I say, "WHAAAT?" And if that same teacher says a "C" to an American person, they say, "You have to work harder at it." They expect a better grade from them, a B or an A. They expect from us to get at least a D or a C, to pass the class. Well, I guess it's our fault that we Latinos have that reputation. But I get mad because I'm not like that. I work hard.* (Anna Marie, female adolescent)

Other adolescents corroborated that teachers often had lower expectations for Latino students, and regularly gave them extra time or the answers for assignments. As noted in the above comment from the bicultural female, the adolescent perceived the exceptions granted by the teacher as discriminatory. In contrast, highly assimilated adolescents found such exceptions (e.g., deadline extensions) as a helpful consideration. Adolescents' reactions seemed to vary by their level of investment in getting a strong education. Anna Marie was highly invested in her education and wanted to compete with American peers. She found the extra time and lower expectations she perceived from teachers to be condescending. At the same time, we interviewed other adolescents who were invested in meeting minimal requirements for graduation. These adolescents perceived the extra time and lower teacher expectations to be helpful.

Of course, not all teachers had low expectations for immigrant students. Schools can also be an important place where a mentor can emerge to positively influence Latino students. Anna Marie, the bicultural adolescent who found her teacher's lower expectations for Latino students to be racist, said that her principal (who previously taught her English) was a critical mentor. He made himself available to advise her, offered her extra resources, checked her report cards, encouraged her participation in an extracurricular activity, and signed forms for her to enter an honors class in Spanish literature.

Although this type of cross-cultural mentoring was relatively rare among the adolescents we interviewed, resilient bicultural adolescents were persistent and tenacious in searching for such mentors. Despite the discrimination that she perceived from other teachers, Anna Marie persevered in seeking out the principal for guidance and support. She put in extra effort to maintain an ongoing relationship with him and acted on his suggestions. Unfortunately, other immigrant adolescents lacked this adult mentoring and disengaged from the school environment. Some adolescents found it easier to embrace the lower expectations they perceived, disengage from the adverse school environment, and put their energy into socializing with their friends.

Latino parents agreed that assimilation and discrimination in the schools was a problem. Initially, parents trusted the messages from teachers as conveyed by the adolescents. At the same time, adolescents understood that their parents were vulnerable and may have tried to protect them from difficulties experienced at school. In most cases, parents held high expectations for their children to make the most of U.S. education, and adolescents did not want to disappoint parents. Under the stress precipitated by monolingualism and discrimination, educational experiences became difficult and unpleasant, prompting some immigrant adolescents to adopt negative coping mechanisms such as hiding poor progress reports and skipping school. Parent academic support was hampered by language difficulties, lack of understanding of school expectations, and values that unquestioningly respected the authority of teachers. In addition, many parents reported being frustrated with the American school system that they did not understand; therefore, they may have sought more control over the system they did understand—the family system.

Adolescents often had to handle assimilation stressors at school on their own, and they coped in different ways. Many spent long hours trying to understand homework assignments in English. This frustrating and solitary work, coupled with decreased time spent with their parents, fueled a sense of loneliness and sadness. For example, Teresa, a female adolescent who was experiencing a period of depression, described having chest pains when she went to school. She believed that she had an illness that had not yet been diagnosed. It is important to note that Teresa had been attending U.S. schools for the previous six years. This assimilation stress that manifested as anxiety and depression was not due to the adjustment shortly after immigration. Assimilation stress can be long-term.

The isolation, anxiety, and sadness immigrant adolescents described are in line with findings from previous acculturation research, which revealed that low-acculturated individuals feel cut off from the host culture, experiencing their new environments as frightening, confusing, and overwhelming (Rogler, Cortes, and Malgady 1991). Such reactions have been linked with psychological difficulties such as depression, social withdrawal, familial isolation, despair, obsessive-compulsive behavior, hostility, anxiety, and post-traumatic stress disorder (Escobar et al. 1986; Miranda, Estrada, and Firpo-Jimenez 2000; Szapocznik and Kurtines 1980; Torres-Matrullo 1976). Unfortunately, few studies have explored intense stressors, such as monolingualism and discrimination, which may cause low-acculturated new immigrants to feel isolated, anxious, and depressed.

Studying the relationships among monolingualism and discrimination in schools and immigrant adolescents' feelings of depression and hopelessness sheds some light on national survey data. Conceivably, these assimilation stressors could make adolescents feel depressed or hopeless. This may serve as a link between our interviews and national survey data. The Centers for Disease Control and Prevention's (CDC) Youth Risk Behavior Surveillance System (YRBSS) examines risk behaviors among more than fifteen thousand high school students using a biannual survey (CDC 2009). Minority populations are oversampled to increase representation. In the 2007 YRBSS results representing more than fourteen thousand students, 42 percent of Latinas and 30 percent of Latino boys reported feeling sad or hopeless almost every day for two weeks or longer in the preceding twelve months. These percentages were significantly higher than those reported by African American or non-Latino Caucasian high school students (CDC 2009). Nearly 10 percent of Latinos did not go to school on at least one day in the previous thirty days because of feeling unsafe at school or on their way to and from school. This was more than double the rate (4 percent) for non-Latino whites. Even more disturbing, 21 percent of Latinas reported having seriously considered suicide, 15 percent have made a suicide plan, and 14 percent reported having attempted suicide; these percentages exceed those from non-Latino Caucasian or African American adolescents of either gender.

The adolescent males we interviewed coped with assimilation stress in different ways. In line with national statistics, these males were more likely to defend themselves by fighting back and becoming disengaged from school. In the 2007 YRBS (CDC 2009), Hispanic high school students reported being in a physical fight (40.4 percent) and being injured in a physical fight (6.3 percent) in the past year with relatively equal prevalence as non-Hispanic, black students (44.7 percent and 5.3 percent, respectively) but with significantly higher prevalence than non-Hispanic, white students (33.7 percent and 3 percent, respectively). Furthermore, Hispanic students (8.7 percent) were significantly more likely to report that they had been threatened or injured with a weapon at school within the preceding year than were non-Hispanic, white students (6.9 percent), and Hispanic students were significantly more likely to skip school because of safety concerns than their non-Hispanic, white peers (9.6 percent vs. 4 percent). Moreover, these patterns remain stable when gender is considered. The 2007 YRBSS data also showed that 32 percent of Latino male adolescents and 26 percent of Latinas reported having property stolen or damaged on school grounds. Such experiences of threats and safety concerns may be related to exposure to discrimination and intimidation.

Monolingualism and discrimination made it easy for adolescents to begin to dislike school, initiating a process of disengagement. It is important to note that this disengagement did not occur because these adolescents were apathetic or lacked ability. Rather, disengagement appeared to be one strategy adolescents, usually boys, used to cope with a string of stressful, negative school experiences. Another way of coping with a threatening school environment was to form or join a gang for protection.

"The wetback" [el mojado], *that's what the whites and the blacks call me at school. Like, I'll be walking down the corridor, and they say this to me. They say, "Go back to your country." My friends and I try to walk together, make as big a group as we can. If you walk by yourself, you get called that name more. When I'm trying to speak the language* [English] *that's difficult. I don't like speaking it. Other students start to laugh when I say something. Even if I say it right, they laugh because of how I say it. I don't like speaking it. It's not my language.* (Alfredo, male adolescent)

There's a teacher at school [a paraprofessional], *she helps the other teacher. If a Latino raises his hand to get permission to go to the bathroom, she refuses to give him permission. But when any other student needs to go to the bathroom, she gives them permission. The students even play with her because they'll ask for permission and then half an hour later, they ask again, and she'll give it to them. But not to Latinos. I just ignore her. We all know she's racist. The other Latinos in that class, they all know. And some of the other students know, too. We all see who she gives permission to. This teacher didn't like me. She didn't like the other Latinos, either. When we've tried to talk with her, she goes like this* [raised his hand over his head with palms opened to gesture "stop"; the other arm is wrapped in front of his waist]. *And I'll say, "We're trying to ask you something." And she said, "No. You guys are talking. There is no talking." And with that, no one can discuss anything with her. So, sometimes, somebody will just get up out of his chair, and she'll ask, "Where are you going?" and he'll say, "To the bathroom," and she says, "You stay right there. Don't move."* [Made a sound in his throat like gasping for air.] *There's been times when someone doesn't listen to her, and she writes a slip, and sends him to the principal's office* [shook his head]. (Jaime, male adolescent)

One day, the teacher asked a boy to help me. But he didn't want to help me. And when we were in line for the bathroom, he was standing behind me and he whispered in my ear, "Te voy a matar" ["I'm going to kill you"]. *And I tried to tell the teacher but when I got home, I told my mother, and she went to the school and told the teacher. The boy was born here, but he's Mexican. I was new here. He thought he could say that to me. It was during my first year at the school here. Another* [Mexican] *girl told me that when she was new here, he was mean to her, too. So, this other girl tried to take care of us new ones.* (Reyna, female adolescent)

I'll always remember how I dreaded getting on the bus. For the first six months of school, even though they'd say stuff to me and I didn't know what they were saying, you could tell what they said by the looks on their faces. They didn't want me in the bus. They didn't want me in their town. To them, it was their bus [emphasized the word "their"]. *I wasn't welcomed. If I had had the greatest day at school, and then, a bad day on the bus, it didn't really matter how great the day had been. The best day at school would turn into a bad day altogether, because of what happened on the bus. I'd go home, and feel like I had a horrible day. I never talked about it, I don't think. We* [he and his family] *just knew that it happened. We were just so tired of it. By the end of the day, we were all worn out about it, I think. At home, we could just feel safe. This is our place to be, and let's keep everything else out of it. It doesn't happen so much now, like it did at the beginning. We've been kind of accepted now. It's not such a big deal like it was. Now* [after six years] *we know when they're just playing around and they really don't mean it. Now we can kind of tell.* (Manuel, male adolescent)

My friends are probably a negative influence although they protect me from fights. At school, this black guy wanted to fight me. So, I fought him. Then the principal suspended me for three days. Aaugh. It was my first year. I had a lot to learn. Now, well, if someone wants to fight me, my friends will take care of him. They'll find him in town. They have cars. I don't. They tell me, "We'll take care of him." Ah, I could fight anyone, but I can't in school. And I don't have a car. (Jaime, male adolescent)

Latino friends played a small role in this situation. Many of the immigrant adolescents felt comfortable with Latino friends because they understood the difficulties and dynamics of the immigration experience. One adolescent said that she could express herself better in Spanish and enjoyed the familiar, comfortable feeling she had when she was with Latino friends. However, her father discouraged her from spending too much time with these friends because they did not study and were considered a poor academic influence. He wanted his daughter to compete academically with Americans. This female adolescent, who had a strong bicultural identity, enjoyed reminiscing with Latino friends and debating which country was better. At the same time, she did not want to behave the way her Latino friends did at school (i.e., some were truant, or failing classes), and tried to distance herself from the "bad reputation" the Latino students had for not studying. Another adolescent found that his Latino friends were less troublesome than the friends he had in Mexico. Although his Latino friends in America tried to influence him to break his curfew, they did not steal as his friends in Mexico had.

Interestingly, the most highly assimilated adolescents did not report having Latino friends. For example, one adolescent was Colombian and did not like the Mexican students in school. This lack of Latino friends led her to spend more of her time with American friends, which led to high levels of conflict with her parents.

Forming friendships with American peers was very helpful for accelerating the exploration and adaptation phase of bicultural development; however, these cross-racial friendships often brought rapid assimilation. According to nearly all of the immigrant adolescents, their American friends did not interact well with their Latino family and friends. This disconnection compartmentalized the adolescents' worlds of family and friends. Balancing the two worlds played out in different ways. A bicultural Colombian adolescent maintained a high sense of familism, believing that American friends were for academic competition but not true social support. In contrast, another highly assimilated Colombian adolescent craved more time with American friends and had frequent arguments with her parents. The comment below provides an example of an interaction between this mother and daughter.

Maria (female adolescent): *My mother wants me to do things the Colombian way, always.*

Zunilda (female parent): *Your friends have put the American culture right here in front of you* [raised hands together, fingers closed, to front of face, placing them about eight inches away from face]. *This is all you see. But I'm like standing back to the side, watching all this. Seeing you look only in this front direction.* [Turned to interviewer.] *She says her friends* [American friends] *make their own decisions. She tells me that*

her friends don't talk to their mothers. Don't tell them what they're think-
ing about, how their day went, about their friends. I want her to keep
talking to me about these things. But she's talking less to me, more to her
friends.

This tension between the Latino influence in the family and the American influence from friends was the root of intense struggles between parents and their children. Latino parents thought American adolescents had too much freedom and were a source of danger for their children, which led the parents to adopt increasingly restrictive protection strategies. Latino adolescents saw that their American friends had more freedom and thought those friends had more fun than Latino adolescents. This perceived disparity made the Latino adolescents resent their parents' restrictive policies and yearn for more freedom.

Many immigrant adolescents found creative ways to deal with overt discrimination and monolingualism, and to do so while staying out of trouble (that is, physically fighting) in school. Latino adolescents purposefully walked through the school hallways as a group to prevent verbal assaults. Reyna tried to tell her teacher that she had been threatened, and she followed up by telling her mother about the threat. Manuel found refuge in his home with his family. The coping styles articulated by the immigrant adolescents in our study were similar to those discussed in prior qualitative studies. Flores-Gonzales (2002) examined how thirty-three Puerto Rican adolescents coped with the pressures they encountered in one high school in Chicago. Applying role theory to her ethnographic data, she found that the adolescents constructed a *school kid* identity that supported their role as students. These school kids were dutiful and obedient in school, family, and community settings, seeking affirmation and rewards for positive behavior. The school kid role was viable and led to success to the extent that the adolescent was able to avoid or deflect messages or roles (i.e., being labeled disruptive in school) that conflicted with this positive identity. In contrast, *street kids* were unable to form school kid identities and took on non-school-kid roles and identities. Street kids engaged in behaviors and sought rewards outside of conventional norms. Flores-Gonzales concluded that these adolescents have this identity thrust upon them and maintain it for lack of access to other roles.

Among the adolescents we interviewed, the effects of monolingualism and discrimination in the school setting alienated and isolated the immigrant adolescents from the larger school environment, and blocked some of them from participating in valued roles (e.g., Flores-Gonzales's school kid role). The majority of adolescents used negative encounters and experiences to fuel their personal resilience. Their aversive experiences pushed them to surpass the low expectations they felt others held for them. Instead of acquiescing to these lowered expectations, the Latino students worked hard to be considered school kids by deflecting negative messages and constructing valued positive roles.

Sometimes they think that because they're from this country they're better than you because they're from here, better than us who came from Mexico. I think that's not correct, but they have some rights that we don't have because this is their country. It's possible that that's why they feel that way. But it's not right because it doesn't matter where we're from. No one is better than anyone else. Like when you first get here, you can't pronounce things correctly and they laugh at you. Every time they laughed, they gave me more strength; strength to keep going and get better with each passing day. Well, I think that, in a way, this helped me because it gave me more strength to improve with each passing day. It made me stronger. (Juana, female adolescent)

With the language, if you do not know it, you cannot speak to other people because you do not know how. Or they make fun of you because you do not know it. But you tell yourself that one day you will learn it and be able to communicate with everyone. That is one way. The only thing that you can console yourself with is the thought that you are going to learn the language some day, and I am going to learn it well. Latinos [students] *are intelligent but they do not understand, and then, do not want to develop that intelligence. I know that we are intelligent but at times we do not believe in ourselves and that is why we do not continue studying. Maybe it is something that changes when they come here, and they don't believe in themselves anymore. I think that it is something that happens here. Maybe it is the lack of support. Sometimes it happens in Mexico, but when you get here and see that it is more difficult for Hispanos to get scholarships, and if one person tells you "no," and another says "no," then you believe the next one is going to say "no," and you don't do it. You just stop trying. If you hear "no" over and over again, then you think they are all going to say "no," and I know it is not like that, but that's what you start to think. But no, because when one door closes, another has to open, always. If someone says "no," someone else can say yes. In several conferences I have gone to, they tell you that if someone says "no," you have to keep insisting until someone will say "yes." I think this is true.* (Eva, female adolescent)

Kids would laugh at me because I didn't know how to speak English, and they would laugh and say bad things to me. And [paused a few seconds], *because I didn't understand English, they would call me "fat"* [said in a quieter voice]. *And* [paused a few seconds], *they would say other bad things to me in English because I couldn't understand them. When I started slowly understanding, they would say these things to me and I would begin to say to them, "No"* [shook her head, lowered her vocal pitch, which made her sound more serious]. I also started telling the teacher but since I still [emphasized the word "still"] *couldn't speak English, I'd call my* [Mexican] *friend. Later, they started calling me, "Cry baby." I wouldn't cry. It was because I told the teacher every, every* [emphasized "every"] *time they said something to me. Then they started calling me, "tattle teller." And I said to them, "I may be a tattle teller and a cry baby, but I am not a person of rude behavior."* (Reyna, female adolescent)

English is my second language [emphasized the word "second"]. *People don't expect me to join jazz band. People don't expect me to play tennis. People don't expect me to take honors classes, AP Environmental Science classes. Well, I guess people don't expect me to be at the top third of my class* [voice pitch dropped]. *To me, it's primarily at school, where I have met and surpassed these expectations from people. I always try to prove people wrong about what they see, and what they expect from who they see. I love to see people's facial expression when they see me at a band concert. I love the faces when people see me at a Beta Club meeting. I just love that. It's a look of shock, a look of surprise. It's as if they're saying, "I didn't know. I didn't know Hispanics could be this way. I thought they were all about being at home, or out dancing"* [started to laugh and shake his head]. *It makes me want to do better* [emphasized the word "better"] *every time I see those expressions. It pushes me.* (Manuel, male adolescent)

Suarez-Orozco and Suarez-Orozco (2001) found that social mirroring had a particularly strong effect on immigrant adaptation. Social mirroring concerns the public perceptions, racial distortions, day-to-day interactions, and ascribed identities that characterize immigrants' relations with members of the dominant culture and the messages immigrants receive from the dominant culture media. For example, Suarez-Orozco and Suarez-Orozco (2001) reported that "fully 65 percent of our participants had a negative association to the sentence 'Most Americans think [people from the child's culture of origin] are _____ ' " (97). In the overall model of adaptation for immigrant children and adolescents developed by these researchers, negative social mirroring is an important factor outside the home, while inside the home, immigrant parents try to reflect positive social mirroring and deflect negative social mirroring. The excerpts from our interviews presented above show that social mirroring was a crucial process for immigrant adolescents. In addition, the participant comments illustrate the ways immigrant adolescents actively deflect negative social mirroring. Although parents help as much as they can, the adolescents and their Latino peer groups had to independently develop coping skills to deal with negative social mirroring. The inner strength required to deflect negative social mirroring was summarized in the following statement by Manuel.

> *I would like to say that teenagers like me, if we don't get caught up trying to be someone that we're not, we're just not, we can try to live up to expectations of what we* [emphasized the word "we"] *expect ourselves to be. If you come from Mexico, you know that there are no calculators down there. It's all mental, all done mentally. We know that we can do it, all mentally. I find that when I got handed a calculator in class, it became like a crutch for me. It was like they were handing me a crutch. So I try to figure it mentally, like they do in Mexico. When I start depending on that calculator, I say to myself, "What am I doing? I know that I can do this mentally, like they taught us in school* [in Mexico]." *It became automatic. I know that I can do it. Those expectations that are put on us by other people here, they're put on, but they don't know us* [emphasized the word "know"]. *They don't know the potential here* [pointed index finger at the center of his forehead]. *They might expect you to get an 80 on a test, and they'll congratulate you* [emphasized the word "congratulate"]. *No, you want to go for the extra points. What are we doing staying with an 80? You know, I have to remind myself. When I got a 100 on a test, I have to remind myself to stay at that level because you know, no one reminds you. Being more than you're expected to be* [emphasized the word "expected"]. *It's not hard, it's just that you have to want to, to be better than what's expected. We already know we can do it, we come from Mexico.*
> (Manuel, male adolescent)

To summarize, monolingualism and discrimination pose serious, ongoing challenges to school success for immigrant adolescents. The language barrier not only required these students to put forth extra effort but also made the female adolescents susceptible to growing feelings of isolation and depression. Males countered discrimination by physically fighting back. Sixty percent of the male adolescents we interviewed had been suspended from school for fighting. We believe that monolingualism and discrimination experiences gradually eroded the positive attitudes toward school and education that many adolescents brought with them to the United States. In the long run, monolingualism and discrimination may prove so problematic that immigrant adolescents disengage from school, and perceive of dropping out of school as a viable means of maintaining their personal dignity. When immigrant adolescents consider the institutional barriers to their getting ahead in school, some adolescents choose to help their families by dropping out and going to work full-time. For many immigrant students, school does not seem to be a place where they feel welcomed or have a sense of belonging.

Monolingualism and Discrimination at Work

The changing economy has dramatically increased the need for advanced education and training. "By the 1990's, education levels in the U.S. workforce had increased dramatically. By 1994, only 17 percent of adult men were high school dropouts and the average worker had over thirteen years of education. But among men who were high school dropouts and worked full time, full year, the average weekly wages had fallen to $400 per week. High school dropouts earned 22 percent less in 1993 than they did in 1979" (Blank 1997, 60-61). It is clear that this new economy views education as the silver bullet for advancement in the United States.

In our interviews, we found that immigrant parents were willing to take low-paying, low-status jobs in manufacturing, construction, hotel housekeeping, restaurants, or poultry processing plants. There were a few exceptions, a father who worked in accounting at a furniture company or a computer programmer. Work opportunities were nonexistent in some parts of Central and South America, and available jobs paid considerably less than U.S. wages. Mexican parents were willing to take whatever work opportunities they could find because they saw work as a necessary sacrifice to get their children ahead. Immigrant parents were willing to work long hours in physically exhausting jobs to ensure their children had better opportunities. However, the parents were not prepared for the pervasive assimilation effects of monolingualism and discrimination they encountered in the workplace.

To adapt here? Well, it's been by working. Work kills all your concentration on what used to be. By working, you don't realize anything but what is in front of you, the job ahead of you. I concentrate so much on myself and on my job. That's how I adapted. You learn about the ways here at your job. They [the Americans] are the privileged ones, us, no [voice tone and volume dropped lower and softer]. Here, we come to work the jobs they don't want. Here, we take those jobs. An American isn't going to wash dishes because he speaks English. He'll go work in the cafeteria line. The Hispano, no.

Whatever they put in front of him [the Hispano], *he'll grab. In construction, it is more difficult. Where the concrete is made is where the Hispano is working. The others, no. And he does it like this, watch* [gestured with his entire arm and hand a circular motion]. *With only one or two times that they tell him, he's learned how to do the job. It is the Hispano that moves to get that job done. But to have what the Americans have, well* [shrugged], *those are the privileges that the Americans have. The American cannot hold up in the heat. They'll get the work in the shade or in the building. The Hispano, no.* (Miguel, father)

I worked with an electric company for ten years now. I have seen how they throw a lot of work on the Hispanos, especially the new ones that just start the job. They think that the Hispanos are going to work for a short time, so they throw them all the work. They have to do things that they don't even know how to do. No one has showed them, "Look, this is how you do that" [gestured with his hand]. *So, when they* [the Hispanos] *can't do it, they tell them, "Get out of here." The others love it when Hispanos are working there. They don't have to do much work then. The Hispanos do all the work. I think that's why it's important to do the job well at the beginning. Otherwise, you won't hold the job* [crossed his arms across his waist]. *That's the way it is. That's the way it is. I notice that the manager at my work gives me some of the most unpleasant, difficult jobs, jobs that the others don't do. With not knowing much English, I can't defend myself, like I would if I were in my own land. That's the way it is here.* (Victor, father)

The themes that arose concerning assimilation in the workplace were remarkably similar to those voiced by adolescents about school. Monolingualism was the greatest obstacle to advancement and recognition. The oppression of monolingualism created an atmosphere in which immigrants had to teach themselves new tasks by watching others without effective instruction or the opportunity to ask questions or get feedback. Discrimination was once again pervasive as coworkers told immigrant workers to go back to their countries, and that they did not belong here.

If I knew English, with the work I know, in another place, I would be checking what is being done badly by others, and correcting that, and checking what is done correctly [supervising]. *I would be less stressed if I had a job like that. Knowing English and everything else that I have* [work skills], *I know I would have it "softer"* [easier], *like we say over there* [in Mexico]. (Ramon, father)

I was trained as an accountant in Mexico, keeping the books, budget, pay-roll for a business. That's what I knew how to do, and I got work here after awhile, doing the same thing. Numbers are the same in both languages. English did not stop me from working in my trade. If I hadn't had that skill before coming here, I would be out there [pointed to the front yard], *mowing, trimming. I wouldn't have learned this skill here because of my difficulty with the language* [English]. *Yes, yes, there is discrimination here. Oh, yes. It's here because when I first came, they would seriously tell me to return to where I came from. Now, nine years later, they still say, "Return to your country," but the difference is that those who know me at work will say it as a joke. But they still* [emphasized the word "still"] *say it. They'll say it like a joke, so I answer, "You will all cry if I left because then you will have a very hard job to do."* (Guillermo, father)

Well, at first, at work, there was some of that [discrimination]. *Yes. It was like racism because I would go and ask permission to do something at work, and the boss wouldn't give me permission. But now, I ask to do something and he lets me do it. I prepare the ten trays of Mexican food. Now, nobody tells me what to do. I know what to do, how to do it. I know how to do all that. I get right to work. Nobody watches over me. Nobody criticizes my work. I concentrate on my work. And there is no problem. I used to work in a restaurant in Mexico, and I learned how to make tamales, moles, chorizos, marinades for the beef steaks, barbeques. Everything. I worked with the tortilla machine. I learned how to make tortillas with the machine. I know how to do all of that. But my boss didn't want me to do anything that I already knew how to do. He wouldn't give me permission. At first, no. He thought that I didn't know* [about Mexican food preparation]. *When he finally saw that I can do this, then he stopped telling me "no." Now, I prepare all the soups for them along with my ten pans* [of Mexican food]. *By watching, I have even learned how to make the desserts that the Americans eat. I've learned how to prepare all the dishes in that kitchen. All of them* [waved his arm in front of him to emphasize "all the dishes"]. *I saw how the blacks prepared the food, and they did it very well except that they would burn the food. They were busy talking to each other or smoking their cigarettes. I just concentrate on my work, make sure the food doesn't burn. One stays focused on what one is doing at work.* (Miguel, father)

Similar to their adolescents' experiences in some schools, some parents were chastised for speaking Spanish at work. These parents also commented on injustices in race relations that they perceived or observed in the workplace.

At the last job that I had, I went in to work. They had changed my depart-ment, and so a group of Hispanas was talking about this change, and the son of the manager of the plant yelled at us for talking in our language, saying, "No! You're in America now." I was angry when he showed us no respect. And I looked at him, and I said in Spanish, "Yo hablo espanol cuando yo quiero." [I speak Spanish when I want to.] He understood what I said because he understands a little Spanish. He left laughing, but I stayed angry. He had no reason to yell at us. We were on our break. That was a time I most felt discrimination. It was directly at us, and for what? We were doing nothing wrong. Now I'll talk with him when he talks to me, but I don't start conversa-tion with him. (Diocelina, mother)

Frankly, most of us are illegal, but we work. Nobody says anything to the black workers, but if a Hispano isn't working for ten minutes, then they're yelling at us, punishing us. And to them [the black workers], they don't tell them anything. And I see it, we all see it. They'll be talking on the phone, socializing, for half an hour, an hour. This is a big difference. A big difference. The black worker would burn himself on the pan. "Oh, I've burned myself. I can't work." And he would sit in the kitchen with an ice pack through the serving time, talking. Sometimes, they go home and we wouldn't see them for a week. A week! After eight days, the manager calls. "No, no, no, I'm sick now. My head hurts." And they'd be out for another four, five days. But the Hispano is there, every day. Ready to work. "Give me more work for a little more money," we say. That money's well earned. We come to work [said de-terminedly]! We come to work [emphasized the word "work"]. We come everyday. That's the difference between us and these [African American] people [voice softened]. (Miguel, father)

Again like their adolescents, parents demonstrated resiliency under the stress of this adversity.

Well, I would say that I have achieved something here by learning a little English, and working. If I spoke English better, I would have a better job in no time. But living here is not impossible. One can achieve here for oneself and for one's children. (Ramon, father)

Workplaces were important contexts for assimilation for parents. Mono-lingualism and discrimination in parents' workplaces functioned just as these assimilation mechanisms did in school for immigrant adolescents. Our findings on monolingualism and discrimination at work extend Su-arez-Orozco and Suarez-Orozco's (2001) discussion of social mirroring to

show that Latino parents not only have to shelter their children from negative social mirroring but also need to deflect toxic messages from employ-
ers and coworkers. This dual process is oppressive and stressful, but immigrant parents reported meeting the challenge with some success.

Monolingualism and Discrimination in Church

Many of the immigrant families were Catholic. Others had become involved in evangelical Christian churches or as Jehovah's Witnesses. Across
all sects of religious institutions, immigrant families' experiences at church
provided an important counterpoint to their experiences at school and at
work. Unlike schools and workplaces, churches handled acculturation issues by accommodating differences. Services were provided either completely in Spanish or in a mixture of Spanish and English components.
Outside of their homes, the church was the only place where immigrant
families saw their traditions acknowledged and practiced. Religious holidays like Todo Santo (Holy Week in November) or the procession of the
Virgin of Guadalupe were celebrated at some Roman Catholic churches
much as they are in Mexico or Colombia, providing immigrant families
with a sense of belonging and a place to unite together as a community.
Parents and adolescents felt that people at church tried to understand their
customs, encouraged them, and helped them with concrete needs such as
finding a home. Overall, churches fostered a welcoming atmosphere; many
actively recruited Latino families to bolster their congregations. For Latino
families, this was a refreshing change from being told that they did not
belong. Consequently, the majority of families we interviewed expressed
strong gratitude and loyalty to their church affiliations.

Immigrant families also valued the interactions they had with other
church members. When sons and daughters went to church, several mothers noticed that their adolescents were becoming more involved with their
American peers, especially in music youth groups, which taught adolescents how to read music and play instruments. Parents, especially mothers,
confided their problems in priests, and accepted their guidance and support. The relationship with priests was unlike any other relationship outside of their homes.

Here at home I speak Spanish and I am here with my parents and everything,
and we have our foods, our customs, but when you go out, you have to change
the language, and everything is different. When they speak to me, I don't under-
stand at school, at some stores, on the street. When I came here, I also learned
that you are not with your traditions like you were in Mexico. We all had the

same traditions there. But here, only at the church, do we see our traditions again. I felt badly before I started going to church because I felt like they [Americans] were out there, and I was in here [in her home]. They are celebrating something, and I am here in my house, separated from them. (Maria Dolores, female adolescent)

Right now, what they are trying to do is get her [Teresa, adolescent daughter who is depressed] to sing in the church choir. So, they are trying to have her sing because she likes to sing. It's a little hard to get into the choir because everybody wants to sing. But this would be good for her. In the choir, they teach them how to sing. They teach them the notes of the song. They teach them the guitar, the piano. They teach them! Ai, this church is so good to us. So good. They've helped us find work, find this house. Whatever I ask of them [the church], they help us. (Diocelina, mother)

In a more abstract, existential way, involvement at church and religious faith in general provided inspiration to fuel personal resilience. Faith offered meaning and context to life's struggles. Religious beliefs helped the immigrant families cope with assimilation stressors and difficult postimmigration changes and losses. Many parents and adolescents prayed that all would turn out well in the end. Some participants were confident that all would turn out well, and they felt that the Virgin of Guadalupe and God were above everyone, watching over them, and protecting them.

Someone asked me once if my life has been difficult, my life with my husband who was so cruel to us, who was an alcoholic, a drug addict, my son dying so young, and I said, yes. But I know that God has a plan for me. When my husband left us with no money, nothing, for a period of time, I said to my daughter, "Let it be what is meant to be. We will survive. The Virgin of Guadalupe will never abandon us." (Sulema, mother)

Now that she [daughter] will be finishing high school, she won't be able to continue studying. That's another problem. If I had papers, if I were legal here, then, there would be good chances that she could study [at the university]. But as it is, I see the situation as very difficult. I talk to El Señor [God] from my heart, and I ask that He finds us a way for our children to continue studying. These are the problems we face here, as Hispanos. (Miguel, father)

We lived for many years without God, but no more. It has an influence on the children. In my [birth] family, we are seven kids, and my parents did not fight in front of us. We never saw that. I asked my mother how they [her parents] *managed to put a good face in front of us kids every day. She told me that God was in their lives. And so, I said, "No more." And now, we walk with God. You know, in my family* [of origin], *we had a lot of trust. When we were little, my father would sit us on his lap and explain things to us, and teach us. When I was seven years old, he gave me a great lesson. Great lesson! We lived on a ranch, and he would show us things. Before planting season, he would give each of us some seeds in our hands. He said, "Come here, little mother, come here. See this seed?* [pointed into her open hand] *See this light?* [pointed up to the sun] *Even if you cover the light* [cupped both hands to cover the seed] *or the light gets covered, the seed will always grow towards the light. Always. You remember this, and even though you do not see the light, the seed will grow towards it.* (Diocelina, mother)

To borrow Diocelina's metaphor, these immigrant families were trying to grow towards the light even as they struggled with the darkness brought on by assimilation stressors. Churches helped to provide concrete assistance, spiritual guidance, interpersonal connections, and much-needed respite from the difficulties presented by monolingualism and discrimination that dominated other parts of their lives.

Conclusions

For most Latino immigrant adolescents, and many parents, the relationship to the host culture was underpinned by a consistent push to assimilate. Assimilation was prompted by two powerful mechanisms, monolingualism and discrimination. Monolingualism required immigrant adolescents and their parents to learn English if they were to fit into and advance in school and work. In this way, monolingualism was a strong form of interpersonal and institutional discrimination against Spanish speakers. Discrimination regulated belonging, enforcing conformity with U.S. norms, appearance, and behaviors. Discriminatory messages were disseminated by U.S. students and coworkers who repeatedly told immigrants to go back to their country. Assimilating individuals anticipated greater belonging, but this was an elusive goal because discrimination did not stop.

Seeing the Mexicans who have lived here a long time, and seeing them go through the same thing that we're going through is hard. Makes me think, does it get easier for us? (Diocelina, mother)

We wish we could have told her that it does get easier, but, based on our interviews with immigrants who had resided in the United States for varying lengths of time, we do not think that discrimination abates over time.

Monolingualism and discrimination served a purpose in promoting assimilation. In promoting cultural change, these obstacles certainly contributed to female adolescents and parents feeling anxious, fearful, isolated, and depressed. Male adolescents felt isolated and fearful as well, but they also grew angry and were ready to physically defend themselves. We will pursue these themes further in chapter 5 when we discuss how research has found culture-of-origin involvement (e.g., separation) and host cultural involvement (e.g., assimilation) to be connected to health, mental health, and adjustment.

Immigrant families found a refuge from the stress of monolingualism and discrimination in their interactions in church. Religious faith and spirituality were important coping mechanisms to handle daily assimilation stress. Churches responded to the Latino community differently from other institutions where we found monolingualism and discrimination to be common. In contrast, churches reached out in a more bicultural way to immigrant families. Many churches provided services in Spanish, supporting immigrant families with tangible assistance and other forms of guidance. Latino families became loyal and grateful, heightening their involvement and devotion. This illustrates an alternation model for cultural involvement, making bidirectional changes so that ethnic and host cultural groups can successfully adapt to one another. This bicultural model does not rely on assimilation or rejection. Having considered culture-of-origin involvement and host cultural involvement separately in the last two chapters, in chapter 4, we turn our attention to how Latino immigrant adolescents and their parents view biculturalism.

4

Balancing between Two Worlds
The Integration Stage of Bicultural Development

For me, my drawing [see figure 4.1] represents how I feel sometimes. How I feel confused, and how I feel about living here. I feel confused about living here away from my family, but I try not to think too much about that. It's as if I were raised here, you understand? I live here, but in reality, I feel confused because I like it here, but I also need and miss my other country. The longer you're here the more confused you get, because you don't know if it's better to be here how we are now, or if it would be better to be over there. Sometimes it's more confusing. You sacrifice having family close because you can't have everything in both places [Mexico and the United States]. It's hard. It's very hard to be in one place but want to be in another. Difficult. Difficult. And . . . umm, very confusing, because it's something you can't choose. Your parents chose it. It's difficult when you remember what you did there when you were with your family. It's difficult when you think about being in Mexico, but you are here. It's difficult on holidays like Christmas and the month of festivities, and New Year's, and all that.

—Juana, female adolescent

Figure 4.1 shows Juana's cultural map. The drawing illustrates her conflict and confusion about living between cultures. Her worlds are bifurcated, separate, and difficult to reconcile, representing a lower level of bicultural identity integration. Over time and with effort, this becomes easier for most bicultural adolescents as they navigate between the cultural systems with more fluidity and are able to integrate disparate cultural messages. In this chapter, we highlight the stages of bicultural identity development and discuss how different environmental systems (family, friends, peers) influence the process of becoming bicultural.

Fig. 4.1. Juana's cultural map

In this chapter, we use alternation theory as a guide in exploring the cultural capital, opportunities, and challenges that immigrant families face in living between two cultures. Alternation theorists argue that there is great value in the individual's maintaining her or his culture-of-origin while acquiring a second culture (Berry 1998; Feliciano 2001). Alternation theory is in strong contrast to the assimilation model, in which linear, one-directional change is emphasized. Alternation theory highlights integration of divergent norms, traditions, customs, and languages rather than assimilation from one culture to another (Gonzales et al. 2004).

As we discussed in chapter 1, acculturation was first defined as "phenomena which result when groups of individuals having different cultures come into continuous first hand contact with subsequent changes in the original culture patterns of either or both groups" (Redfield, Linton, and Herskovits 1936, 149). This original definition stressed continuous, long-term change and allowed for a bidirectional process, in which two interacting cultures could make accommodations. Contact between members of different cultural groups would precipitate cultural changes, with neither of the cultures lost or replaced by the other. Consequently, acculturation suggests cultural accommodation but does not assume assimilation.

According to Berry (1998), acculturation has two criteria: whether the acculturating individual or group maintains a positive relationship with the culture-of-origin, and whether the acculturating individual or group establishes a positive relationship to the host culture. In contrast, assimilation theory posits that a positive relationship to the dominant society is established without retention of ethnic identity. However, in alternation theory, the individual establishes a moderate-to-strong positive relationship to the host culture while also maintaining a moderate-to-strong positive relationship to the culture-of-origin.

Alternation theory is aligned with the original Redfield et al. (1936) definition of acculturation that allows for dynamic bidirectional adaptations to occur in either or both cultures. Assimilation theory is aligned with subsequent modifications to this definition that hypothesized that unidirectional change is imposed by the dominant onto the nondominant group. In the following sections of this chapter, we describe Latino immigrant families' relationships to their culture-of-origin. Then, we explore their relationship to the U.S. host culture. The combination of these two cultural forces leads to a detailed discussion of biculturalism. We examine benefits and challenges inherent in developing bicultural skills, paying special attention to the ways in which bilingualism and peer networks facilitate bicultural development.

Fully exploring the range of dynamics that characterize acculturation processes in general and biculturalism in particular is an ongoing challenge. Research in this area has traditionally emphasized quantitative epidemiological studies but has largely ignored qualitative methodologies that can explore the intricate complexity of biculturalism and the acculturation experience (Rogler, Cortes, and Malgady 1991). Biculturalism is a fascinating concept for qualitative inquiry because it involves complex issues in identity development. The process of becoming bicultural is not well researched and lends itself to this type of inquiry. The positive effects of biculturalism focus on the multiple cognitive and affective processes that help the individual withstand the negative impact of acculturation stress. It is ironic that qualitative research methods have not been commonly used in this research area, especially because the concept of biculturalism is dynamic, nonlinear, and multidimensional.

Biculturalism is commonly thought of as balancing two worlds or two cultures; however, the Latino adolescents we interviewed thought that they had three worlds to balance. Their Latino world was primarily driven by family influences and dynamics within the home. This family world supported their bicultural identity development, but was particularly invested in the adolescent's maintaining a sense of familism and pride in her or his culture-of-origin. The second world was the American world that was dominated by school and American friends. These American influences were strongly assimilationist, pushing the adolescent to become increasingly integrated into American culture. The need to learn the English language (i.e., become bilingual), and anti-Latino discrimination further supported this assimilation push. The third world was characterized by the adolescent's emerging sense of self. This emerging world represented the internal process for integrating disparate influences and making personal identity decisions. One Colombian female adolescent described her experience balancing these three worlds in the following way when asked to interpret a drawing she made.

> Anna Maria (female adolescent): *Here's my world* [pointed to the "me" circle on drawing paper]. *I can look down on them* [referring to the "friends" and "family" circles, separate and below the "me" circle]. *Family and friends and I see the differences* [pointed to circles]. *And before I make any decisions, I go to my new world, and that's just me, up there* [pointed to the "me" circle].
> Interviewer: Okay. So, look at this. Family and friends don't really connect.
> Anna Maria: [interrupted] *They are not alike at all.*

The family world this adolescent referred to represented her Latino influences whereas all of her friends were American. There was no overlap between these worlds, and the Latino and American worlds did not interact well. A young Mexican boy described similar dynamics in the following exchange with the interviewer.

> Interviewer: Tell me about this idea of living Mexico-America. Describe it.
> Luis (male adolescent): *Like, in your house, you live like Mexican. Your father and mother speak Spanish. My uncles speak Spanish. Nothing of English. And outside, like American. Outside is America, where I have to speak English. In my classes, with teachers. Everything outside is in English. Except some of my friends.*
> Interviewer: Where do you spend the majority of your day?
> Luis: *At school, the American place. From eight a.m. and I get home at four. But many of my friends speak Spanish at school.*
> Interviewer: So, do you feel more like in one culture than in another?
> Luis: *Yes, more in American culture. The school is pure American. The way they run the school. How things are done, like, like the classes. How the classes are. The teachers, how they teach, what they teach. The language everybody speaks. How the other students are.*

The following sections discuss each of these worlds in detail.

Relationship to Culture-of-Origin

As described in chapter 2, the Latino immigrant parents and adolescents we interviewed took pride in their nationality and preserved their customs, traditions, values, and language. In other words, they were acculturating without assimilating. By acculturating, we specifically mean that they were coming into continuous first-hand contact with U.S. culture in their schools and workplaces, where cultural changes were occurring. In chapter 3, we discussed the assimilation pressures of discrimination and monolingualism, and the way these mechanisms functioned in the acculturation process. While these pressures certainly affected immigrant families, parents and adolescents did not respond to assimilation pressures by letting go of their culture-of-origin customs, traditions, language, or behaviors.

> *I believe that one never, when one lives with one's family here* [in the United States], *one never leaves one's culture behind in order to learn another culture. You either learn from the other culture, or you learn how to manage both cultures, but you don't leave your culture behind. Never, you never leave your other culture behind. I think that one can live a whole lifetime here, and you will never ever let go of these* [Mexican] *customs. Even if sometimes you don't do them, they're always in your head. The customs are part of me.* (Nohemi, adolescent female)

> *We reflect often on what we were, and what we are now. It bothers me a lot when some people who have been here for a long time no longer want to speak Spanish. It seems foolish to me. I tell my kids to do the opposite. They should be able to speak two languages, and speak them very well. People need to know where they come from, and it's necessary that they know how to live, know how to share, know how to talk. These are important things that one ought not to forget.* (Adriana, mother)

> *I am not American because of my color, my language. My country is another country. I would never let go of how I feel when I see the* [Mexican] *flag. It's different. When they take out the* [American] *flag, people here salute it. In Mexico, I did* [salute] *with the Mexican flag. But here, no, I don't salute the American flag. I just stay standing with respect. The teacher and other students have asked me why I don't salute the* [American] *flag. I've told them I cannot salute this flag because it is not from my country.* (Alfredo, adolescent male)

There was a strong consensus among parents and adolescents, males and females, that it was critical to maintain culture-of-origin customs, tra-

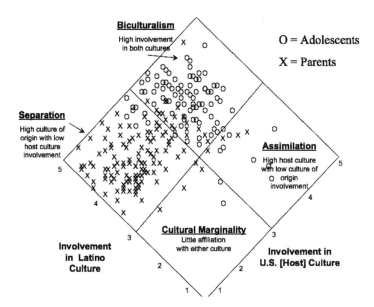

Fig. 4.2. Biculturalism scores from LAHP for Latino immigrant families (N = 323)

ditions, language, values, and national identity. Cultural identity was an indelible part of their being that could not be eroded by assimilation pressures. We asked parents and adolescents, "In what ways are you _____ [Mexican or Colombian, etc.]?" and they immediately provided numerous responses. With our next question, "In what ways are you not Mexican or Colombian?" there were few responses and some parents were offended, quickly retorting, "But I *am* Mexican." Their reactions illustrated the stability of their culture-of-origin identities even after years of living in the United States. Along with their national identities, immigrant families maintained their cultural traditions and rituals in their homes and churches. They spoke Spanish, practiced family-oriented and communal values, prepared traditional foods, and tried to re-create holiday celebrations as they remembered from their country-of-origin.

Figure 4.2 provides a scatterplot of the distribution of the Latino adolescents (immigrant and U.S. born) and parents (all foreign born) in the LAHP study on a measure of bicultural involvement. This chart uses adolescents' responses on the Bicultural Involvement Questionnaire (Szapocznik and Kurtines 1980) to graph Latino cultural involvement and non-Latino (United States) cultural involvement. The BIQ's Latino cultural involvement and non-Latino cultural involvement subscales each consist of twenty items rated on a five-point Likert scale. Scores are averaged to compensate for missing data on any individual items, resulting in a range from one to five on each dimension, with higher scores denoting greater cultural involvement. Results shown in figure 4.2 clearly illustrate that most adolescents were maintaining high levels of culture-of-origin involvement. Almost all of the immigrant and U.S.-born adolescents participating in LAHP would be considered either in the Separation category with strong cultural identities or in the Bicultural category with a balanced involvement in both cultures. Biculturalism was substantially more common than assimilation, even considering that 20 percent of the adolescent were born in the United States. This quantitative data supports the qualitative findings we report throughout this chapter.

Relationship to the U.S. Host Culture

Outside of their homes and churches, Latino parents and adolescents came into contact with U.S. culture and experienced the assimilation pressures of discrimination and monolingualism (see chapter 3). These pressures pushed them to learn English and take on American behaviors, customs, and values. Critics of acculturation research point out that many studies examine acculturation but few articulate actual differences between the culture-of-origin and the U.S. host culture (Hunt, Schneider, and Comer 2004). Unless those differences are established, acculturation is meaningless. The families we interviewed described a host of differences between their cultures-of-origin and U.S. culture, including differences in traditions, customs, values, social behaviors, laws, food, clothing, the physical environment, language, and climate.

> I'm Mexican because I maintain my Mexican nationality. But you know they always say, if I was there [in Mexico] at this age, I'd be different than I am here. I've always thought that this is a country of both a new future and of ruin. It's like saying . . . let's see, how can I explain this to you? For instance, here [in the United States], they always talk to you about marijuana and cocaine, and they scare you. In Mexico, you would say to your friends, "I'd never do that." Here, it's very normal. You use marijuana? That's okay. You use cocaine? That's okay. So everything is very different. For example, in Mexico, the girls, they would get up to a certain age where they didn't know what it was like to be with many boys. Whereas here, they're all very liberal. They think it's okay if they get involved with the first guy that comes along simply because they want to. In Mexico, you are taught to be more particular

when you're choosing a boyfriend. These are things that are very different. Here in the U.S., if you want to be out all night, you just worry about mom and dad not finding out and that's enough. But in Mexico, it's a very serious thing, and you know that. (Nohemi, female adolescent)

I was born there, I am from there. I feel Colombian because of the traditions that I have because there are different traditions there. And because I grew up in Colombia and it is very different from growing up here, because I don't know, it is very different in everything. In communication, the language, and because here, there is more money and more work than in Colombia. There is less there, and it is different. We played outside, with my friends, cousins. Here, we play inside, by ourselves. Here at home I speak Spanish and I am here with my parents and everything, and we have our foods, our customs, but when you go out, you have to change the language, and everything is different. I feel very different here [in the United States] *with my Colombian culture because when I am at home, it is almost like being in Colombia for me, but when I leave my house, it is different. The people are different and they are not like me because here, there are Hispanics, but they are not the majority. So, when I go out, I see that the people are not like me, they speak a different language, they look different and all. When I am here at home, I can communicate with my parents, with my sisters, and when I'm not* [at home], *I am more alone.* (Maria Dolores, female adolescent)

She's changed just a little. Mainly through the language [English], *more than anything else. And in her classes, she is studying much more than compared to how she studied over there* [in Mexico]. *She arrived timid, but here, she has seen everything. Everything! She is less timid now. Her timidness has left her. It has to be that way, I think, because the customs here* [in the United States] *change people. She has seen things at school that she would not have seen in her old school. How the students address the teachers. How they say they haven't done their homework. How they* [the students] *talk about going anywhere they want, and their parents let them. How the students are encouraged to express their opinions. The school is very different than the school she attended before* [in Mexico]. *She attends various classes with different teachers, and over there, she had one teacher who taught all the subjects in the same classroom. Here, each teacher has her specialty class, over there, no. There was no class for physical education. There are many more students here. Most of the students she doesn't know. At her other school* [in Mexico], *she knew most of the students. She even gets her lunch at school, free. The benefits are many here* [in the United States]. *This is something I really like, that there are benefits for the children* [emphasized the phrase, "for the children"]. *None of the children go hungry at this school. How the school loves their children here! When they see a child who is waiting to get home, they'll bring the child home themselves. That is something you don't see in Mexico. They'd tell them to start walking home. That's the way they get home, walking. Here, it's not like that. Not here. And for everything, they ask for permission! For everything, they ask for permission. They send us a note, and they explain that they want to take the children to a park, and how the children will get there. They ask for my permission by authorizing the note. With permission from the parents, they avoid problems with the children. In this way, the school respects the parents very much.* (Miguel, father)

Well, it is strange to live between two cultures that are very different. For example, here [in the United States] *it's very liberal. They* [Americans] *are liberal, the children and the parents. In Mexico, no. In Mexico, they respect each other a lot. But here, no. Here, the children, after a certain age, can do what they want. They even leave their homes because they are no longer minors. But in Mexico, no. You keep your children at home because of the advice you give them. If I tell my son, "Look son, you must keep respect towards your parents regardless of your age, because this is our custom, and we will always be your parents." And even if he comes here, we have gotten him accustomed to this type of respect towards his parents. Even though, he will see other adolescents do things different here, they leave home or do anything they want after a certain age, no. One must stand firm in the ways one has been taught.* (Petrona, mother)

There were marked differences between the two cultures. The process described by these immigrant families corresponded with the original notion of acculturation, that is, contact between two autonomous and independent cultural groups occurred and cultural changes were taking place. Parents and adolescents actively maintained their culture-of-origin values, customs, and traditions while being involved in U.S. culture outside their homes. Following alternation theory, these moderate-to-intense relationships with both cultures suggested that parents and adolescents were living between two cultures.

Biculturalism—Living between Two Cultures

Biculturalism is the ability to navigate between two different cultures. This ability should evolve through a series of stages, moving from bifurcated cultural contact to a fully integrated bicultural identity. During these stages, family members, school personnel, and Latino and American friends strongly influence the development of bicultural identity. Immigrant adolescents were placed in a difficult situation where they had to adjust to a system that was completely foreign to them while balancing disparate messages from people who occupied important roles in their lives (e.g., parents, teachers, friends). Even though school and friends outside the home pressed the adolescent to assimilate, parents consistently reminded their children that they could never change their Latino blood; what was internal to them was unchangeable.

The adolescents were in different phases of the bicultural identity development process. It is useful to place their descriptions of what it is like to be bicultural next to one another. Clara, a low-assimilated (e.g., Separated/Enculturated adaptation style) Mexican adolescent, described her situation:

With Americans, I just speak English. With Mexicans, I just speak Spanish. But I feel Mexican. I am Mexican, even though I'm living here. I am very, I am very, how do you say? I like to have fun. That's what I enjoy, talking and sharing stories, telling jokes with people. But not really with the Americans. They are serious. They don't stand around talking for much time. They say what they need to say, and leave. I like being with people, but not really with the Americans. (Clara, female adolescent)

In contrast to Clara's experience, a highly assimilated Colombian female was moving away from her culture-of-origin influences to embrace the U.S. way of life. There was significant stress between this adolescent and her less-assimilated parents. For example, she grew excited when we discussed differences in attitudes toward dating.

In Colombia, you bring the guy to your house. They talk to your parents. Here [voice pitch went up], *they don't. They're kinda more free* [shrugged shoulders]. *In that way, it's, it's like, like, like, the boy comes to the house for the parents* [in Colombia]. *Here, no* [held index finger up]. *If the boy comes to the house, it's for the girl* [pointed to herself with index finger that was held up]. *Like, they do homework together, listen to music, like they chill together. They don't have to talk to the parents* [emphasized the word "have"]. (Camila, female adolescent)

A final comment from a bicultural Colombian female showed she was very conscious of the strategies she used to move between the two cultural systems.

It depends on where I'm at. In my house, I consider myself fully Latina. I'm with the family, and they are Latino. When I'm with my friends, I'm Latina because they're Latinos. When I'm with Americans, I change totally to American. And when I'm with both, I guess I'm bicultural [smiled]. (Juliana, female adolescent)

Parents and adolescents we interviewed did not typically use the word "biculturalism." Therefore, we stopped using the word after the first interview so we could observe how they would describe the process of participating in two cultures. Most participants described biculturalism as "living between two cultures" or "two worlds." In general, parents and adolescents were in favor of living between two cultures.

I've always thought that living with two cultures is a very nice thing. I've always thought it's a very nice thing because I think that if I could pick a lifestyle, I'd like to meet many people from other cultures. So I don't dislike it here. On the contrary, I'd like to know more about their culture, understand them more, communicate more with them, and be able to spend more time with them. I think it would be nice to be able to share in their culture, and then always be able to go home to your own culture. At home, I'm with my mom and dad in our culture, and just as soon as I go out with my friends or with my next-door neighbors, I'm already sharing in another culture. I think that's really cool. (Sylvia, female adolescent)

Well, ideally, [living between cultures] *is a beautiful thing because one comes with one's culture and customs, and you come here, and you can grab other customs, the ones you like. It's another culture. It's something more.* (Petrona, mother)

The [American] *kids are telling her this is how it is, and this is how we do this or that. And the language* [English], *she's really using the language now. But she is not losing the customs that she has brought with her. Those customs, because she remembers them, she holds on to them. Had she been little when we brought her here* [to the United States], *her customs would be erased by these new customs. She knows the life she had in our homeland, and that has helped her maintain her customs. But she has taken on all the customs from here, while keeping her customs from there* [Mexico], *and it is like she's in between the two. She's in between the two customs, and that appears to be fine with her. She's not forgetting what she's brought with her. If she were younger, I think she would forget. Her customs, she will never forget them.*

She knows her customs. They've become a part of her because she was older when she left our country. (Miguel, father)

For me, no, [I do not live with two cultures] *because I feel Mexican, and I will always be Mexican, even if I don't live in Mexico. Sometimes I have to live with two cultures. It isn't real hard, but it isn't easy, either. Since I'm learning English, I can go places and ask for what I need. I am not like them* [her parents]. *When I need to ask someone where something is, I don't get stuck with English like they do. I can ask, and they really can't. I've had to go through many* [emphasized the word "many"] *situations in my life where I had to learn it* [English], *and I had to say it well. And yes, that* [emphasized the word "that"] *is hard. I know lots of words in English, but I prefer being with other* [female] *Mexicans. I feel better being with other* [female] *Mexicans.* (Teresa, female adolescent)

Benefits of Living between Two Cultures

Alternation theory researchers have found that maintaining moderate to high levels of participation in both the host culture and the culture-of-origin creates the fewest psychosocial problems for the acculturating individual and provides the basis for the best adjustment (see chapter 6; LaFromboise, Coleman, and Gerton 1993). Researchers suggest that biculturalism, or having the ability to navigate competently within two different cultures, is the optimal end point for the process of cultural acquisition (Berry 1998; Feliciano 2001; LaFromboise et al. 1993; Suarez-Orozco and Suarez-Orozco 2001). For the immigrant individual and her or his family, alternation theorists support the *integration* of cognition, attitudes, and behaviors from both the culture-of-origin and the host culture, which is also called the culture of acquisition. This integration may result in bilingualism, the development of multiple identities, and cognitive frame switching, which is the individual's ability to shift between cultural scripts to match environmental demands. An example of this cultural shifting is immigrant adolescents behaving "American" at school and "Latino" at home (Dolby 2000; Suarez-Orozco and Suarez-Orozco 2001; Trueba 2002).

As described in detail in chapter 6, researchers report that bicultural individuals display an array of positive qualities, such as reporting higher levels of quality of life, affect balance, and positive psychological adjustment (Lang et al. 1982); high levels of social interest and low levels of depression (Miranda and Umhoefer 1998); wider repertoires of achievement styles in their educational pursuits (Gomez and Fassinger 1994); lower acculturation stress and more family pride (Gil, Vega, and Dimas 1994); less school dropout (Feliciano 2001); and lower levels of family conflict and more commitment, help, support, cohesion, and adaptability among family members (Miranda, Estrada, and Firpo-Jimenez 2000; Smokowski, Rose, and Bacallao 2008).

Suarez-Orozco and Suarez-Orozco (2001) discussed the construction of identity in immigrant adolescents. In one of the largest qualitative studies of immigrant families, these researchers tracked more than four hundred children of immigrants from a variety of Latin American and Asian cultures living in either Boston or San Francisco. They identified three adaptation styles that are similar to the three upper quadrants—assimilation, separation, and biculturalism—depicted in figure 1.2. The first adaptation style is *ethnic flight*, which, similar to assimilation, occurs when adolescents align with the dominant culture and separate from their culture-of-origin. The ethnic flight strategy can help the adolescent "make it" or be accepted in mainstream American society, but it often comes at a significant cost to the adolescent's social and emotional functioning. The second adaptation style, *adversarial*, is similar to separation and occurs when an immigrant adolescent rejects or responds in opposition to host culture norms, behaviors, and attitudes, thus creating an adversarial identity. Being disparaged and disenfranchised can push immigrant adolescents into creating marginalized individual and group identities that reject mainstream norms and values. Like Flores-Gonzales's (2002) "street kids" discussed in chapter 3, adversarial adolescents may seek ethnic gang affiliation for protection and pursue unconventional reward structures because other opportunities are blocked. The final adaptation style, which is seen as the most promising, is *transcultural identity* formation. This bicultural identity style fuses aspects of both cultures and serves as a bridge, or cultural broker, between the disparate cultural systems.

As compared to other adaptation and acculturation styles, bicultural individuals experience less stress and anxiety because they have skills to handle stressors and to access resources from both cultural systems (Rashid 1984). Bicultural individuals appear to benefit from the ability to shift their socio-cognitive perceptual schemas to fit situational demands. This cultural frame switching is more highly developed in bicultural individuals than it is in their low- or highly-assimilated peers, and allows them to cope successfully with a wide range of culture-laden situations (Haritatos and Benet-Martinez 2002). When bicultural individuals perceive environmental stimuli connected to the host culture, such as a flag or a teacher they know who is from the United States, these cues prompt a shift in their cognitions so that they begin to think in the appropriate cultural framework.

In a situation in which environmental cues from the culture-of-origin dominate, bicultural individuals shift back to their original way of thinking. Overall, bicultural individuals maintain a positive relationship with both cultures without having to choose one or the other; they participate in the two different cultures by tailoring their behavior to the situation at hand (LaFromboise and Rowe 1983; LaFromboise et al. 1993; Bacallao and Smokowski 2009). Adolescents in our study gave examples of how they adjusted their behavior according to environmental cues.

> *It just means, speaking one way to a group of people and then, going home, and speaking another way to your family. It means going to a football game and then, going to church. It means being different because at school, work, it's all the American life. At home, church, they expect the Hispanic way of living. That's just the way it is. At first, I found that people looked at me funny sometimes, and I'd get home and wonder, "What happened?" And I found myself holding on to my mom like I'll do at home, but we weren't home. We were at the mall. [Paused for a few seconds.] I had a meeting at school. My mom came. People saw us, I was hugging her. That's normal to us. But I saw some people looking. Hispanics express more to their families, I think. But it was looked at funny because she was my mom, and these were my friends, and they were like thinking, "What are you doing?" And then, I started realizing what I was doing wrong, or what I was doing like a Hispanic but in an all-American place. And then you learn what not to do in school, and what you can do at home or at church. You learn how to act one way, and as soon as you step out, you turn it on the other way.* (Luis, male adolescent)

The adolescents' experiences of bicultural identity were split, depending upon what the situation demanded. This ability to shift between cultures showed that their sense of identity was fluid. Parents and adolescents agreed that there were important benefits to being bicultural.

> *The idea of living in two cultures is a good thing for this country because the Hispanic needs to adjust to the ways of the American. We live in a country that has different customs than ours, and if one does not adjust to these customs, one is forever sad and longing to be back in one's country. It holds one back from advancing in this rich country. So many opportunities for work, education, buying a house. To have the two cultures is to open oneself to all the opportunities in this country. To have only my Colombian culture is to limit myself in these opportunities. This is much, much easier for the children to do than for their parents. [My daughter] can go anywhere she wants and doesn't have to depend on anyone to interpret. She is, she is free in this*

country, in that sense. If you can't speak the language of the country, you are not free, really. One becomes more vulnerable. Olivia is free of all these constraints. She knows the freedoms of this country, and she can use them. (Sergio, father)

It is difficult for me, because at times you are part of one and also part of the other. You do both things of both cultures. Sometimes you like one thing about one culture better, and at other times you prefer to do something like the way the other culture does it. So, it is like half and half. That's difficult. Some things in one culture, I am in favor of, but other things [in that same culture], I am against. I like it that the [United States] schools give scholarships for studying, so you can keep studying. They [Americans] give you support like for food [at school]. In my culture, they give you help, but not economically. It is a different kind of help. (Eva, female adolescent)

Well, if we could live with two cultures, we could move more in the middle of the two. We would have two languages, not one. We would have two ways of doing things, like working hard at school and resting with your family at home, listening to the two countries' music, eating Mexican food and American food, celebrating their holidays and our holidays. What I'm saying is that the rhythm of our lifestyles would change. We would not have only our Mexican rhythm, but it would be mixed with something American. That would change our lifestyle, but I see it as a way of Americanizing. But yes, yes, it would change our Mexican lifestyle [said in a serious tone]. (Guillermo, father)

BILINGUALISM

Bicultural competencies are strongly associated with language use. Several studies have found that immigrant youths fluent in both their culture-of-origin language and English do better in school than those who speak one language (e.g., English-alone or limited-English speakers; Stanton-Salazar and Dornbusch 1995; Rumberger and Larson 1998; Feliciano 2001). Bilingual youth also display fewer emotional or behavioral problems, less delinquency, and lower levels of aggression than nonbicultural peers (Toppleberg et al. 2002).

In our interviews, bilingualism also emerged as a key component of living between two cultures. Learning English, or "the language," as participants referred to it, was both the largest obstacle in the acculturation process and one of the greatest assets adolescents would gain from living in the United States. Parents supported adolescents' development of bilingual skills, which they recognized would enhance their children's career opportunities in their country-of-origin.

I see a better future for my children in Mexico because in Mexico they could be bilingual teachers. They could work at a school with good pay, because they will take the language back with them, the real thing from here in the United States. The language is what they will gain here. Since they know how to read and write Spanish perfectly, they have that opportunity to be bilingual teachers. In Mexico, they need bilingual teachers. The goal is to return in maybe five or six years. (Adolfo, father)

We have more of a plan, more of a security over there [in Mexico] *with the ranch than we do here* [in the United States]. *Here, who knows what we'll be doing, and for how long. Only God knows. We don't know. In Vera Cruz, we have more of a knowing what we will do.* [Family owns a ranch in Mexico.] *At a ranch, there is always work. But for now, he can go to school. He does not need to go to work. I'll tell you, if he studies that language* [English], *over there in Mexico, he will be able to find plenty of work with that language. To be bilingual, that will promise him work. There's a lot of Americans visiting Vera Cruz, and they speak only one language* [held up one index finger]. *He's learning the language. But you know, to be back in one's own land, that's a very comforting feeling. But we'll see what he decides to do when he turns eighteen.* (Victor, father)

What happens is that because we come from the border, they will have better jobs in the United States because they will be able to work in the factories and the agencies that are run by Americans but are on the border. They will have both languages. They will have more doors open to them if they finish their studies here. I would like them to finish all of their schooling here. University, too. (Petrona, mother)

Since it is a border, they would be able to find better work there because they speak the two languages, English and Spanish. They could live in Mexico and work in the U.S. They would be well prepared to start businesses over there [in Mexico]. (Luis, father)

In addition to bettering employment prospects, bilingual skills were also associated with other benefits. Parents were proud of their adolescents' bilingual skills, and said speaking two languages would increase the adolescents' social status in their countries by signaling they were educated in the

United States. Adolescents who spoke both languages were able to make a wider network of friends, develop diverse social skills, perform better in school, and navigate within U.S. environments. Bilingual adolescents also gained a new status within their families because they were able to help their parents with translation and were valued by the family as cultural brokers.

Being bilingual is a very beautiful thing, and a very good thing. She helps us so much with the language because if there is something from school that I don't understand, or if I take her to the doctor, she can tell the doctor what I say. When she is sick and I take her to the doctor, I tell her in Spanish what to tell the doctor, and she tells him what I say. She helps me with everything, with everything. She has never told me that she won't help me. Do you know what she says about speaking both Spanish and English? She says, "Mami, if I don't speak English, I won't be able to work anywhere. And if I don't speak Spanish, they won't give me the job as fast as someone who does." (Sulema, mother)

My parents didn't really have to adapt because of us [the children]. *We are there as their mediator between the two cultures, and when they need something, they'll say, "Can you help us out?" We don't tell them that we need this or that. We go to the bank, the doctor, the store. We help them. Like at the bank, they'll say, "Say this for us." So they really didn't need to adapt too much. They live their way here, and when they want something from the outside, they come to us, and that's just how it is. We help them out.* (Manuel, adolescent male)

Becoming bilingual and living between two cultures also provided parents and adolescents with the opportunity to create something new—a mixture of features from both cultures and both languages.

Living between cultures is entertaining because you learn your culture and you learn other cultures, and you mix the cultures, and you can make something new out of one and the other, or you can pick the way that you like how things are done. (Reyna, female adolescent)

I always try to look at the good. Both cultures have good and bad things. The Mexican culture also has things that are not very good. An example is having many festivities with little money. It is a tradition that we have, to waste money on fireworks and having many celebrations with much food and drink. Here, Americans don't have festivities like we have over there [in

Mexico]. *These are things that harm the economy, more than anything. So, I try to take the good from both cultures* [reached out with both hands in different directions]. *I take what is good for me from both.* (Adolfo, father)

It's two different ways of living your life. If you live one way, you'll be greatly discriminated in one. You have to know how to change modes, like immediately. There's no way to live one lifestyle. It's really living two lives. You can't really live one life because if you do, then people look at you strangely for whichever one you're not living. You have to be able to look at a situation and see where you are at, what people you are with, what place are you at, what are the right ways of acting, what to say, what not to say, what language to say it in, how to say it. Yeah, sometimes it even gets as detailed as what you wear. In one culture, what you wear is not right for the other. Sometimes you have to even change opinions [emphasized the phrase "change opinions"]. *I do it to stay out of trouble.* (Manuel, male adolescent)

Manuel provided a good example of the integration that signifies a high level of bicultural identity development. This bicultural identity integration comes with a practiced fluidity in shifting cultural perspectives, understanding the norms required and appropriate in disparate contexts and situations, and changing behavior to match situational expectations. The benefits of biculturalism manifest most clearly at this advanced stage of integrative cultural development.

Adolescent females realized there were new options in the United States that were not as readily available in Mexico, where traditional values emphasized marrying and starting a family. Being able to choose from a wider range of religions or occupations entailed more decisions about how they wanted to live their lives.

[Mexican parents] *do not want us to behave like Americans . . . that we are Mexicans . . . in other words that we don't become so liberal but rather that we remain like we were before we left Mexico. So we do not change our way of being. One example is that I am accustomed to the majority of people in Mexico being Catholic and believing in God and Jesus Christ, but all of a sudden it is different here. There are Pentecostals and Jews, and that is different. That is difficult because you do not know anymore if everyone is the same or different from you, and how do you decide? That is so different. There are many different types of people and religions in this country. And it makes you think; which religion do you want, you think is best, and which one do you want to follow. There are so many options in this country.* (Eva, female adolescent)

A woman, well especially in the place where I used to live [in Mexico], *sometimes we don't aspire to anything, and we simply say: "I'll finish la prepa* [high school]; *I'll marry, have kids, and dedicate myself to the home." Whereas my ideas have changed here, because now I say, "I want to do this* [waved one hand to one side and then her second hand to the other side], *I want to do that before I marry* [emphasized the word, "before"], *before I start a family, or before I dedicate myself to the home." I don't necessarily want to be stuck somewhere taking care of kids, because in reality I think there's time for everything, but that's not the only thing I want for my life. Not anymore.* (Nohemi, female adolescent)

Challenges Inherent in Living between Two Cultures

Along with these advantages, living between two cultures also causes challenges. Many options and multiple identities bring confusion and complexity. For example, maintaining strong ties with two cultural systems can cause contradiction, tension, and social strain (Haritatos and Benet-Martinez 2002), especially during the early stages of bicultural identity development, before different cultural messages have been integrated. Veronica Vivero and Sharon Jenkins (1999) suggest that cross-cultural tensions (i.e., the stress of trying to adapt to contradictory social norms, values, and communication processes) may result in cultural homelessness. We think this bifurcated confusion occurs in the beginning stages of bicultural development but is resolved with time and effort. Even so, the cultural frame switching that is thought to enhance the social and cognitive repertoires of bicultural individuals may also lead to social and emotional confusion when the tensions between cultural systems are too intense for the individual to integrate.

Consistent with these thoughts about cross-cultural tensions, some of the parents and adolescents we interviewed expressed social and emotional confusion as a result of living between two worlds. Bilingual individuals reported that at times it was difficult to decide which language to speak or which cultural values to support. This difficult decision making, often in the presence of or under the pressure of their peers, was complicated by the fact that many of the adolescents missed their country-of-origin and felt caught between the two cultures.

I think it is difficult when you speak Spanish and every one stares at you, and those that speak English tell you not to speak Spanish. So you wonder whether to speak Spanish or not. You start to question your own language.

It is complicated to decide which of the two languages to speak at school, and sometimes you decide to speak some words in Spanish but most in English so that everyone understands. That is complicated, deciding which language to speak [at school], *because some speak English and some speak Spanish, and you don't know what to do. Normally, I'd just speak Spanish if the others speak Spanish. Sometimes you speak English with the Americans and they tell you to speak Spanish with them, or not speak Spanish to them and only speak English. My Hispanic friends have agreed to speak Spanish among ourselves, even though we know we have to practice English. If the majority* [of people around me] *is American, then we speak the English we know. If the majority are Hispanics, among ourselves, we speak Spanish, but if we are talking with them, then English. If they are with us, so as not to make them feel bad, then we must speak English so that they know what we are saying, so they do not think we are talking about them.* (Sylvia, female adolescent)

There are times that we say, "Now, let's do something that they [the Americans] *do to have fun." We do that every now and then. But we have our culture. More often* [living with two cultures is difficult] *when our children request more permission to go with their friends, more liberties. They'll say, "No, here, Mama, it's different." And they insist that it's different* [in this culture], *and that is when it's hard. We try to say, "But no, we have our culture, our way of thinking from our land, and we want to maintain that." But it is difficult living with two cultures.* (Diocelina, mother)

Conflicts sometimes arose when an adolescent knew customs and values from two cultures that were difficult to integrate. Adolescents understood the values from both cultures and needed to form personal opinions when the cultural ideologies clashed.

It's difficult being bicultural when you have to like, when you have to like, you have different opinions in each culture. You have to defend different points of view. Like knowing things from both cultures, it puts me against some things that each culture does because I know how things are done in the other culture. In Colombia, a child is supposed to work. Being in this country now, I'm against that. My Colombian people there are okay with that, that children can work to help the family. I ask my friends over there about their work. To me, as an American, I am against that. But as a Colombian, I can understand that many of the children have to help out at the house, with their families because they're poor. (Angel, female adolescent)

Peer Networks and Living between Two Cultures

Few studies have explored the role that peer networks play in acculturation processes. Peer influence should not be ignored or underestimated because such influence is critical in facilitating or hindering cultural adaptation. In the families we interviewed, interactions with peers were arguably the most complex aspect of living between two cultures. While it was clear to adolescents that their family home and church represented their Latino culture and that school and work represented U.S. culture, interactions with peers were ambiguous. Latino and non-Latino American peer networks were often separated, and each of these subsystems had positive and negative nuances. Some adolescents chose their niche while others had no friends or floated between divergent groups. In the sections below, we describe characteristics of Latino and non-Latino American peer networks.

LATINO PEERS

It was often harder for adolescents to make friends in the United States than in their country-of-origin. For example, the extended family networks in Mexico often included cousins of the same age. Large extended families, together with shared language and town centers within walking distance, often made for a dynamic social life. In contrast, immigrant adolescents in the United States cited the need to be driven everywhere as a major obstacle to making and maintaining friendships. Most adolescents said they saw friends only at school—a place where speaking Spanish was sometimes discouraged—or spoke to them over the telephone.

Immigrant adolescents joined Latino peer groups more readily than non-Latino peer groups. Difficulties speaking English limited opportunities for making friends within non-Latino American groups or with Latinos who did not speak Spanish. Experiences with Latino peers were mixed. Immigrant adolescents said that Latino peers sometimes said ugly things, were bothersome, rebellious, and mean. In addition, Latino peers were often mentioned as having a negative influence because they teased the newly immigrated Latinos about being responsible in school, urged them to break family curfews, and did not believe in themselves. One female adolescent thought that her Latino peers who had been in the United States longer thought they were better than Latino newcomers. Another female adolescent reported having her life threatened by a U.S.-born Mexican boy who was asked to translate for her in school. One male adolescent was becoming involved with Latino peers who were in a gang and who led him into risk-taking behaviors. He associated with them for protection from racist American peers.

*My friends are probably a negative influence although they protect me from fights. If someone wants to fight me, my friends will take care of him. They want me to go to some of their parties. They like to drive to abandoned houses. Then we party in there. These houses, you can't get to without a car. Some of them are farther back from the road, lots of woods around. The po-*lice found us once [head dropped slightly, paused]. *They must've heard talk of the party. They checked to see if we had marijuana. Each person, every one was checked. They drove me home, told the boss* [his father] *where they found me. I got in trouble* [shook his head] *with him. I told him I didn't have marijuana, and the police, they didn't find any on me. They brought me home and he* [his father] *understood enough* [of what the police had told him]. *They're not my friends. I do a few things with them. When they have parties, they invite me. That's how it is here. I don't do too much with them. They're not my friends* [shook his head again]. (Jaime, male adolescent)

Other immigrant adolescents often had a positive relationship with Latino peers, and Latino peers who became friends were valuable sources of support. These peers helped the newcomers adjust by interpreting in class and explaining English instructions. These Latino friends understood the acculturation process and what it felt like to not understand the language, the school system, or the curriculum. These peers provided emotional support and talked about common difficulties such as having conflicts with parents or being unable to continue their studies because of their documentation status.

I don't have many [Latino friends]. *I only have one because in my school, there are not many Hispanos. I have a friend who came here a year ago* [from Honduras]. *In August, it will be one year, and she speaks English, and she helps me a lot. I ask her how to say things in English, and she helps me because she knows. She tells me to go and ask the teacher, and the teacher gets happy because I am learning. My friend understands me very well.* (Maria Dolores, female adolescent)

When you are talking in English, and you don't pronounce one word correctly, that's it. You realize that you can't express yourself as a Mexican, as easily as you can in Spanish. When I'm with my [Latino] *friends, we mix the two* [languages] *because when you can't say a word in one language, you can say it in the other.* (Jaime, male adolescent)

Mexican friends supported me, supported me a lot in my studies. I can talk to them, and they'll tell me, "Don't feel sad, Reyna" They tell me that I shouldn't feel sad. I'm not the only one who has suffered. It helps. It was a little difficult because arriving here with no English, not knowing the schools. I couldn't do the homework. It was all very difficult. In the classroom, I could only ask a [female] friend. I would guess at the words the teacher was saying, and aaah, it was very difficult to adapt here. But God is good, and the other Mexican girls in my class helped me. (Reyna, female adolescent)

They've always been there at times when I've felt bad. They listen to me, help me with my problems. My friend. Her name is Inez. She's Mexican. Inez is the one who most listens to me, who doesn't get tired of me. She has patience with me. I see her at school every day. Sometimes, I see her at church. Or sometimes, I invite her to my house. We'll sit here and do our homework together. Like that, we'll pass the time. She is always on my side. She always helps me. I trust her. She's the same age as me, fourteen. I hardly ever go to her house because I don't have a ride, and her father drinks and he's a cocaine addict. My father won't let me go there. She comes to my house. (Teresa, female adolescent)

Her friends are only Hispanics. She has her little group. They're all Mexicans and with them, she is in her element, with her [emphasized the word "her"] *language. Her language* [repeated softly]. (Diocelina, mother)

One of the most striking observations occurred when adolescents compared their peer networks in their country-of-origin to their new Latino peers in the United States. Latino peers in the United States appeared to be a healthier influence than peers in the countries-of-origin. One adolescent said he would probably be in jail with his friends if he were still living in Mexico.

I think better here. I believe that I'll have a better future now than what I thought I had in Mexico. The school helped, but mostly, I think it's because I have [Latino] friends here. In Mexico, I didn't have many friends. And the friends I had, it was because we did bad things together. Here, I can have friends and not have to do bad things to keep those friends. I have a lot more friends here. That has helped me, and has changed how I think about my future. In Mexico, I went to school. The school started earlier, ended at 2:30. I'd come home to spend time with my friends. We did some bad things like stealing, mostly stealing. Hub caps off cars, things like that. I had to do it because I'd be with them. The friends I have here are better. They're not bad. Because I'm fat, I had those friends [in Mexico]. Because the others, I couldn't be friends with them. They called me bad names. The bad friends accepted me as long as I did bad stuff with them. (Juan, male adolescent)

There were parallel themes for parents. Although adult Latino peers were sometimes described as not helpful or biased against newcomers, overall adult Latino peers assisted parents in understanding U.S. culture, offering information, resources, and advice concerning the way things are done in the United States.

There are certain persons that have lived here a long time and speak the same language as us, and they have helped us a lot. They explain things to us, how things are here. (Guillermo, father)

It is good when other Mexican families offer their help. And we accept it. They have been here longer, and they know how things are. (Luis, father)

Overall, Latino peers provided critical support, serving as cultural mentors who understood the difficulties and the benefits inherent in the acculturation process. There was a natural fit between immigrant parents and adolescents and Latino peers. In contrast, the fit with non-Latino American peers was problematic and difficult to establish.

NON-LATINO AMERICAN PEERS

Few immigrant Latino adolescents had non-Latino American peers as friends. More often their interactions with non-Latino American peers were marked by racial discrimination against immigrants and hampered by language differences. In all of the ecological systems (family, churches, workplaces, schools), American peers were reported as being the most discriminatory, rejecting immigrants and devaluing biculturalism. To support this assertion, table 4.1 presents responses from LAHP adolescents to questions concerning how different people and social systems in their lives valued living between two cultures. This table shows that adolescents perceived the least support for going between different cultures from non-Latino Anglo friends, and from people in their neighborhoods, in their towns or cities, and in the United States in general. At the same time, Latino adolescents, their families, teachers, Latino friends, ministers, and church congregations supported going between different cultures.

Non-Latino American peers had different customs, language, and behaviors that made immigrant adolescents feel as if they did not belong with this group. Further, immigrant parents discouraged their children from

TABLE 4.1

Biculturalism Support from Different Ecological Levels—Adolescents Only

	Not at all		Some		Very much
1. How much do you value going between different cultures?	8%	—	25%	17%	50%
2. How much does your family value going between different cultures?	8%	8%	17%	8%	58%
3. How much do your teachers at school value going between different cultures?	9%	27%	9%	9%	45%
4. How much do your Latino friends value going between different cultures?	8%	8%	25%	8%	50%
5. How much do your non-Latino friends value going between different cultures?	25%	8%	33%	—	33%
6. How much does your minister value going between different cultures?	—	—	9%	18%	73%
7. How much does your congregation value going between different cultures?	—	9%	27%	18%	45%
8. How much do people in your neighborhood value going between different cultures?	17%	17%	8%	33%	25%
9. How much do people in your town value going between different cultures?	8%	8%	76%	—	8%
10. How much do people in the United States value going between different cultures?	—	8%	50%	25%	17%

befriending American adolescents because they perceived them as liberal role models for bad behavior.

> *The most difficult part of adapting is to have friends. We hardly have any American friends because they'll say, "You're Mexican, and you're invading our territory." For me, yes, it hurts a little, but it doesn't affect me too much.* (Teresa, female adolescent)

> *It's that I don't really spend time with American friends. I don't really have American friends. Just people I work with. For instance, how to behave outside of my house. All of the friends that we have that are American, they're very different. Their customs are very different. And I think that no matter how much I hang out with them, I think that in my head there will always be that concept that their behavior is wrong, and even if in that environment, what they do is good, it's never going to be good to me because I have different customs, and they are my customs* [emphasized the word "my"]. (Nohemi, female adolescent)

> *The relationship with her classmates is not pleasant. That is the most difficult experience that she has had, having problems with the black race, because she has had unpleasant friction with them, and that has made her feel badly.*

That is the strongest experience she has had. And the language barrier. But not as much as the problems with her classmates. (Adolfo, father)

I was playing American football, and someone was right here [gestured to his side], *and if I tried to tackle him, he'd start hitting me, but hitting hard. It happened more than once. I left him alone. I'd let him run. I did that because I didn't want him to hit me. This other time, we were at the football field, playing American football, and this guy started fighting with me* [vocal pace quickened]. *He joined the game. He usually doesn't play with us. And as the game was going on, he started punching me. I hit him back. The police came. It had turned into a fight. The others there had called the police.* [Mother interjected: "Tell why he was fighting you. What did he tell you?"] *Because I didn't know English. Yes. That's what he told the police. He told me to go back to Mexico.* (Alfredo, male adolescent)

Some [American peers] *are bad, some are good. The bad ones, when I first got here, would talk to me, and I did not understand them. Maybe they were making fun of me. The good ones are not like that, they would tell me words in Spanish and I felt fine because I knew they were not calling me things. They were trying to talk to me.* (Maria Dolores female adolescent)

As Maria Dolores's comment indicates, not all interactions with American peers were negative experiences. A few of the immigrant adolescents were able to press through these negative experiences to build friendships with non-Latino Americans. When these friendships occurred, they were quite helpful to the immigrant adolescents. American peers helped immigrant adolescents find their way around school, showed them how things were done, explained the difference in U.S. customs, and provided English-language assistance. These friendships were reciprocal, with non-Latino American peers displaying interest in learning Spanish and understanding the immigrant adolescent's culture-of-origin. In this way, some American peers were cultural emissaries.

I have one [American] *friend. Walker is his name. He lives around here* [in the large apartment complex]. *He looks more Mexican than American. He knows a lot of Spanish words but he doesn't speak it. But he wants to practice* [speaking Spanish]. *He's always asking me how do you say this, how do you say that. He likes to talk with me in Spanish, the words he knows. He's learning it. One day, we were here, talking, listening to music, and my mother came in. Walker stood up, said, "Buenas tardes."* [The mother laughed, saying, "I remember that! First time I heard him speak in Spanish!"] *He likes our language, wants to learn it.* (Juan, male adolescent)

American friends have supported me by taking me into their group and learning from them, and explaining to me how to do things here, and why they behave the way they do, things like that. Like for St. Patrick's Day, they tell me what they are going to do, what it is, what to say. They tell me to dress in green, and I learn from them how to behave, what they do. (Eva, female adolescent)

One of the benefits of being bilingual and bicultural was being able to interact with an array of social groups. Having the cultural capital and enhanced social network that came with being able to navigate successfully within the new cultural system tended to decrease adolescents' feelings of isolation and increase their sense of well-being.

I'm here and there. I never hang out in one place, one group. I have friends everywhere. I don't feel like I can, uhm, like I can [paused a few seconds] fit in the way they do, like in a certain group. I feel like I can't agree with how just one group thinks. I really feel like I have to do what's right for me. I have something to say to them, and we talk [shrugged]. I move on. I don't dislike any of the groups. I don't. It's just that I don't fit into any one group. That's how I get to know the groups. It doesn't matter if they speak Spanish or English. (Manuel, male adolescent)

If I had a problem, I would listen to advice from both Mexican and American friends, and see which is better for me because my Mexican friends would handle the problem differently, less liberal than the American friends. But I would want to hear their advice [from American friends], even though I probably wouldn't do it. (Eva, female adolescent)

Interestingly, immigrant parents made no mention of having American friends. They described American coworkers, ministers, or members of their church congregations as being helpful and kind. However, immigrant parents did not gain the benefits, such as English-language assistance, that came with having American friends. The lack of American friends, along with being older when they arrived in the United States, may partially explain why parents were generally less bicultural than their adolescents (see figure 4.2). Through their friendships with American peers, some adolescents gained experience, practice, and guidance with English language skills and knowledge concerning host culture customs. These friendships with American peers were key elements in promoting bilingual and bicultural development. This support was lacking for parents; they relied on their children.

To summarize, Latino and non-Latino American peer social networks were sources of both negativity and discrimination on the one hand and support and cultural mentoring on the other. Immigrant parents and adolescents found a comfortable match with Latino peers who knew their customs, values, language, and acculturation challenges and benefits. While some Latino peers were considered to be mean and poor role models, generally they were positive sources of understanding, emotional support, assistance, and guidance for immigrant adolescents and their parents. Non-Latino American peers were less available because of language barriers and xenophobic attitudes. Making American friendships, however, was an important component for immigrant adolescents' bilingual and bicultural skills development.

Conclusions

To summarize, Latino families strongly encouraged biculturalism, placing the primary support for alternation theory in the adolescent's home. Because American influences outside the home, especially school and American friends, emphasized assimilation, Latino parents tended to counteract this influence by reinforcing familism and practicing restrictive parenting strategies. Latino parents tried to protect their children from the dangers that they perceived existed for their children in the American environment. Parents associated these perceived dangers with American friends, drug use, and increased independence.

Adolescents were left trying to mediate among three worlds (see figure 1.3): their Latino world, their American world, and their internal world of an emerging self in which they made personal decisions. It was a challenging balance and an ongoing process. Our interviews demonstrated that immigrant adolescents were acculturating without assimilating. Adolescents maintained strong culture-of-origin identities that were strengthened by nationalistic pride and reinforced by practicing their culture-of-origin customs, values, and traditions in their homes and churches. At the same time, meeting U.S. cultural and linguistic demands at work and in school placed immigrant parents and adolescents between the two cultural systems. As alternation theory suggests, this mixture of cultural messages prompted adolescents and parents to integrate some U.S. customs, language, or social behaviors into their daily lives, increasing bilingualism and biculturalism.

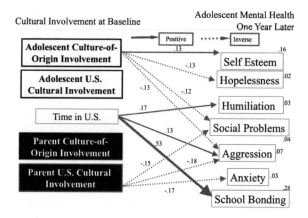

Fig. 4.3. Cultural involvement and adolescent mental health. N = 281, Chi-Square = 42.5, DF = 33, p = .124, Normed Chi-Square = 1.29, CFI = .987, RMSEA = .032 (.000 to .057)

Unsupportive Latino and non-Latino American peers made the acculturation process more difficult by discriminating against new immigrants and encouraging adolescents to engage in risk-taking behavior. Supportive Latino and non-Latino American peer networks served as essential sources of guidance, offering cultural mentoring and English-language assistance.

Bicultural development is a complicated undertaking. Our quantitative analyses show that immigrant adolescents and parents benefit from doing the opposite of what is comfortable (Smokowski, Buchanan, and Bacallao 2009). As shown in figure 4.3, immigrant parents who are immersed in their culture-of-origin benefit from becoming involved in the new U.S. culture. Latino adolescents who had a parent with higher levels of U.S. cultural involvement reported feeling less anxious, being less aggressive, and having fewer social problems one year later. Meanwhile, as compared to assimilated adolescents, those adolescents who avoided the strong push to assimilate and maintained a high involvement in their Latino culture-of-origin had higher self-esteem, less hopelessness, less aggression, and fewer social problems (measured at one-year followup). The benefit of maintaining culture-of-origin involvement was particularly salient for U.S.-born adolescents, who often lose cultural assets that immigrant adolescents hold dear.

Bicultural identity development was a lengthy process that required persistence, patience, and practice. However, once developed, bicultural skills brought wide-ranging benefits rarely seen in other protective factors in social science research (see chapter 6). Our analyses of quantitative and qualitative data from the LAHP study show that bicultural development is a complex process with a particularly difficult initial stage in which the two cultural systems seem to be diametrically opposed, leaving adolescents in a bifurcated ecology, balancing between home and school. Resilient adolescents often seek out cultural mentors who guide them through the subsequent exploration and adaptation phase of bicultural development. Over time, language barriers fall and cultural frame switching becomes fluid and integrated, bringing the two cultural systems together into a new synthesis created by the bicultural individual. High levels of bicultural identity integration, allowing the individual to smoothly navigate between cultural systems, mark the integration stage. Ultimately, new bicultural skills nurture the adolescent's self-esteem, build socio-cognitive processing abilities, and preserve key cultural assets, such as familism, which usually deteriorate in the heat of the assimilation melting pot.

5

Cultural Adaptation Styles and Health

Risks of Staying Separate or Assimilating

When I came to the U.S. at fifteen, my life was changed. I didn't know how to speak English and the Americans would talk to me, and I couldn't express myself. When I started school it was so difficult communicating with the teachers and expressing myself. I couldn't express myself. I learned somewhat how to understand English. Then, I began to make friends. That didn't help. They'd invite me to go out, and I neglected my studies. It got worse because I couldn't really study. I was only doing stuff with my friends. I still don't know how to speak English very well. All my friends are Mexican. If we made a movie of my life, the movie ends with me not finishing school [high school], but I get married and start a family with four or five children.

—Bonifacio, seventeen-year-old Mexican male

In chapters 2 and 3, we took an intimate look at the dynamics of culture-of-origin involvement within the immigrant family's home and host-cultural involvement outside of home. Staying separate or assimilating both posed different challenges for immigrant adolescents. In this chapter, we consider how these different cultural adaptation styles are related to health, mental health, and adjustment.

More than five decades of both qualitative and quantitative empirical research have demonstrated the association of acculturation, especially high and low levels of acculturation (e.g., Separation and Assimilation), with physical health and mental health status (Rogler, Cortes, and Malgady 1991; Organista, Organista, and Kurasaki 2003). Many authors hypothesize a link between acculturation and social maladjustment, psychopathology, and substance use (e.g., see Szapocznik and Kurtines 1980; Gil, Vega, and

Dimas 1994; Al-Issa and Tousignant 1997; Delgado 1998). Researchers have posited disparate relationships between acculturation and social maladjustment, and have proposed positive, negative, and curvilinear associations. In other words, acculturating is thought to improve, decrease, or have a complex relationship with minority health (LaFromboise, Coleman, and Gerton 1993). However, the theoretical frameworks introduced in earlier chapters of this book posit different relationships between acculturation and maladjustment. Briefly, assimilation theory assumes that the relationship between acculturation and health outcomes is positive and linear; that is, health improves as immigrants become more "Americanized." In contrast, alternation theory assumes a nonlinear, perhaps curvilinear, relationship wherein some acculturation is beneficial but the benefits decrease at higher levels of acculturation, especially when ethnic identity is left behind in favor of assimilation.

Assimilation and alternation theories have both inspired several decades of research and knowledge development. Neither theory has been able to marshal enough empirical support to dominate the other. Lloyd Rogler, Dharma Cortes, and Robert Malgady (1991) reviewed thirty investigations to determine whether consensus existed on the link between acculturation and mental health. Their review found evidence supporting each of the proposed relationships—positive, negative, and curvilinear—between acculturation and mental health. The relationship depends upon the specific mental health issue (e.g., drug use, aggressive behavior, depression, anxiety) that is under scrutiny.

Considering the lack of consensus, and the resulting competition and potential confusion in choosing programs and policies stemming from these theories, it is particularly important to understand what these approaches bring to acculturation research. Figures 5.1 and 5.2 combine the cultural adaptation styles and theoretical frameworks from figure 1.2 with the empirical findings generated from research on acculturation and health. These figures capture major findings related to research on acculturation and health, and present the same basic information, but in different visual formats. The key findings are summarized in the following two points:

1. As acculturation progresses from low levels of assimilation (e.g., Separation) to high assimilation levels, alcohol use increases, especially binge drinking and alcohol use by females; psychiatric problems proliferate; and familism (by definition, familism is an especially strong sense of family cohesion and the cultural emphasis on family life being at the center of a person's world) decreases.

2. Compared to low and high levels of assimilation, biculturalism has been found to be associated with more positive health behavior and psychological attributes. This research will be reviewed in chapter 6.

What these figures do not convey is that researchers have found important mental health differences between foreign-born Latino immigrants and U.S.-born Latinos. Behaviors for U.S.-born Latinos are captured in the high assimilation category in these figures. We explain each of these points in more detail in the sections that follow.

In general, higher levels of assimilation are associated with negative health behaviors and mental health difficulties for both adolescents and adults (Rogler et al. 1991; Miranda, Estrada, and Firpo-Jimenez 2000; Smokowski, David-Ferdon, and Stroupe 2009). In comparison to their less acculturated peers, Latinos who have become more assimilated to the host culture display higher levels of alcohol and drug use, less consumption of nutritionally balanced meals, and more psychiatric problems (Amaro et al. 1990; Marks, Garcia, and Solis 1990; Vega et al. 1998; Alegría et al. 2008).

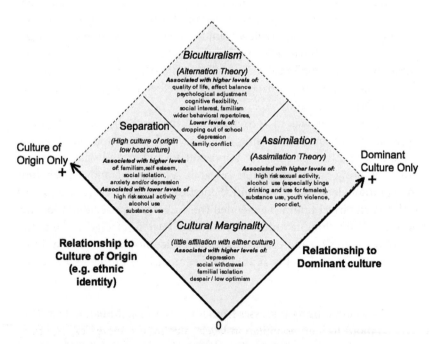

Fig. 5.1. Acculturation theories and major research findings (M. Bacallao and P. R. Smokowski, "Entre Dos Mundos/Between Two Worlds: Bicultural Development in Context, *Journal of Primary Prevention* 30[3–4] [2009]: 421–452)

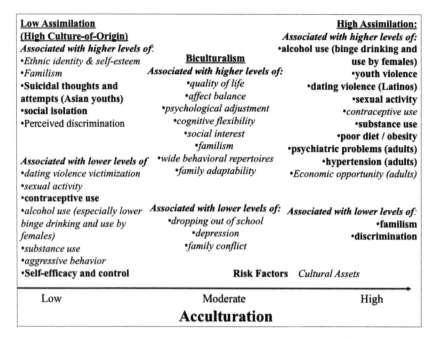

Fig. 5.2. Acculturation and mental health

Acculturation and Health in Adolescents

Acculturation and Substance Use

Research on the links between assimilation and substance use for Latino adolescents has provided inconsistent results. Some studies have reported that high levels of assimilation were predictive of substance use (Dinh et al. 2002), whereas other research has found the reverse (Carvajal et al. 1997; for reviews, see De La Rosa 2002; Gonzales et al. 2002). Findings of path analyses conducted using longitudinal data from 286 Latino adolescents living in either North Carolina or Arizona (65 percent foreign born) showed that acculturation stress (acculturation stress was defined by John Berry 2006, 43, as "a response by people to life events that are rooted in intercultural contact," that is, the strain placed on people due to the challenges inherent in the acculturation process) negatively influenced relationships with family and friends, which in turn affected adolescent mental health problems and substance use (Buchanan and Smokowski 2009). The key mediators in the pathway from acculturation stress to substance use were parent-adolescent conflict, internalizing problems, and externalizing problems.

Acculturation and negative adolescent behavior is commonly related to assimilation markers such as place of birth (termed "nativity"), length of time in the host country, and language facility and use. Research has found that U.S.-born Latino adolescents display levels of alcohol and substance use that are consistently higher than those of foreign-born Latino adolescents (Gil and Vega 1996; Vega and Gil 1998; Gil, Wagner, and Vega 2000). The longer foreign-born adolescents live in the United States, the higher their rates of alcohol or substance use (Gil et al. 2000). Consistent with this finding, other research has shown that Latino adolescents who primarily speak Spanish are less likely to use alcohol and drugs than English-speaking Latino adolescents (Zapata and Katims 1994; Welte and Barnes 1995).

Acculturation and Youth Violence

Most research on acculturation and adolescent health behavior has focused on youth violence and aggressive behavior. Violence is "the intentional use of physical force or power, threatened or actual, against oneself, against another person, or against a group or community, that either results in or has a high likelihood of resulting in injury, death, psychological harm, maldevelopment, or deprivation" (Dahlberg and Krug 2002, 5). Adolescent *interpersonal violence* includes violence between unrelated youth who have a romantic or intimate relationship (i.e., dating violence), as well as violence between unrelated youth who may or may not know each other in other contexts and environments (i.e., youth violence). Similar to acculturation, adolescent interpersonal violence has been assessed in multiple ways across studies. Dating violence has also been assessed in a variety of ways, including verbal, emotional, and physical abuse and sexual assault. Researchers investigating youth violence assess violence involvement using measures such as gang membership, bullying, physical fighting, carrying weapons, verbal threats, aggressive behavior, externalizing symptoms, and serious criminal activity, including homicide or assaults. *Self-directed violence* is a subcategory of violence that includes a person's tendency to intentionally inflict self-harm that may or may not shorten or end life. Measures of suicidal ideation, plans, and attempts and suicide-related deaths are regularly used in this area of inquiry.

In their literature review on acculturation and mental health in Latino youth, Gonzales and her colleagues (2002) identified ten studies that examined the link between acculturation and youth violence. Of those studies, six showed that higher assimilation levels were associated with increased delinquency and stronger relationships with antisocial peers (Buriel, Calzada, and Vasquez 1982; Wall, Power, and Arbona 1993; Vega et al. 1993; Fridrich and Flannery 1995; Vega et al. 1995; Samaniego and Gonzales 1999). This association between assimilation and aggressive behavior surfaced across studies even when simple proxy measures of acculturation (e.g., generational status, language use, or nativity) were used as markers for more complex acculturation processes (Gonzales et al. 2002). In contrast, two other studies did not find a link between assimilation and aggression problems (Knight, Virdin, and Roosa 1994; Dumka, Roosa, and Jackson 1997); however, these investigations examined the variables of parent assimilation and adolescent externalizing behavior, and found no significant relationship between those variables.

Recently, Paul Smokowski, Corinne David-Ferdon, and Nancy Stroupe (2009) conducted a comprehensive review of studies examining the relationship of adolescent acculturation and youth violence. Among the studies reviewed, the association between acculturation and Latino youth violence outcomes was examined in sixteen studies; thirteen of these investigations examined the perpetration of violence as the outcome, and three studies examined fear of being a victim of violence as the outcome. The results favored a significant positive association between assimilation and youth violence. Nine of the thirteen studies reported that higher adolescent assimilation (defined in different ways according to time spent in the United States, generational status, language use, or multidimensional survey measures) was associated with increased youth violence (Buriel et al. 1982; Sommers, Fagan, and Baskin 1993; Vega et al. 1993; Vega et al. 1995; Brook et al. 1998; Samaniego and Gonzales 1999; Dinh et al. 2002; Bui and Thongniramol 2005; Smokowski and Bacallao 2006; Schwartz, Zamboanga, and Jarvis 2007). To provide a closer look at the quality of studies in this area, table 5.1 presents detailed information about the studies that link acculturation and violence in Latino youth.

Alongside studies on the deleterious effects of assimilation, research efforts have focused on stress precipitated by adapting to a new cultural system. Acculturation stress has been linked to several negative outcomes for Latino youth, including mental health difficulties (Gil, Vega, and Dimas 1994); suicidal ideation (Hovey and King 1996); delinquent behavior (Samaniego and Gonzales 1999); and behavior problems (Vega et al. 1995). Researchers have consistently demonstrated links among acculturation stressors such as language conflicts, perceived discrimination, parent-adolescent culture conflicts, parent-child acculturation gaps, and negative health behavior in youth.

TABLE 5.1

Studies Examining the Association between Acculturation and Interpersonal and Self-Directed Violence among Latino Youth

Study and Topic Area	Sample	Acculturation Measures	Violence Measures	Results
Sanderson, Coker, Roberts, Tortolero, & Reininger (2004) *Dating Violence*	4,525 9th graders (51% female); 100% Mexican American from Texas	Language use, parent birthplace, salience of ethnicity, ethnic discrimination	YRBS dating violence victim	• English-speaking-only females were significantly more likely to experience dating violence than peers speaking both English and Spanish in home. • Spanish-speaking-only females were significantly less likely to experience dating violence than peers speaking both English and Spanish in home. • For females, parent birthplace outside of US was significantly associated with a reduced likelihood of dating violence relative to peers whose parents were born in US. • For females, ethnic discrimination significantly positively associated with dating violence. • For females, high salience of ethnicity significantly associated with low dating violence victimization. • For males, language use, parent birthplace, salience of ethnicity, and ethnic discrimination not associated with dating violence.
Decker, Raj, & Silverman (2007); Silverman, Decker, & Raj (2007) *Dating and Sexual Violence*	6,019 9th–12th graders (100% female); 76% White; 10% Hispanic; 7% African American; 3% Asian; 2% Other/mixed from Massachusetts (%'s vary slightly across articles)	Language use, immigrant status	YRBS sexual assault victim and dating violence victim	• Hispanic girls reported significantly lower prevalence of sexual assault prior to the past year and dating violence victimization relative to peers. • Sexually active, immigrant Hispanic girls reported significantly higher prevalence of sexual assault prior to the past year and sexual assault in past year relative to peers. • Sexually active, immigrant Hispanic girls were significantly less likely than peers to report dating violence victimization. • No significant association between language and sexual assault or dating violence for Hispanic youth.
Buriel, Calzada, & Vasquez (1982) *Youth Violence*	81 13–16-year-olds (100% male); 100% Mexican American from California; Generation status: 33% 1st, 33% 2nd, 33% 3rd	Generation status	Delinquency	• 3rd-generation adolescents had significantly higher delinquency rates than 1st- or 2nd-generation adolescents. • 1st- and 2nd-generation adolescents did not significantly differ on delinquency.

Study	Sample	Measures	Outcome	Findings
Sommers, Fagan, & Baskin (1993) *Youth Violence*	1,077 12–19-year-olds (mean age 15.7; 100% male); 100% Puerto Rican from New York	Combined language familiarity and usage, ethnic interaction, identification, and background, and cultural lifestyle and traditions; familism; immigrant status	Interpersonal violence	• Highly acculturated adolescents and adolescents with low familism were significantly more likely to engage in violence. • No significant differences in interpersonal violence between immigrant versus US-born youth. • For immigrant youth, acculturation did not significantly predict interpersonal violence but lower levels of familism significantly predicted higher violence. • For US-born youth, higher acculturation and lower familism were significantly predictive of higher interpersonal violence.
Vega, Gil, Warheit, Zimmerman, & Apospori (1993) Vega, Zimmerman, Khoury, Gil, & Warheit (1995) *Youth Violence*	1993: 1,843 6th–7th graders; 100% Cuban from Miami 1995: 2,360 6th–7th graders; 69% Hispanic; 18% Non-Hispanic White; 13% African American from Miami; Of Hispanic youth: 71% US born, 43% Cuban, 12% Nicaraguan, 7% Columbian, 6% Puerto Rican, 32% other	Language and acculturation conflict, perceived discrimination, birthplace, perception of closed society	Youth reported delinquency; parent reported CBCL; teacher reported TRF	• Among Cuban youth, language conflict, acculturation conflict, perceived discrimination, and perception of a closed society were positively associated with delinquency • Among Cuban youth, birth inside the US and higher perception of a closed society predicted delinquency. • No significant differences between Hispanic subgroups. • Among foreign-born Hispanic youth, those with higher language conflicts had significantly higher CBCL and TRF problem behaviors. • Among US-born Hispanic youth, those with higher language conflicts, perceived discrimination, and perception of a closed society had significantly higher TRF problem behaviors.
Brook, Whiteman, Balka, Win, & Gursen (1998) *Youth Violence*	882 16–25-year-olds (mean age 20; 56% male); 52% African American; 48% Puerto Rican from New York	Family church attendance, country of origin, familism	Delinquency and physical violence	• Family church attendance was significantly inversely associated with delinquency/violence at 5-year followup. • Having been born in the US significantly associated with higher levels of violence. • Familism was not significantly associated with delinquency/ violence at 5-year followup.

(continued)

TABLE 5.1 (*continued*)

Study and Topic Area	Sample	Acculturation Measures	Violence Measures	Results
Samaniego & Gonzales (1999) *Youth Violence*	214 7th–8th graders (mean age=13.5; 57% female); 100% Mexican American; 44% born in Mexico; Generation status: 43% 1st, 30% 2nd, 26% 3rd	Combined language use and generation status	National Youth Survey delinquency scale	• Acculturation significantly positively correlated with delinquency. • Effect of acculturation on delinquency mediated by family conflict and inconsistent discipline. Acculturation positively related to family conflict and inconsistent discipline, which were positively related to delinquency. • Effect of acculturation on delinquency mediated by maternal monitoring. Acculturation negatively related to monitoring, which was negatively related to delinquency.
Carvajal, Hanson, Romero, & Coyle (2002) *Youth Violence*	1,119 6th–7th graders (mean age 12; 53% female); 63% Latino, 37% non-Latino White from northern California; Of Latino youth: 62% Mexican American; Generation status of Latino youth: 13% 1st, 40% 2nd, 26% 3rd, 21% 4th or more	Bidimensional Acculturation Scale Latino orientation and Other Group orientation subscales	Injury or threat victim, physical fight	• Latinos and non-Latino youth did not significantly differ on reports of being injured or threatened or fighting. • Acculturation was not significantly associated with any violence measures.
Dinh, Roosa, Tein, & Lopez (2002) *Youth Violence*	330 4th–8th graders (50% male); 100% Hispanic from southwest US; 33% born outside US; Home language: 44% Spanish, 35% English, 21% equal Spanish and English; Survey language: 76% English, 24% Spanish	Latent factor of immigrant status, home language, language used to complete survey	Problem behavior proneness latent factor based Arizona Criminal Justice Survey (gang, substance use), Denver Youth Survey (peer delinquency), YSR (conduct problems)	• Level of acculturation of Hispanic youth significantly positively related to their problem-behavior proneness one year later. • Relationship between acculturation and problem behavior mediated by parental involvement. Youth with higher levels of acculturation reported lower levels of parental involvement, which predicted higher problem behavior proneness.

Study	Sample	Acculturation measure	Outcome	Findings
Yu, Huang, Schwalberg, Overpeck, & Kogan (2003) *Youth Violence*	15,220 6th–10th graders (53% female); 58.6% White; 19.3% Hispanic; 17.5% Black; 4.6% Asian from national sample; Of Hispanic youth: 24% foreign born, 27% English in home, 27% other home language, 46% mixed home language	Language use	Bullied victimization for race or religion	• Relative to English-only speaking Hispanic peers, Hispanic youth who spoke another language at home were significantly more likely to be bullied.
Brown & Benedict (2004) *Youth Violence*	230 9th–12th graders (52% male); 94% Hispanic; 4.4% White; 1.8% Other from Texas; 52% speak Spanish at home, 48% speak English at home	Language use	Fear of weapon-associated victimization	• Spanish-speaking youth significantly more fearful of weapon-associated victimization than English-speaking peers.
Bui & Thongniramol (2005) *Youth Violence*	18,097 12-21-year-olds (51% female); 62.6% White; 22.2% Black; 7.4% Asian; 7.8% Other races; 17.5% Hispanic from national sample; Generation of overall sample: 8% 1st, 15.2% 2nd, 76.8% 3rd	Immigration generation	Violent delinquency	• 2nd- and 3rd-generation Hispanic youth were 60% and 88%, respectively, more likely to report violence than 1st-generation Hispanic peers. • No significant differences were found between 2nd- and 3rd-generation Hispanic youth.
Bird, Canino, Davies, Duarte, Febo, Ramirez, Hoven, Wicks, Musa, & Loeber (2006); Bird, Davies, Duarte, Shen, Loeber, & Canino (2006) *Youth Violence*	2,491 5-13-year olds (mean age=9.2; 52% male); 100% Puerto Rican from San Juan (54%) and South Bronx, New York (46%)	Child and Parent report of Cultural Life Style Inventory Bidirectional Scale (language preference, other ethnic characteristics)	DISC-IV disruptive behavior disorders subscale was given to children and adults	• Child and parent acculturation and parent-child acculturation gap not associated with disruptive behavior disorders.

(continued)

TABLE 5.1 (*continued*)

Study and Topic Area	Sample	Acculturation Measures	Violence Measures	Results
Gonzales, Deardorff, Formoso, Barr, & Barrera (2006) *Youth Violence*	175 11–15-year-olds (mean age=12.9; 51% female); 100% Mexican from southwest US; 38% born in Mexico; 62% born in US	Adolescent, maternal, and family linguistic acculturation	CBCL mother report conduct disorder subscale; YSR adolescent report conduct disorder subscale	• Latino youth acculturation positively related to adolescent-reported conduct problems but unrelated to mother report. • Maternal acculturation positively related to adolescent- and mother-reported conduct problems. • Direct relationship between family acculturation and conduct problems not significant. • Effect of family acculturation mediated by family conflict. • Effect of maternal acculturation mediated by interparental conflict. Pathway led from higher maternal acculturation to higher interparental conflict to higher mother-reported problems.
Smokowski & Bacallao (2006) *Youth Violence*	481 11–19-year-olds (mean age=15; 54% female); 61% Mexican; 39% Other Central/South American countries from North Carolina (69%) and from Arizona (31%); 80% born outside of the US	Adolescent and parent report of BIQs Culture-of-Origin Involvement and US Culture Involvement subscales; Adolescent report of acculturation conflict with family	YSR aggression scale	• Latino youth with a stronger culture-of-origin involvement had significantly lower levels of aggression. • Direct relationship between adolescent US cultural involvement and acculturation conflicts and aggression not significant. • Effect of acculturation conflicts mediated by familism and parent-adolescent conflict. Pathways led from more acculturation conflicts to lower familism to higher aggression and from more acculturation conflicts to more parent-child adolescent conflict to higher aggression. • Effect of parent US cultural involvement mediated by parent-adolescent conflict. Pathway led higher US cultural involvement to lower conflict to lower aggression.
Schwartz, Zamboanga, & Jarvis (2007) *Youth Violence*	347 6th–8th graders (approximately 50% male); 58% Mexican, 42% Puerto Rico, Honduras, Chile, Cuba or other Hispanic countries;	Acculturation Rating Scale for Mexican Americans-II; MEIM; SAFE-C (acculturative stress)	Externalizing symptoms	• Direct relationship between US orientation, Hispanic orientation, and ethnic identity and externalizing symptoms not significant. • Relationship between ethnic identity and externalizing mediated by self-esteem. Pathways led from higher ethnic identity to higher self-esteem and from higher self-esteem to lower externalizing.

	86% US born, from western Michigan			• Relationship between acculturative stress and externalizing mediated by self-esteem. Pathways led from higher stress to lower self-esteem and from higher stress to more externalizing symptoms. • US orientation indirectly related to externalizing symptoms through acculturative stress and self-esteem.
Swanson, Linskey, et al. (1992) *Self-directed*	4,157 11–19-year olds (50% female); 57% Mexican from Mexico; 43% Mexican American from Texas	US resident	Suicide thoughts	• Mexican youth residing in US had significantly higher rates of suicidal ideation than peers living in Mexico. • Living in the US significantly predicted more suicidal thoughts.
Vega, Gil, Warheit, Zimmerman, & Apospori (1993) *Self-directed*	5,303 6th–8th graders (100% male); 28% Cuban; 29% Other Hispanic; 14% African American; 14% White, non-Hispanic; 9% Nicaraguan; 3% Haitian, 3% Caribbean black from Miami, Florida	Acculturation stress (language conflict, acculturation conflict, perceived discrimination, perceived closed society)	Suicide attempts	• Controlling for suicide ideation and attempts at Time 1, use of psychoactive drugs or cocaine interacted with higher acculturation stress (all four measures) to predict higher rates of suicide attempts among Cuban students and Other Hispanic students one year later. • Controlling for suicide ideation and attempts at Time 1, use of alcohol interacted with higher acculturation conflicts and use of cigarettes interacted with language conflicts to predict significantly higher rates of suicide attempts among Other Hispanic students one year later.
Hovey & King (1996) *Self-directed*	70 14–20-year-olds (mean age=16.8; 57% female); 77% Mexican; 4% Central American; 4% South American; 2% Spanish from southern California; generational status: 23% 1st early (<12), 66% late 1st immigrants (>12), 11% 2nd	Acculturation stress	SIQ-JR	• Acculturation stress significantly positively associated with suicidal ideation among Latino youth. • More acculturation stress was a significant predictor of increased levels of suicidal ideation.

(continued)

TABLE 5.1 (*continued*)

Study and Topic Area	Sample	Acculturation Measures	Violence Measures	Results
Ng (1996) *Self-directed*	61 adolescents (mean age=15.1; 66% female); 100% Mexican American from Texas; 85% US born; 15% Mexico born	Time living in US	Pierce Suicide Intent Scale	• Relative to a low suicide intent group, the high suicide intent group lived in the US for a significantly shorter period of time.
Rasmussen, Negy, Carlson, & Burns (1997) *Self-directed*	242 8th graders (mean age=13.7; 57% female); 100% Mexican American from Texas	Acculturation Rating Scale for Mexican Americans	SIQ-JR	• Acculturation not independently predictive of suicide ideation. • When examined in combination with depressive symptoms and low self-esteem, high acculturation was significantly and positively predictive of suicide ideation.
Hovey (1998) *Self-directed*	54 students (mean age=16.8; 52% female); immigrant Mexican American from southern California	Acculturation stress; time living in US	SIQ-JR	• Acculturating stress was significantly positively associated with suicidal ideation. • Time living in the US unrelated to suicidal ideation.
Olvera (2001) *Self-directed*	158 6th–8th graders (mean age=12; 54% female); 56% Hispanic; 21% Anglo; 14% mixed; 1% African American from Texas	Spanish language preference; immigration/ generation status	DSD	• Hispanic youth had significantly higher suicidal ideation than Anglo youth. • Hispanic ancestry significantly predicted suicidal ideation. • Spanish-language preference unrelated to suicidal ideation. • Having US-born mother significantly decreased the risk for suicide.

Note: Unless noted, acculturation and violence measures completed only by participating youth. BIQ=Bicultural Involvement Questionnaire; CBCL=Child Behavior Checklist; DISC-IV=Diagnostic Interview Schedule for Children–IV; DSD=Diagnostic and Statistical Manual Scale for Depression; SAFE-C=Societal, Attitudinal, Familial, and Environmental Accultura-tive Stress Scale for Children; SIQ-JR=Suicidal Ideation Questionnaire–Junior; TRF=Teacher Report Form; US=United States; YRBS=Youth Risk Behavior Survey; YSR=Youth Self-Report

Studying the link between acculturation and delinquent behavior in a sample of 1,843 Cuban boys and girls, William Vega and his colleagues (1993) found a significant positive correlation of .35 between acculturation conflicts and self-derogation. Correlations range from –1 to 1, with higher positive or negative numbers signaling a stronger relationship. In this study, there was a moderately strong tendency for children who experienced acculturation conflicts to also report self-derogation. These researchers showed that conflicts inherent in the acculturation process were associated with more negative feelings about oneself. Perceived discrimination displayed a statistically significant interaction with peer approval of drugs and with self-derogation. Language conflicts also had a significant interaction with teacher derogation and peer drug use. Moreover, this study found that acculturation factors, such as perceptions of discrimination and language conflicts, had a direct positive association with delinquent behavior. This association between acculturation factors and delinquent behavior was stronger than the impact family variables had on delinquent behavior.

In an investigation of acculturation stressors with a predominantly Cuban sample of 2,360 adolescents living in Miami, Vega and his colleagues (1995) found that only language conflicts were associated with adolescents' total behavior problems as reported by the parents and teachers of immigrant adolescents. However, among the U.S.-born Cuban youth, language conflicts, perceived discrimination, and perceptions of a closed society were associated with behavior problems reported by teachers. Furthermore, Dinh and her colleagues (2002), whose assessment of 330 Latino youth represents one of the few longitudinal studies in this area, found that higher levels of assimilation predicted statistically significant higher levels of problem-behavior proneness (i.e., gang involvement, peer delinquency, conduct problems) in youth reports collected one year after baseline measures were established. Similarly, Ebin and colleagues (2001) reported that high assimilation levels had a positive association with problem behaviors and a negative association with health-promoting behaviors. Foreign-born Latino adolescents exhibited fewer problem behaviors than U.S.-born Latino adolescents. Likewise, Coatsworth and colleagues (2005) studied the acculturation patterns of 315 Latino youth and found that when compared with less-assimilated participants, high-assimilated youth reported significantly greater numbers of problem behaviors and less parental monitoring.

Recently, we and our colleague Roderick Rose conducted one of the most exhaustive analyses of acculturation and Latino adolescent aggressive behavior (Smokowski, Rose, and Bacallao 2009). In this study, we examined reports of youth's aggressive behavior that were obtained from both the adolescents and their parents. This multiple-reporter approach provides

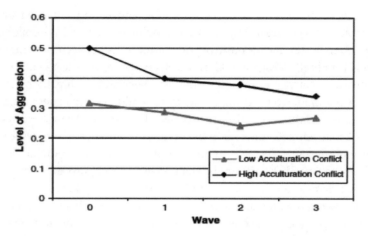

Fig. 5.3. Adolescent aggressive behavior by parent-adolescent conflict (Latino Acculturation and Health Project, Paul R. Smokowski, Roderick Rose, and Martica Bacallao, "Acculturation and Aggression in Latino Adolescents: Modeling Longitudinal Trajectories from the Latino Acculturation and Health Project," *Child Psychiatry and Human Development*)

more confidence in the study results because the results are more objective than relying on the accuracy of adolescents' reports alone. Furthermore, we followed the sample of 256 adolescents for two years, collecting data every six months. This approach provided four data points for us to use in examining the longitudinal trajectory of aggressive behavior, improving upon the cross-sectional snapshot that many studies have considered in the past.

The overall trajectory of Latino adolescent aggression displayed a statistically significant negative trend best characterized by a quadratic curve. Over time, adolescent aggressive behavior decreased and leveled out near the end of the study period. This trend is illustrated in figure 5.3. In the analyses, we delineated significant risk factors related to aggression levels, showing that gender, age, parent-reported acculturation conflicts, and adolescent-reported parent-adolescent conflicts were associated with higher levels of adolescent aggression. The influence of acculturation conflicts is shown in figure 5.3. Latino adolescents whose parents reported high levels of acculturation conflict displayed higher levels of aggressive behavior at every time point, and although their aggression decreased over time, the levels did not decline as much as in those youth who had low levels of acculturation conflict. Parent reports of acculturation conflicts were a significant risk factor associated with more aggressive behavior for foreign-born youth, but not for U.S.-born youth.

In another recent analysis of the pathways to Latino adolescent aggression, we and our colleague, Rachel Buchanan, constructed the model shown in figure 5.4. Based on 286 foreign- and U.S.-born adolescents participating in the Latino Acculturation and Health Project (Smokowski, Buchanan, and Bacallao forthcoming), this model shows that perceived discrimination and acculturation conflicts were significantly related to aggressive behavior at baseline. This heightened aggressive behavior led to lower levels of adolescent self-esteem and familism, and higher internalizing of problems (e.g., anxiety and depression), more parent-adolescent conflict, and more relationships with delinquent peers six months later. The baseline aggression associated with acculturation stressors was also directly connected to increased levels of aggressive behavior one year later. In addition to promoting baseline aggression, experiences of perceived discrimination and acculturation conflicts positively predicted parent-adolescent conflict and adolescent substance use six months later.

Four research reports were unable to find a significant direct association between assimilation variables and youth violence perpetration (Carvajal

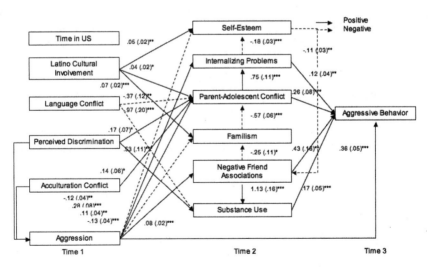

Fig. 5.4. Pathways from acculturation stress to adolescent aggression. Chi-Square = 81.202, 45 df, *p* = .001; Normed Chi-Square = 1.804; CFI = .964; RMSEA = .053 (.034–.071). (Paul R. Smokowski, Rachel Buchanan, and Martica Bacallao, "Acculturation Stress and Aggressive Behavior in Latino Adolescents: Examining Mediation Pathways in the Latino Acculturation and Health Project," *International Journal of Child Health and Human Development*, in press)

et al. 2002; Bird, Canino, et al. 2006; Bird, Davies, et al. 2006; Gonzales et al. 2006; Schwartz, Zamboanga, and Hernandez Jarvis 2007). In a sample of 175 Mexican youth and their mothers living in the southwestern United States, researchers found the direct relationship between family linguistic acculturation and adolescent conduct problems was not significant. However, the findings showed that an indirect relationship was mediated through family conflict (Gonzales et al. 2006). Similarly, self-esteem was found to mediate the relationship between acculturative stress and externalizing symptoms in Latino youth from Michigan (Schwartz, Zamboanga, and Hernandez Jarvis 2007). Overall, 85 percent of existing studies—that is, twelve of fourteen studies—on Latino adolescents have shown assimilation or acculturation stress to directly or indirectly predict aggressive behavior.

Nine articles shown in table 5.2 have focused on acculturation and youth violence of Asian/Pacific Islander youth. Four studies included large multiethnic group investigations (Yu et al. 2003; Shrake and Rhee 2004; Bui and Thongniramol 2005; Willgerodt and Thompson 2006). The other five articles (Go and Le 2005; Le and Stockdale 2005; 2008; Le and Wallen 2007; Ngo and Le 2007) analyzed the same sample of 329 Chinese and Southeast Asian youth recruited from two public schools and five community-based organizations in Oakland, California. The majority of the youth in this sample were second-generation status (i.e., U.S.-born), except for Vietnamese youth, who were nearly equally divided between first and second generations. In acculturation research, first-generation immigrants are those who were born in a foreign country. Adolescents who were born in the United States and have foreign-born parents are considered second-generation immigrants. Much of what we know about Asian/Pacific Islander youth violence comes from one moderate-sized sample from one city in California. Although it remains important to synthesize this knowledge, caution is clearly warranted in generalizing these findings to the general Asian/Pacific Islander population.

Several themes in the Asian/Pacific Islander youth literature parallel those already described for Latino adolescents. Assimilation, individualism (a measure similar to U.S. cultural involvement), acculturation stress, and experiencing/perceived discrimination remain important risk factors for aggression and violence. Among Filipino youth, second-generation adolescents had significantly higher delinquency than first-generation youth (Willgerodt and Thompson 2006), but there were no differences relative to third-generation age peers. After examining data from 217 Korean American students in Los Angeles, Eunai Shrake and Siyon Rhee (2004) reported that Korean American adolescents' experience of perceived discrimination

TABLE 5.2

Studies Examining the Association between Acculturation and Interpersonal and Self-Directed Violence among Asian American/Pacific Island Youth

Study and Topic Area	Sample	Acculturation Measures	Violence Measures	Results
Decker, Raj, & Silverman (2007); Silverman, Decker, & Raj (2007) *Dating and Sexual Violence*	6,019 9th–12th graders (100% female); 76% White; 10% Hispanic; 7% African American; 3% Asian; 2% Other/mixed from Massachusetts (%'s vary slightly across articles)	Language use, immigrant status	YRBS sexual assault victim and dating violence victim	• No significant association between language use or immigrant status and sexual violence or dating violence among Asian youth.
Yu, Huang, Schwalberg, Overpeck, & Kogan (2003) *Youth Violence*	15,220 6th–10th graders (53% female); 58.6% White; 19.3% Hispanic; 17.5% Black; 4.6% Asian; Of Asian youth: 58% foreign born, 27% English in home, 26% other home language, 46% mixed home language	Language use	Bullied victimization for race or religion	• Relative to English-only-speaking Asian peers, Asian youth who spoke another language at home were significantly more likely to be bullied. • Mixed language use at home was not a risk factor.
Shrake & Rhee (2004) *Youth Violence*	217 13–18-year-olds (mean age=15.8; 57% female) 100% Korean American from Los Angeles; 52% Korean born, 46% US born	Ethnic Identity and Attitudes toward Other Groups subscales of MEIM; perceived discrimination	Externalizing scale of YSR	• Ethnic identity and Attitudes toward Other Groups significantly negatively associated with externalizing for Korean youth. • Perceived discrimination significantly positively associated to externalizing. • High ethnic identity significantly predicted lower levels of externalizing. • High perceived discrimination significantly predicted higher levels of externalizing.

(continued)

TABLE 5.2 (*continued*)

Study and Topic Area	Sample	Acculturation Measures	Violence Measures	Results
Bui & Thongniramol (2005) *Youth Violence*	18,097 12–21-year-olds (51% female); 62.6% White; 22.2% Black; 7.4% Asian; 7.8% Other races; 17.5% Hispanic from national sample; Generation of overall sample: 8% 1st, 15.2% 2nd, 76.8% 3rd	Immigration generation	Violent delinquency	• No significant differences in violence by immigration generation for Asian youth.
Go & Le (2005); Le & Stockdale (2005); Le & Wallen (2007); Ngo & Le (2007); Le & Stockdale (2008) *Youth Violence*	329 10–18-year-olds; 34% Cambodian; 20% Chinese; 26% Vietnamese; 20% Laotian/Mien; 2nd generation: 81% Chinese, 88% Cambodian, 53% Vietnamese (%'s vary slightly across articles)	MEIM factors of Ethnic Identity and Ethnic Belonging; Individualism and collectivism cultural orientation; intergenerational/intercultural conflict (acculturative dissonance); acculturated behavior	General measure of serious delinquency; Denver Youth Survey serious delinquency; serious violence; violence victimization	• Chinese youth were significantly less seriously delinquent relative to Cambodian, Laotian/Mien, and Vietnamese peers. • Individualism positively related to, and collectivism negatively related to, serious delinquency, with partial mediation through peer delinquency and with model invariant across Asian groups. • Acculturated behavior, collectivism, and intergenerational/intercultural conflict interacted with certain stressors (emotional hardship, physical abuse, emotional abuse) to predict Denver Youth Survey serious delinquency; significance of interactions varied by Asian ethnic group. • Acculturative dissonance was significantly predictive of serious violence, with full mediation through peer delinquency. • Ethnic identity not significantly associated with serious violence. • Ethnic identity was a positive predictor of delinquency for male Cambodian youth but not for female Cambodian youth. • Ethnic belonging unrelated to delinquency for Cambodian youth.

Study	Sample	Measure	Outcome	Findings
Willgerodt & Thompson (2006) *Youth Violence*	1,003 7th–12th graders (50% male); 40% White; 39% Filipino; 21% Chinese from national sample	Immigration generation based on youth and parent place of birth	Delinquency	• Filipino youth had significantly higher delinquency than Chinese and White peers. • Among Filipino, 2nd generation had significantly higher delinquency than 1st generation. No difference relative to 3rd-generation peers. • Among Chinese youth, no significant difference in delinquency by generation status.
Yuen, Nahulu, Hishinuma, & Miyamoto (2000) *Self-directed*	3,644 9th–12th graders (52% female); 62% full or part Hawaiian; 8% Japanese; 6% Filipinos; 3% Caucasian; 21% other from Hawaii	Hawaiian Culture Scale–Adolescent	Lifetime suicide attempts	• Hawaiian youths had a higher suicide attempt rate than non-Hawaiians. • Hawaiian cultural orientation was a significant positive predictor of lifetime suicide attempts among Hawaiian youth but unrelated to suicide attempts among non-Hawaiian youth.
Lau, Jernewall, Zane, & Meyers (2002) *Self-directed*	285 4–17-year-olds (mean age=12.9); 39% Chinese; 32% Southeast Asian; 14% Korean; 13% Japanese; 2% Filipino from California; 13% suicidal, 87% non-suicidal	Combined English proficiency, primary home language, age of immigration, proportion of life in US	Consensus of two raters' review of medical charts for a history of suicidal ideation and self-harm	• Suicidal group had significantly fewer US-born Asian youth and were significantly older when they immigrated to the US relative to the nonsuicidal group. • Suicidal and nonsuicidal groups did not differ on language. • Japanese and Korean youth more acculturated than Chinese and Southeast Asian youth. • Lower acculturation significantly predicted higher suicide risk. • Significant interaction between acculturation and parent-adolescent conflict. When conflict is high, less acculturated youths were at higher risk of suicide than the more acculturated group. When conflict was low, there was no significant difference in risk for the two acculturation groups. • No significant ethnic group differences in predicting suicide.

Note: Unless noted, acculturation and violence measures completed only by participating adolescent. MEIM=Multigroup Ethnic Identity Measure; US=United States; YRBS=Youth Risk Behavior Survey; YSR=Youth Self-Report showed a strong positive effect on both internalizing (anxiety and depression) and externalizing aggressive problem behaviors. In the sample of 329 Southeast Asian youth from Oakland, Thao Le and Gary Stockdale (2005) found that individualism (used as a measure of assimilation) was positively related to self-reported delinquency, with partial mediation through peer delinquency. Similarly, Hieu Ngo and Thao Le (2007) reported that increased levels of assimilation, intergenerational/intercultural conflict, and individualism placed youth at increased risk for serious violence (e.g., aggravated assault, robbery, rape, and gang fights). Assimilation, individualism, and intergenerational/intercultural conflict enhanced the impact of certain stressors (e.g., emotional hardship, physical abuse, emotional abuse) to predict violent behavior. In a third study using the same sample, acculturative dissonance (a measure of the amount of conflicting cultural messages adolescents experience) was found as significantly predictive of serious violence, with full mediation through peer delinquency (Le and Stockdale 2008).

Acculturation and Dating Violence Victimization

Although three studies have investigated acculturation and dating violence, two of those studies used the same sample of participants (Decker, Raj, and Silverman 2007; Silverman, Decker, and Raj 2007). All three studies indicated that both being an immigrant and being less assimilated acted as protective factors against dating violence victimization (Sanderson et al. 2004; Decker, Raj, and Silverman 2007; Silverman, Decker, and Raj 2007). For instance, after examining data from more than forty-five hundred Latinas in southern Texas, Sanderson and her colleagues (2004) concluded that greater assimilation may be associated with greater prevalence of dating violence victimization, but that association was moderated by gender. For females, parental birthplace outside of the United States and high salience of ethnicity were significantly associated with a reduced likelihood of dating violence victimization. A Latina's making a report of ethnic discrimination was also strongly associated with increased dating violence victimization.

In a dating violence study with a large multiethnic sample from Massachusetts (Decker, Raj, and Silverman 2007; Silverman, Decker, and Raj 2007), among both the adolescent females identifying as Hispanic and the Latinas who reported being sexually active, immigrant females were found to be at reduced risk for dating violence but at higher risk for sexual assault as compared to nonimmigrant Hispanic females. However, the language spoken at home was not a relevant factor for adolescents regarding their vulnerability to dating violence. This lack of a significant effect for language spoken at home is at odds with results from Sanderson and her colleagues (2004), who indicated that females who spoke only Spanish were significantly less likely to experience dating violence than peers who spoke both English and Spanish in the home. In addition, females who only spoke English were significantly more likely to experience dating violence than peers who spoke both English and Spanish in their homes (Sanderson et al. 2004). Although this initial evidence suggests that low-to-moderate acculturation levels might be a cultural asset against dating violence victimization, especially for females, more studies are needed to confirm these assertions.

Recently, two articles were published that reported on attempts to examine acculturation and dating or sexual violence in Asian/Pacific Island youth. The same research group produced both of the articles (Decker, Raj, and Silverman 2007; Silverman, Decker, and Raj 2007). Using a multiethnic sample of 6,019 ninth and twelfth graders from Massachusetts, both of these studies found no significant association between language use or immigrant status and sexual violence or dating violence among Asian youth. Although this lack of association is noteworthy, these analyses used simple markers of acculturation, and only 3 percent of the sampled adolescents were Asian (approximately 180 youths out of 6,019). Therefore, we cannot draw firm conclusions about acculturation and dating and sexual violence in Asian/Pacific Islander youth until more research has been conducted.

Acculturation and Self-Directed Violence

Seven empirical studies have examined the link between acculturation and self-directed violence for Latino youth. Three of these studies found that acculturation stress and strain was significantly positively related to suicidal ideation (Hovey and King 1996; Hovey 1998), or interacted with cocaine and crack use to predict suicide attempts among Latinos (Vega et al. 1995). In their study of seventy Latino males in a California bilingual program, Joseph Hovey and Cheryl King (1996) reported that acculturation stress explained 9 percent of the variance in depression and 6 percent of the variance in suicidal ideation, representing a medium to large effect size for this predictor. Two additional studies that measured acculturation differently also found a positive association between acculturation and suicidal behavior. Jeffrey Swanson and his colleagues (1992) found that Mexican youth residing in the United States had significantly higher rates of suicidal ideation than peers living in Mexico, and that U.S. residency significantly predicted more suicidal thoughts. In a study of 242 Mexican American eighth grade students, Katherine Rasmussen and her colleagues (1997) examined acculturation as assessed by the Acculturation Rating Scale for Mexican Americans and found that assimilation, when combined with depressive symptoms and low self-esteem, significantly and positively predicted suicide ideation. Further, female participants had significantly higher suicidal ideation scores than male participants.

Two studies failed to support the association between high assimilation levels and suicide risk among Latino youth. Bernardo Ng (1996) found the opposite relationship, with low assimilation demonstrating an increased risk of suicide. Ng examined medical records from sixty-one Mexican American adolescents and reported that living in the United States for a shorter period was a characteristic of the group with high suicide intent. Differences across samples may contribute to these conflicting findings. For example, the Ng study sample included youth who had been previously admitted to a psychiatric facility, whereas the other studies examined general, nonclinical samples of youth. In a study of 158 Latino middle-school students, Olvera (2001) also failed to support an association between high assimilation and suicide, but for different reasons than the Ng study. Olvera did find a trend ($p = .06$) for Spanish-language preference to predict increased risk for suicidal ideation, but this link did not reach conventional levels of statistical significance ($p < .05$).

Self-directed violence in Asian/Pacific Islander adolescents is an understudied topic. We found only two articles that focused on acculturation and suicidality for this group, and these studies indicated that low acculturation levels may be a risk factor for suicidal behavior in Asian/Pacific Islander adolescents. In a large survey of 3,094 youth in Hawaii, which encompassed 15 percent of Hawaiian high-school students in the state, Noelle Yuen and her colleagues (2000) examined the association between Hawaiian cultural orientation and lifetime suicide attempts. Hawaiian youths had a higher suicide attempt rate than non-Hawaiians. Strong Hawaiian cultural orientation was a significant risk factor for suicide attempts and was a better predictor than ethnicity (i.e., Hawaiian versus non-Hawaiian).

Anna Lau and her colleagues (2002) analyzed suicidal ideation and self-harm in a sample of 285 Asian American children and adolescents who had received outpatient treatment in a mental health clinic. The study used a variable for acculturation that was a composite consisting of proficiency in English, language spoken at home, age at immigration, and proportion of life spent in the United States. The results indicated that youths who were less acculturated were at greater risk of suicidal ideation and attempts. However, there was a significant interaction effect between acculturation and parent-adolescent conflict, which significantly predicted suicidal ideation and attempts. When parent-adolescent conflict was high, the group of less-assimilated youth was at higher risk of suicidal ideation and attempts than the more assimilated group. When conflict was low, there was no significant difference in risk for the two acculturation groups.

Our investigation (Smokowski and Bacallao 2007) found a similar effect for Latino youth in which the relationship between assimilation and internalizing symptoms was moderated by parent-adolescent conflict. Although intriguing, these mediation pathways and moderating relationships need to be replicated in future studies.

A study conducted by Kevin Yoder and his colleagues (2006) examined enculturation and suicide in a sample of 212 American Indian youth who lived on or near three reservations in the upper midwestern United States. Enculturation was first assessed with three subscales that measured the target youths' involvement in and identification with the American Indian culture; this enculturation score was then used to predict suicidal ideation. Results from a bivariate model showed that enculturation was not a significant predictor, but it became significant (with an inverse association) in multivariate models. As levels of enculturation or ethnic identity increased, reports of suicidal ideation went down. In the final multivariate model, enculturation was the second strongest predictor variable of suicidal ideation after drug use. In addition, perceived discrimination was also a significant predictor of suicidal ideation. Although this study found that enculturation was a significant cultural asset, three out of the four extant studies on acculturation and suicidal behavior in American Indian/Alaskan Native youth reported that ethnic identity, cultural identity, or "traditionality" did not have a significant relationship with suicidal ideation or attempts (Howard-Pitney et al. 1992; Novins et al. 1999; Freedenthal and Stiffman 2004). For example, using a sample of 144 urban-reared and 170 reservation-reared American Indian adolescents, Stacey Freedenthal and Arlene Stiffman (2004) demonstrated that cultural identity was not a significant predictor of suicidal behavior. These few and contrasting findings underscore the importance of conducting more collaborative research in American Indian/Alaskan Native communities. National data indicate that suicidal behavior is a serious public health concern for this ethnic minority group, but we have little empirical evidence mapping risk and protective factors for American Indian/Alaskan Native interpersonal or self-directed violence.

Acculturation and Internalizing Problems Such as
Depression and Anxiety

Several studies have examined the relationships among acculturation
and internalizing symptoms (anxiety and depression) and self-esteem.
Using data from the National Longitudinal Survey of Adolescent Health
(Add Health), Kathleen Harris (1999) found an inverse relationship between nativity and well-being. Both first- and second-generation immigrants reported healthier well-being compared to youth with three or more
generations of family members born in the United States. Using the same
Add Health data set, Kathryn Harker (2001) also found that first-generation, foreign-born adolescents reported greater psychological well-being
than subsequent generations. Mexican, Puerto Rican, and Filipino adolescents reported the highest incidence of depression and the lowest levels of
psychological well-being as compared with adolescents from other racial
and ethnic groups. Harker found that the psychological well-being of first-
generation adolescents was significantly improved (i.e., buttressed) by assets including parent supervision, lack of parent-child conflict, religious
practices, and social support.

In a third Add Health analysis on adolescent well-being across immigrant generations, Anne Driscoll, Stephen Russell, and Lisa Crockett
(2008) found that self-esteem scores improved across generations, depression scores stayed the same, and delinquency and alcohol use increased.
These researchers have implicated changes from authoritarian to permis-
sive parenting styles in bringing about these differences in adolescent well-
being.

Using a different data set (i.e., the National Educational Longitudinal
Study [NELS]) and different indicators of psychological well-being, Grace
Kao (1999) reported the opposite relationship: as compared with third-
generation Latinos, both first- and second-generation immigrants displayed
lower levels of self-efficacy and control. These conflicting generational effects are important to understand; however, generation and nativity are the
most sociological measures of acculturation, telling us about cohort differences rather than person-centered individual and family processes.

Cross-sectional studies of individuals and families, rather than generational cohorts, have linked measures of acculturation (e.g., English language fluency) and acculturation stress to depression and anxiety (Hovey
and King 1996; Katragadda and Tidwell 1998). Although neither of these
early empirical studies found a relation between their measures of assimilation and participants' self-reports of depression, both studies found
that acculturation stress was positively related to depression and suicidal

ideation. One study identified perceived family dysfunction and negative expectations for the future as significant predictors of both acculturation stress and depression (Hovey and King 1996).

The vulnerability of low-assimilated adolescents may predispose them to victimization, anxiety, alienation, and depression. Stella Yu and her colleagues (2003) found that, relative to youth who spoke only English at home, Latino adolescents who primarily spoke a language other than English at home were at elevated risk for psychosocial risk factors such as alienation from classmates and being bullied. In their study of 2,528 junior and senior high students in Texas, Saundra Glover and her colleagues (1999) reported that socioeconomic status, family composition, and linguistic fluency had a greater relative impact on the Youth Self-Report Anxiety subscale than all other factors. Being born outside of the United States and having low English-language fluency were risk factors predicting adolescent anxiety. Scott Carvajal and his associates (2002) examined a sample of 1,119 high school students from northern California, and reported that Latinos in the marginalized acculturation group (e.g., those with fewer attachments and adaptations to Latino and other cultures) displayed less desirable mental health outcomes (e.g., higher incidence of depression and low optimism) as compared with the bicultural group.

Other studies have identified language conflicts and racial discrimination as significant acculturation stressors. In a study of 5,264 multiethnic Latino high school students, Ruben Rumbaut (1995) concluded that English-language competence was associated with lower rates of depression. Andrea Romero and Robert Roberts (2003) reported that lower self-esteem and higher numbers of stressors, including various types of discrimination, predicted depressive symptoms. Another investigation in a sample of 1,843 Cuban adolescents found a significant correlation between acculturation conflicts and self-derogation (Vega et al 1993). Seth Schwartz, Byron Zamboanga, and Lorna Hemandez Jarvis (2007) reported finding a strong inverse relationship between acculturation stress and self-esteem. In this study, self-esteem mediated the effect of ethnic identity on externalizing problems. This research revealed that problems inherent in the acculturation process were associated with lower self-esteem. In turn, lower self-esteem appears to be an important mediator between acculturation variables and behavioral outcomes.

In our Latino Acculturation and Health Project, we examined internalizing behavioral problems and self-esteem in 323 Latino adolescents living in North Carolina (Smokowski and Bacallao 2007). Our findings from multiple regression analyses revealed that two risk factors—perceived discrimination and parent-adolescent conflict—were highly significant predictors of adolescent internalizing problems and low self-esteem. Familism—the cultural emphasis on family life being at the center of an individual's world —was a cultural asset found to be associated with fewer internalizing problems and higher self-esteem.

Illustrated in figure 5.5, our latest analyses explored the pathways linking acculturation to self-esteem and internalizing problems from baseline data collection to one year later. Path analyses on data from a sample of 288 Latino adolescents (average age fifteen years; 66 percent foreign born) showed that acculturation conflicts and perceived discrimination were risk factors for both internalizing problems at baseline and parent-adolescent conflict six months later. The adolescents who had been in the United States the longest time reported more internalizing problems. In turn, internalizing problems at baseline, which were associated with acculturation stressors, had a wide-ranging impact, increasing feelings of humiliation, parent-adolescent conflict, and adolescent relationships with delinquent peers six months later and, one year later, resulting in higher internalizing problems and lower self-esteem.

Acculturation and Adolescent Sexual Behavior

Acculturation levels have also been linked with adolescent sexual health. U.S.-born and highly assimilated Latinas are at greater risk for poor birth outcomes, such as having preterm births or low-birth-weight infants (Driscoll et al. 2001). The poorer birth outcomes among U.S.-born and highly assimilated women may be due to negative views of the pregnancy and lack of support from the fathers (Driscoll et al. 2001). As compared to U.S.-born and highly assimilated peers, foreign-born and less-assimilated adolescents have lower rates of sexual activity. However, when foreign-born and less-assimilated adolescents report being sexually active, they are also less likely than highly assimilated peers to use contraceptives or have an abortion if they become pregnant (Ford and Norris 1993). Consequently, birth rates for foreign-born and less-assimilated youth are higher than those for U.S.-born and highly assimilated peers, even given the lower rate of sexual activity among foreign-born, less-assimilated adolescents. The higher birth rates for the foreign-born and less-assimilated teens are driven primarily by decisions not to use contraceptives or to have abortions (Driscoll et al. 2001). The association between sexual health and acculturation is complex and requires more research to understand underlying processes.

Overall, the association between acculturation and negative behavior appears to be related to nativity (i.e., place of birth), length of time in the host country, and language facility and use. Research has found that U.S.-

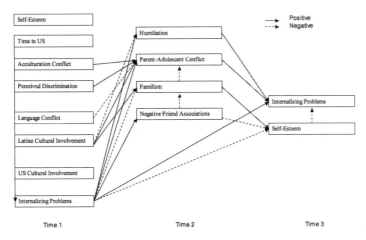

Fig. 5.5. Pathways from acculturation stress to subsequent internalizing problems and self-esteem. Time points are separated by six months. All paths are statistically significant. Chi-Square = 73.07, 57 df, *p* = .07; Normed Chi-Square = 1.28; CFI = .98; RMSEA = .031 (.000–.051). (Paul R. Smokowski, Martica Bacallao, and Rachel Buchanan, "Mediation Pathways from Acculturation Stressors to Adolescent Internalizing Problems: An Ecological Structural Model for Latino Youth, *Journal of Community Psychology*, in press)

born Latino adolescents display levels of alcohol use, substance use, and mental health disorders that are consistently higher than those of foreign-born Latino adolescents (Gil and Vega 1996; Vega and Gil 1998; Gil, Wagner, and Vega 2000; U.S. Department of Health and Human Services 2001). The longer foreign-born adolescents live in the United States, the higher their rate of alcohol or substance use (Gil, Wagner, and Vega 2000) and internalizing problems (Smokowski, Bacallao, and Rose 2010). Consistent with this finding, research has also shown that Latino adolescents who primarily speak Spanish are less likely to use alcohol and drugs than Latino adolescents who are primarily English speakers (Zapata and Katims 1994; Welte and Barnes 1995).

Acculturation and Health in Adults

The relationship between acculturation and adults' physical health and mental health has received considerable research attention. A number of studies with large, nationally representative samples of Latino and Asian

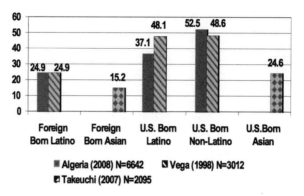

Fig. 5.6. Lifetime prevalence of any psychiatric disorder by nativity and race/ethnicity

adults have estimated prevalence rates for a range of psychiatric disorders. Differences in acculturation are typically indexed by nativity, with foreign-born immigrants and U.S.-born minority groups being compared to each other and the differences discovered between these groups being commonly attributed to acculturation. This approach is often taken by researchers conducting long surveys with large numbers of participants in the sample. The most sophisticated of these studies also compare foreign-born and native minority groups to U.S.-born non-Latinos to determine whether prevalence rates vary by race or ethnicity and nativity. A sample of these studies is provided in figure 5.6.

Figure 5.6 illustrates the so-called *immigrant paradox*. This term has been coined to describe the seeming incongruity that, despite experiencing significant socioeconomic disadvantages and social hardships during and after immigration, immigrants tend to report better physical and mental health than U.S.-born respondents. U.S.-born Latinos report rates of physical and mental health disorders similar to those of U.S.-born non-Latinos, which might signal both a generational trend toward assimilation and the health-promoting effect of indigenous cultural factors for first-generation immigrants. A number of research studies have found that the immigrant paradox was salient for Latinos in a host of physical health and mental health outcomes: lifetime and twelve-month prevalence rates of psychiatric disorders (Burnam et al. 1987; Swanson et al. 1992; Escobar 1998; Vega et al. 1998; Alegría et al. 2008), drug use (Pumariega et al. 1992), dual diagnosis of psychiatric disorders and substance abuse (Vega et al. 2009), intermittent explosive disorder (Ortega et al. 2008), obesity (Bates et al. 2008), binge eating and bulimia nervosa (Alegría et al. 2007), hypertension

(Winkleby et al. 1998), cardiovascular disease mortality (Sundquist and Winkleby 1999), and infant birth weight (Zambrana et al. 1994; Guendelman and Abrams 1994). The immigrant paradox also applies to psychiatric disorders and obesity in Asian immigrants, although information is much more limited and the effects are not as profound as they are for Latinos (Takeuchi et al. 2007; Bates et al. 2008).

A positive linear relationship between assimilation and problematic behavior can be seen in alcohol use for Latino adults. Six out of seven studies on Latino alcohol consumption and abuse included in Rogler, Cortes, and Malgady's (1991) review found that assimilation was associated with increased alcohol use. For instance, Theodore Graves (1967) found that assimilation was consistently associated with high rates of alcohol consumption and deviant behavior in Mexican Americans with low socioeconomic status. Audrey Burnam and colleagues (1987) found U.S.-born Mexican Americans had higher prevalence of alcohol and drug abuse and dependence than Mexican-born participants. Similarly, a national probability sample of Latinos also found high rates of frequent heavy drinking in assimilating young Latino men (Caetano 1987). Moreover, Caetano's study found that the association between assimilation and alcoholism was even stronger for women, with highly assimilated women being nine times more likely to drink heavily than low-assimilated women. Gilbert (1987) also found that women in later generations of immigrants tended to move from light to moderate drinking.

William Vega and colleagues (1998) examined substance use in a sample of 3,012 Mexican adults living in Fresno County, California. They reported that high assimilation levels and U.S. nativity were significant risk factors for illicit drug use. The combined influences of being born in the United States, being highly assimilated, and living in an urban area increased the odds of illicit drug use by 7.38 times for men, and 29.26 times for women. In the Vega study, high levels of assimilation and stress that stemmed from an individual's experience of discrimination increased the person's odds of being clinically depressed. Increased alcohol and drug use may be a maladaptive coping mechanism for handling this stress and symptoms of depression.

Some researchers suggest that the immigrant paradox occurs because the healthiest members of the sending society (Mexico, for example) are most likely to emigrate, making foreign-born immigrants a self-selected group of particularly hardy people. In a rare transnational study, Breslau and his colleagues (2007) explored this hypothesis by comparing psychiatric data from 2,362 Mexican residents who had not emigrated with similar data from seventy-five Mexican immigrants living in the United States.

The results showed that Mexican residents reported rates of lifetime mood and anxiety disorders that were less than half the rates for Mexican immigrants in the United States (lifetime anxiety: 10.7 percent Mexican residents, 24.7 percent Mexican immigrants in United States; lifetime mood: 9.3 percent Mexican residents, 19.3 percent Mexican immigrants in United States). Twelve-month rates for anxiety and mood disorders in Mexican residents were one-third the rates for Mexican immigrants in the United States (residents' anxiety 7 percent versus 21.9 percent for immigrants; residents' mood disorders 4.8 percent versus 13.6 percent for immigrants). The lopsided sample sizes between the groups of Mexican residents and Mexican immigrants in the United States are a limitation of this study. The small group of seventy-five Mexican immigrants living in the United States may not be a representative sample. Rates for a larger sample of Latino immigrants, not exclusively Mexican, from the National Latino and Asian American Study ($n = 2,554$) were 15.4 percent for a lifetime mood disorder and 15.7 percent for a lifetime anxiety disorder (Alegría et al. 2008); lower than the seventy-five Mexican immigrants in the Breslau study, but still substantially higher than the Mexican residents in the Breslau study. Even though more transnational studies like this are needed, these data refute the idea that healthier individuals are choosing to emigrate, leaving those with more problems behind.

Javier Escobar, Constanza Nervi, and Michael Gara (2000) reviewed studies on Mexican adults to assess the link between immigration and mental health. They concluded that

> Mexican-born immigrants, despite significant socioeconomic disadvantages, have better mental health profiles than U.S.-born Mexican-Americans. . . . The elevated rates of psychopathology of U.S.-born Mexican-Americans may be related to easier access to abused substances and an elevated frequency of substance abuse among the U.S. born. (64)

Conversely, foreign-born Mexicans who have immigrated to the United States may be protected by traditional family networks and may have different expectations about what constitutes success in the United States.

Why Would High Assimilation Be a Risk Factor?

Various hypotheses have been put forth to explain the relationship among high assimilation, substance use, and health and mental health problems. Assimilation theorists interpret findings on these problems as evidence that immigrants are taking on behaviors that are tolerated in the host culture. A behavior adaptation hypothesis helps to explain this dynamic, stating that acculturating individuals are taking on behaviors that are tolerated, or even supported, by the host society (Castro et al. 1996). For instance, immigrant youth initiate alcohol and substance use to fit into and identify with American peer groups. Women markedly increase their alcohol consumption as traditional Latina gender role constraints against such behavior are eroded (Caetano 1987; Rogler, Cortes, and Malgady 1991). Obesity tends to increase as immigrants adopt the dietary habits of the United States population, eating fast foods with high saturated fat levels.

In addition, acculturating individuals may adopt "American" attitudes toward many behaviors such as alcohol, drugs, or fast food, and disregard their previously held culture-of-origin attitudes about these behaviors. Of course, Americans are not a homogenous group and have diverse attitudes concerning any of these topics. However, the central issue appears to be that acculturating individuals see what is and is not tolerated in the host society and change their behavioral repertoires accordingly, gradually replacing culture-of-origin behaviors, routines, beliefs, and norms with those from the host society.

This perspective of assimilation is supported by evidence in the research literature on acculturation and health. It appears that significant changes in health behaviors occur across generations that suggest that U.S.-born children of immigrant parents, and later generations, will report health behaviors similar to those of non-Latino white U.S. citizens. Unfortunately, the evidence available also suggests that this cultural adaptation comes at a high personal price. Healthy behaviors characteristic of foreign-born immigrants are often lost in subsequent generations, signaling a strikingly negative aspect of assimilation. In the past, assimilation ideology was concerned with the integration of foreigners into the host society, mainly through education and intermarriage for white European immigrants. This historic context stressed the benefits of assimilation. In light of new evidence illuminating the immigrant paradox, it is critical to consider the negative aspects of assimilation. Along with new educational and economic opportunities, melting pot assimilation may strip immigrants of the healthy behaviors they bring from their countries-of-origin while fostering poor health and mental health functioning that is characteristic of the host society.

Alternately, researchers suggest that negative health behaviors, such as alcohol and substance use, may be undertaken as a strategy for coping with acculturation stress (Gil et al. 2000). Maladaptive behavior is thought to derive from "increased perceptions of discrimination, internalization of minority status, and/or socialization into cultural attitudes and behaviors that have a disintegrative effect on family ties" (Gil, Vega, and Dimas 1994, 45). This maladaptive behavior results in self-deprecation, ethnic self-hatred, and a weakened ego structure in the assimilated individual (Rogler, Cortes, and Malgady 1991). Further, maladaptive coping that includes substance use, aggressive behavior, hypertension, mental health problems, and obesity has been linked to generational differences between acculturating family members. A resilient first generation of immigrant parents tends to focus on perceived increases in their standard of living, leaving them thankful for new opportunities and protected by traditional values. In contrast, the perceptions of subsequent generations (e.g., immigrant children and adolescents, U.S.-born children of immigrant parents) tend to focus more on deprivation because of higher unrealized expectations and aspirations, which has the potential to lead these generations to turn to maladaptive coping strategies (Burnam et al. 1987; Rogler, Cortes, and Malgady 1991). At the same time, negative health behavior patterns increase perceived stress, adding to the difficulties inherent in the acculturation process. Ultimately, coping with acculturation stress with negative health behaviors becomes a self-propelling cycle, causing some U.S.-born Latino and Asian adolescents and adults to become immersed in high-risk behaviors, such as substance use and antisocial behavior, and to experience mental health problems.

Why Would Low Assimilation Be a Risk Factor?

Assimilation theorists predict that not assimilating to American ways is likely to cause problems for low-acculturated individuals living in the United States. Low-assimilated individuals may endure cultural marginality, experiencing their environment as frightening, confusing, and overwhelming (Rogler, Cortes, and Malgady 1991). There is some evidence for this perspective. Researchers have linked low assimilation levels with psychological difficulties such as depression, hopelessness, social withdrawal, familial isolation, despair, obsessive-compulsive behavior, and teen pregnancy (Torres-Matrullo 1976; Szapocznik and Kurtines 1980; Escobar et al. 1986; Miranda, Estrada, and Firpo-Jimenez 2000).

Individuals with a low assimilation level seem to have different trajectories according to the amount of stress they experience. As might be expected, low-assimilated individuals who experience little stress exhibit better adaptation than those who experience high levels of stress. It is thought that these low-stress individuals benefit from traditional cultural protective factors such as high family cohesion (e.g., familism) and strong ethnic identity. Further, these protective factors may lead low-stress, low-assimilated individuals to internalize fewer negative stereotypes and prejudices that ordinarily act as risk factors for poor adjustment (Rogler, Cortes, and Malgady 1991; Gil, Vega, and Dimas 1994).

In contrast, low-assimilated individuals experiencing high levels of stress display low self-esteem, experience acculturation conflicts, and may be cut off from the protective benefits of their culture-of-origin (i.e., extensive family support networks, shared value systems). Moreover, low-assimilated, high-stress individuals often lack the resources and skills necessary to successfully navigate within their new environment and, thus, have a more difficult time coping with negative stereotypes and perceived discrimination than high-assimilated or low-assimilated, low-stress individuals (Rogler, Cortes, and Malgady 1991). Andres Gil, William Vega, and Juanita Dimas (1994) found that low-assimilated adolescents who were U.S. born had a particularly problematic profile of stressors and difficulties. Compared to foreign-born peers, these low-assimilated U.S.-born Latino adolescents were substantially more likely to perceive discrimination and internalize negative self-images and stereotypes. Further, these U.S.-born adolescents had lower levels of family cohesion. This finding is important because family cohesion acts as a protective factor to mediate the relationship between acculturation stress and self-esteem.

Conclusions

According to available evidence, the relationship between acculturation and health may be either the result of the assimilation of unhealthy behaviors or the result of attempting to cope with acculturation stress. More research is needed, especially longitudinal studies, to fully clarify the process that immigrant families go through while adjusting to life in the United States. Our current understanding suggests that both low- and high-assimilation levels (Separation and Assimilation adaptation styles) pose risk for Latino and Asian adolescents and their parents. High assimilation is particularly problematic for health and mental health. In the next chapter, we discuss how biculturalism, which is the integrative style balancing culture-of-origin and the host culture, has been connected to adaptive coping and healthier psychological functioning.

6

The Benefits of Biculturalism

Savoring the Flavors in the Simmering Stew

If we made a movie about my life, it would be called "Being Between Two Worlds." I'm from Mexico and I'm fifteen years old. I now live in the U.S. and I am happy because I am with my family. But, I was sad. In Mexico, I left my friends and a life that I had imagined there. On the other hand, the life that I have now is very fun and interesting. God has given me a family that loves and supports me and that makes me stronger and gives me the motivation to move forward each day of my life. I hope to continue studying and become a good teacher.

—Fernanda, fifteen-year-old Mexican female

My life changed since I came to the United States. When I was in Colombia, I didn't do anything and only spent time in the streets with my friends until really late. But since I came here, I am already doing better in school and I learned that anything can be achieved in life with good effort. Thanks to God that I came to the United States with the help of my stepmother and can move forward. She has offered me the opportunity to learn new things. In the beginning, my mom separated from my dad and we had a lot of problems. There were always fights between my parents but my mother was a woman that no one could change . Then my stepmother came to Colombia to get me and my brother. She took us to the United States. Now I am doing well in school and think about going to college. I have the opportunity because I am almost a resident. I'm going to give it my all.

—Angel, seventeen-year-old Colombian male

Considering the difficulties at both low and high levels of assimilation discussed in chapter 5 (see figures 5.1 and 5.2), some researchers hypothesize that moderate levels of acculturation (i.e., a balance between culture-of-origin and U.S. cultural identity) are the most advantageous for cultural adaptation (LaFromboise, Coleman, and Gerton 1993). Bicultural individuals are those with moderate acculturation levels who have successfully internalized two cultures, that is, both cultures are alive inside of the person. Many bicultural individuals report that their internalized cultures take turns guiding their thoughts and feelings (LaFromboise, Coleman, and Gerton 1993; Phinney and Devich-Navarro 1997; Hong et al. 2000). While it is important to remember that conflicting evidence exists for any of the hypothesized relationships between acculturation and health (Rogler, Cortes, and Malgady 1991), research findings have linked biculturalism with more adaptive, positive mental health outcomes than either separation/enculturation or assimilation cultural adaptation styles (see figures 5.1 and 5.2). Alternation theorists have determined that biculturalism is an important, positive cultural adaptation style within the acculturation process.

Alternation theorists suggest that maintaining moderate levels of acculturation in both the host U.S. culture and the culture-of-origin is associated with the least incidence of psychosocial problems and the best adjustment. Proponents of the alternation or bicultural theory of cultural acquisition contend that there is great value in an individual's maintaining culture-of-origin affiliation while acquiring the second culture. From this perspective, the bicultural individual experiences less stress and anxiety because the person can access skills and resources from both cultural systems to handle stressors (Rashid 1984). Further, individuals who are becoming bicultural maintain a positive relationship with both cultures without having to choose one over the other, which precludes feelings of guilt over preferring one culture. A bicultural individual participates in the two cultures by tailoring his or her behavior to the situation. The two internalized cultures remain distinct and are not necessarily blended together (LaFromboise and Rowe 1983; LaFromboise, Coleman, and Gerton 1993). More important, the new cultural experiences and attitudes do not supplant the established behaviors and attitudes the person has already internalized. Consequently, for the bicultural individual, cultural experiences are cumulative, and assimilation is not inevitable.

Alternation researchers believe that society will eventually adapt to increasing pluralism. In doing so, society will begin to emphasize multiculturalism rather than assimilation. With the greater emphasis on diversity, the multiple identities that come with multiculturalism will then be valued as a new form of cultural capital (Trueba 2002). Other societies, such as Canada and New Zealand, have already moved in this multicultural direction. Trueba (2002) wrote,

The mastery of different languages, the ability to cross racial and ethnic boundaries, and a general resiliency associated with the ability to endure hardships and overcome obstacles will clearly be recognized as a new cultural capital that will be crucial for success in a modern, diversified society, not a handicap. The hypothesis is that oppression and abuse can also generate precisely the opposite—resiliency and cultural capital to succeed. Often, these create the psychological flexibility necessary to assume different identities in order to survive. That is, the mechanisms that marginalize certain persons of color may turn into a cultural capital in other settings. (7-8)

Researchers espousing alternation theory hypothesize a nonlinear relationship (e.g., a U-shaped curve) between acculturation and mental health problems, leaving moderate levels of acculturation to display the least problems and the best adjustment. There is research evidence for this as a hypothesis. In a study comparing low- and high-assimilated Latinos, researchers found that bicultural Latinos obtained higher levels of quality of life, affect balance, and psychological adjustment (Lang et al. 1982). Alexis Miranda and Debra Umhoefer (1998) reported that bicultural individuals displayed high levels of social interest and low levels of depression. In a sample of 252 Latina undergraduate students, Maria Gomez and Ruth Fassinger (1994) found that bicultural women had wider repertoires of behavioral styles than either their low- or high-acculturated peers. Other studies found that bicultural individuals have increased creativity (Carringer 1974) and greater attention control (Bialystok 1999; Bialystok et al. 2004). Veronica Benet-Martinez, Fiona Lee, and Janxin Leu (2006) argue that the more complex U.S. and culture-of-origin cultural representations developed by bicultural individuals relate to their higher levels of both cultural empathy (i.e., the ability to detect and understand others' cultural habits or pressures) and cultural flexibility (i.e., the ability to quickly switch from one cultural strategy or framework to another).

> *In my house, I consider myself completely Latina. When I'm with my friends, I'm Latina because they're Latinos. When I'm with Americans, I totally change to American. And when I'm with both, I guess I'm bicultural!* (Juliana, Colombian female adolescent, age fifteen)

Elsa Rivera-Sinclair (1997) investigated biculturalism in a sample of 254 Cuban adults. She measured biculturalism using the Bicultural Involvement Questionnaire (BIQ) and found that biculturalism was related to a variety of factors, including length of time a person had lived in the United States, age, family income, education level, and general anxiety level. Her findings showed that the study participants who were more likely to report high levels of biculturalism were those individuals who had been in the United States longer, had higher incomes, and had more education. In addition, she found that younger individuals were more inclined to be bicultural than were older persons. Most important, this analysis showed that participants' anxiety levels decreased as their biculturalism levels increased.

Andres Gil, William Vega, and Juanita Dimas (1994) found that bicultural adolescents had the lowest levels of acculturation stress and were less likely to report low family pride as compared with low- and high-acculturated Latino adolescents. For these bicultural adolescents, the acculturation process did not erode levels of family pride—a dynamic that usually takes place as adolescents become highly assimilated.

In our study with 323 Latino adolescents living in North Carolina (Smokowski and Bacallao 2007), we found that biculturalism was a cultural asset associated with fewer internalizing problems and higher self-esteem. Interestingly, we found that it was individuals' high level of involvement in non-Latino culture (i.e., U.S. culture) that fueled the protective effect of biculturalism on internalizing problems. However, the reverse appears to hold true for externalizing problems (e.g., aggressive behavior). We found Latino adolescents who had higher levels of culture-of-origin involvement reported less aggressive behavior, fewer social problems, less hopelessness, and higher self-esteem (Smokowski, Buchanan, and Bacallao 2009). It is fascinating that both dimensions of biculturalism appear to be positively connected to self-esteem. Further, each of the two dimensions, culture-of-origin and U.S. cultural involvement, make unique contributions to healthy adjustment in different areas such as aggressive behavior and internalizing symptoms. This variation in positive contribution helps to explain the wide-ranging protective effect of biculturalism as a cultural asset. Similarly, J. Douglas Coatsworth and colleagues (2005) compared the acculturation patterns of 315 Latino youth and found that bicultural youth reported significantly higher levels of academic competence, peer competence, and parental monitoring.

John Berry and his colleagues (2006) conducted the largest and most elaborate investigation of acculturation and adaptation in immigrant youth in a study that encompassed youth from twenty-six different cultural backgrounds in thirteen countries. In all, 7,997 adolescents participated, including 5,366 immigrant youth and 2,631 host culture youth, that is, youth whose country-of-origin was the host country. The youth in the study ranged in age from thirteen to eighteen years old, with a mean age of fifteen years. These researchers were able to confirm empirically the four cultural adaptation styles discussed in chapter 1. Integration or bicultural-ism was the predominant adaptation style with 36.4 percent of immigrant youth fitting this profile (22.5 percent displayed an ethnic profile; 18.7 per-cent, an assimilation profile, also called a national profile; and 22.4 percent, a diffuse or marginalized profile). This bicultural way of living included reporting diverse acculturation attitudes, having both ethnic and host cul-tural identities, being proficient in both their ethnic language and the host culture language, having social engagements with both ethnic and host-culture peers, and endorsing the acceptance of obligations to family and parents as well as believing in adolescents' rights. This high level of bicul-turalism (i.e., integrative cultural adaptation style) in youth supports ear-lier findings with adult immigrants (Berry and Sam 1997).

In this study, Berry and colleagues (2006) found that the longer youth had lived in the new culture, the more likely they were to have a bicul-tural adaptation style. Further, these researchers found that the integrative cultural adaptation style was associated with both positive psychological adaptation (measured by indicators of life satisfaction, self-esteem, and psychological problems) and positive sociological adaptation (measured by school adjustment and behavioral problems). In comparison, the ethnic cultural adaptation style was linked to better psychological adaptation but worse sociological adaptation, whereas both the national and diffuse styles were associated with poor psychological and sociological adaptation. Al-though boys had slightly better psychological adaptation than girls, they had poorer sociocultural adaptation.

These studies provide mounting evidence that psychological and social benefits are associated with being bicultural. Having established these posi-tive effects, we now review the cognitive and linguistic factors that may be the foundation for the advantages offered by biculturalism.

Biculturalism and Cognition: Cultural Frame Switching

Bicultural individuals appear to benefit from the ability to quickly shift their socio-cognitive perceptual schemas to fit situational demands. This ability, called *cultural frame switching,* is more highly developed in bicultural indi-viduals than in either their low- or high-assimilated peers, and thus allows bicultural individuals to cope successfully with a wider range of culture-laden situations (Haritatos and Benet-Martinez 2002). People process the social cues in their environment, such as others' facial expressions, body language, or tone of voice, on the basis of models that we acquire as we are raised in a certain culture. These models are the interpretive frames we use to respond to our world. Bicultural individuals have acquired two sets of interpretive frames. While frame switching, bicultural individuals shift between interpretive frames rooted in different cultures as they respond to cues in the social environment (LaFromboise, Coleman, and Gerton 1993; Hong et al. 2000). Frame switching may be triggered by different contexts (e.g., moving from home to school or work) or may occur in response to cues or symbols (e.g., hearing a language, seeing a Mexican flag) that have a psychological association with one culture.

Cognitive psychologists now believe that culture is not internalized as a monolithic, overarching worldview that constantly guides cognition, like putting on a pair of colored glasses. Instead, scholars consider cultural models, beliefs, theories, norms, and behaviors as loosely networked in the brain, and these knowledge constructs remain domain specific. These constructs guide cognition when matched to the situation in a given environment (Hong et al. 2000). Thinking of cultural knowledge as domain specific and situational, rather than overarching and continuous, allows for individuals to internalize more than one cultural system. Even pieces of different cultural systems that are conflicting or contradictory can be internalized in the same mind. Cultural frame switching creates a perspective that grasps the relativism and multidimensionality of each cultural system (Gutierrez and Sameroff 1990), which leads to complex representations of both the culture-of-origin and the host culture (Benet-Martinez, Lee, and Leu 2006).

Researchers conducting studies on cultural frame switching think it is possible to activate different parts of a bicultural person's network of cultural knowledge with culture-specific stimuli, called *primes*. Bicultural individuals have two distinct networks of cultural knowledge (e.g., Mexican cultural concepts and beliefs, and the equivalent from the United States culture). Whichever cultural system is most recently activated (i.e., primed) guides the individual's interpretation of environmental events. Consequently, cognitive psychologists conduct cultural frame-switching experiments by priming bicultural individuals with different cultural symbols and evaluating whether the person's interpretations of ambiguous stimuli are guided by the cultural network that was primed.

For example, Anne-Marie Yamada and Theodore Singelis (1999) compared 120 individuals who were segregated into four acculturation-based groups: Bicultural, Western (e.g., assimilated), Traditional (e.g., Separated/Enculturated), and Culturally Alienated. As compared with the other groups, the Bicultural group was the only group that had significantly higher scores on both independent and interdependent self-construal (i.e., an individual's sense of self in relation to others). In other words, the Bicultural group was able to affiliate with values espoused by both the Western and the Traditional groups. This finding illustrated the ability of bicultural individuals to navigate between two cultural systems by switching the cognitive framework they used to process cues from the environment.

Ying-yi Hong and colleagues (2000) conducted a series of cultural frame-switching experiments in Hong Kong. This locale is appropriate for such studies because it is a multicultural territory characterized by Western belief systems embedded within a traditional Chinese culture. In this study, Chinese undergraduate students were randomly assigned to one of three conditions: an American-culture priming condition, a Chinese-culture priming condition, or a control condition. Participants in the American-culture priming condition were shown six pictures of American icons, such as the White House or the American flag, and were asked to answer short questions about the pictures. Chinese-culture priming participants were shown pictures of Chinese icons such as the Great Wall of China and were asked the same short questions that were asked of the other priming condition. Control participants were shown neutral landscapes and were asked the same questions. Next, participants were shown a picture of a group of fish with a single fish at the front, similar to the illustration in figure 6.1. A series of rating scales was administered to see if participants thought the front fish was leading the other fish (an internal cause) or was being chased by the other fish (an external cause). Hong Kong students in the American priming condition were significantly more confident that the front fish was leading compared with their peers in the Chinese priming condition, who were more confident that the front fish was being chased. The responses of the control group were divided between those of the American and Chinese priming groups. The researchers concluded that the priming was effective in influencing Hong Kong youth to explain events by internal causes, an attribute of American ideology, or external causes, a Chinese attribute.

Applying similar research methods and conditions, the same researchers asked 234 Hong Kong Chinese high school students to interpret a story about an overweight boy abandoning his diet when offered cake at a buffet dinner with his friends. Once again, participants in the American-culture priming condition accorded less importance to external social factors than did participants in the Chinese-culture priming condition, with the responses of the nonprimed control participants falling between those of the two primed groups (Hong et al. 2000).

This research into cultural frame switching provides beginning evidence that cultural icons or primes can activate cultural values that guide cognition. Different primes can activate alternate cultural cognitions residing within the same bicultural mind. Most important, language can serve

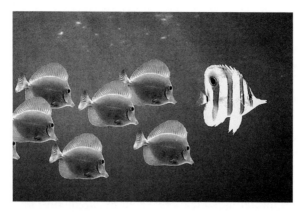

Fig. 6.1. Why is the first fish swimming in front of the other fish?

as a powerful cultural prime. For example, studies have shown that when bilingual Chinese individuals answer questionnaires that are in English, their responses tend to be guided by Western (e.g., U.S.) culture, whereas when the questions are in Chinese, they provide responses oriented toward Chinese culture (Hong et al. 2000). Extending this research, Nairan Ramirez-Esparza and colleagues (2006) examined whether language was a sufficiently strong cultural cue to prime approximately thirty Spanish-English bicultural young adults to change personality attributes. The initial evidence suggested that language use can trigger cultural frame switching. In addition, these researchers found that personality traits such as extraversion, agreeableness, and conscientiousness can shift according to the frame bilingual individuals use to respond to cultural cues in their environment. Consequently, bicultural adolescents may not simply learn to act "Latino" at home and "American" at school, but rather, this cognitive priming effect suggests that their brains are trained to actually think and perceive differently in these disparate cultural contexts.

Cognitive research on bicultural functioning has not been empirically linked to the acculturation process; however, there are important conceptual links requiring further research. For example, Hong and her colleagues (2000) concluded,

> A dynamic constructivist approach lends itself to viewing acculturation as a more active process. The end result, thinking and behaving like a member of the host culture, is seen as a state, not a trait. This state will occur when interpretive frames from the host culture are accessible. We submit that

individuals undergoing acculturation, to some extent, manage the process by controlling the accessibility of cultural constructs. People desiring to acculturate quickly surround themselves with symbols and situations that prime the meaning system of the host culture. Conversely, expatriates desiring to maintain the accessibility of constructs from their home culture surround themselves with stimuli priming that culture. (718)

The idea that acculturation is a state rather than a trait validates our circle model of becoming bicultural that was presented in chapter 1. The cognitive psychology research on cultural priming suggests that a dynamic flow occurs between cultural contexts depending upon the primes available to trigger the bicultural individual's perceptions, cognitions, belief schemas, and personality traits. The evidence suggesting that these cognitive structures shift with the cultural context supports the idea that bicultural individuals have multiple identities that emerge as appropriate responses to environmental situations.

Biculturalism and Bilingualism: Neural Networks and Language Processing

> *I became bilingual. Can't think of why that would be a bad thing at all. Um, because you can communicate with, like, thousands of more people that way!*
> (Cristian, Peruvian male adolescent, age sixteen)

Bicultural competencies are usually strongly associated with language use. Several studies have found that youths who are fluent in both their culture-of-origin language and English typically do better in school than those who speak only one language (e.g. English-only or limited-English speakers; Stanton-Salazar and Dornbusch 1995; Rumberger and Larson 1998; Feliciano 2001). In addition, bilingual youths typically show fewer emotional-behavioral problems, less delinquency, and lower levels of aggression (Toppleberg et al. 2002). For example, Cynthia Feliciano (2001) used 1990 Census data to study the link between biculturalism and school dropout among more than sixteen thousand Mexican eighteen- to twenty-one-year-olds. Using bilingualism as a proxy indicator of biculturalism, her findings showed that bicultural Mexican youths were less likely to drop out of school than either limited-English or English-only speakers. Compared to their bicultural peers, Mexican youths were more than twice as likely to drop out of school if they spoke limited English, and those who spoke only English were 29 percent more likely to leave school. Having bilingual individuals in the household was also a deterrent to dropping out. Mexican youths in bilingual households were 50 percent less likely to drop out of school than those in homes with no bilingual speakers.

Psycholinguistic researchers have provided strong evidence that bilingual individuals are fundamentally different from monolingual speakers, especially regarding the existence of differentiated dual lexicons (i.e., systems of words) and the nature of the connections between those language systems. Moreover, the bilingual speakers exhibit fundamentally different levels of control, such as the control needed to use items from one language versus the other (e.g., searching for a Spanish word rather than an English one; Kovelman, Baker, and Petito 2008). Linguists continue to debate whether bilingual speakers have two separate, distinct language lexicons or one overarching lexicon that is wired in a neural network like that of monolingual speakers but containing both languages.

Neuroimaging studies are contributing new knowledge to the bicultural discussion. Specialized imaging techniques, such as functional magnetic resonance imaging (fMRI), show increased blood flow in certain areas of the brain. The increased blood flow is associated with greater neural activity and is an indication that those areas are responsible for processing certain types of information or stimuli. These types of neuroimaging studies have shown that four specific brain areas are involved in bilingual switching: the dorsolateral prefrontal cortex, inferior frontal cortex, anterior cingulate, and supramarginal gyrus (Price, Green, and von Studnitz 1999; Hernandez, Martinez, and Kohnert 2000; Rodriguez-Fornells et al. 2002; 2005; Quaresima et al. 2002). During rapid switching from one language to another, a bilingual individual's brain functions differently from the brain of a monolingual person. The bilingual individual's brain has undergone structural changes as a result of extensive exposure to two languages, including enlargement of brain areas that process sensory stimuli (Mechelli et al. 2004: Kovelman, Baker, and Petito 2008). This area of the brain (i.e., the inferior parietal cortex) is sensitive to the system of sounds for a given language and appears to be involved in reading languages as well. It makes intuitive sense that this area of the brain would be enlarged in bilingual individuals who process two languages through sound and visual processing of text.

When exposed to both languages from an early age, bilingual individuals use the same brain areas for processing both languages. In contrast, persons who become bilingual later in life set up new brain pathways to process their second language (Dehaene et al. 1997; Kim et al. 1997; Weber-Fox and Neville 1996; 2001; Hernandez, Martinez, and Kohnert 2000; Hahne and Friederici 2001; Marian, Spivey, and Hirsch 2003; Wartenburger et al.

2003). As compared to monolingual speakers, bilingual speakers display an increased density in gray matter in the left inferior parietal lobe (Mechelli et al. 2004). Gray matter density increases most in early, high-proficiency bilinguals, and is lowest in late, low-proficiency bilinguals. Ioulia Kovelman, Stephanie Baker, and Laura Ann Petitto (2008) found that bilingual individuals' behavioral performance and neural activity were different depending upon whether they were processing in English or processing in Spanish. This finding provides new support for the view that bilingual individuals develop two differentiated, monolingual-like linguistic systems in one brain. Viorica Marian and colleagues (2007) also used fMRI studies to reveal different centers of neuron activation associated with the first versus the second language in bilingual individuals. Interestingly, these effects were salient for the processing of words and sounds, but not for visual processing.

These results indicate that late-learning bilingual individuals may have greater difficulty translating between languages because the brain areas they use for processing the two languages are more distant than the neural centers used for finding multiple words in one language. In other words, the brain of the late-learner bilingual speaker may literally be working harder and sending messages farther while searching for words and processing auditory information from two languages. Interestingly, this neurological process can map directly onto our model of bicultural identity development (see figures 1.3 and 1.4). Late-learning bilingual individuals have a more difficult time going between their two languages; the areas of the brain they use are more distant, causing more effort and conflict. Early-learning bilingual individuals have more gray matter in certain areas of the brain and closely integrated neural networks, enabling them to fluidly process or go between their two languages. This is beginning physiological evidence for bilingual and bicultural identity integration.

Development of Bicultural Skills

A successful person is that person who fights against all the obstacles, which are many and very hard, and overcomes them . . . to achieve a future.
(Camila, Peruvian mother)

Not all of the research on biculturalism is as positive as the studies cited above. Maintaining ties with two cultural systems may cause contradiction, tension, and social strain (Haritatos and Benet-Martinez 2002), especially during the early phases of bicultural development. Diane de Anda (1984) was one of the first researchers to point out the importance of an individual's transactions between the larger majority and minority cultural systems in promoting or inhibiting bicultural development. She hypothesized that the amount of stress in bicultural adaptation was largely the result of the following six factors: (1) overlap between the two cultural systems, (2) availability of cultural translators or models, (3) positive or negative corrective feedback provided by members of each culture, (4) compatibility between the individual's cognitive style and styles valued by the majority culture, (5) bilingualism, and (6) degree of similarity in physical appearance between the minority individual and the majority culture. All of these factors contribute to the person-environment fit between the acculturating individual and the dominant host culture. A poor fit can inhibit bicultural development, causing higher levels of stress and strain.

According to these criteria, prior waves of immigrants from Europe and Russia had less stress developing biculturalism or assimilating. The European and Russian immigrants during the first half of the twentieth century had more overlap with the white Anglo majority group. Although there were clear differences in religion, language, and country-of-origin, their cognitive style was not overly divergent from that of the majority host culture. The immigrants also shared light skin tones with the dominant majority, a feature that helped them blend into the host society. In contrast, the new waves of immigrants from Latin America and Asia come from cultures with little overlap to white Anglo-Saxon norms. Corrective feedback, in the form of prejudice and discrimination, is arguably harsher because of darker skin, differences in appearance, and divergent cognitive styles. Overall, these differences make a backdrop for current immigrants' bicultural development that is more difficult than that experienced by the European immigrants of the past.

Socioeconomic status may also impact adaptation styles and bicultural identity development. In her qualitative study of coping styles of immigrant parents, Dorit Roer-Strier (1997) presented professionals (i.e., pediatricians, educators, social workers, psychologists) with three typical coping strategies and asked them to express their opinions regarding the adaptive and risk values of each coping style. Her results indicated that professionals viewed adaptation, risk, and well-being in a variety of ways, which were often conflicting. Evaluations of immigrant parents' coping styles differed according to the profession of the person interviewed. Pediatricians and educators preferred the rapid assimilation model, whereas social workers and psychologists preferred the coping style of the bicultural model. This difference in professional perceptions of what constitutes the "best practice in coping skills" underscores that immigrant families are likely to receive divergent opinions about acculturation from various professionals, creating conflict, stress, and confusion.

Veronica Vivero and Sharon Jenkins (1999) articulated hazards for the developmental processes of multicultural individuals and families. They suggest that cross-cultural tensions may result in *cultural homelessness*, which is a developmental challenge that results from the stress of trying to adapt to contradictory social norms, values, and culture-based communication processes. Thus, the cultural frame switching that is thought to eventually enhance the social and cognitive repertoires of bicultural individuals may also lead to social and emotional confusion early in the cultural adaptation process or when the tensions between cultural systems are too extreme for the individual to integrate.

Dimensions of Bicultural Development

A foundational question underlies the cognitive psychology studies and the brain imaging investigations discussed above: Do bicultural individuals develop separate internalized cultural systems for each culture, or is the bicultural individual's brain wired with one cognitive and linguistic system that responds to both cultural systems? Linguists, neurologists, and psychologists working separately on this question have gradually become interested in within-group differences between bicultural individuals, wondering if disparate types of biculturalism exist.

Teresa LaFromboise, Hardin Coleman, and Jennifer Gerton (1993) have described two biculturalism modes: *alternation*, which involves switching behaviors in response to cultural cues, and *fusion*, which involves the creation of a new integrated cultural system blending the other two. Bicultural individuals using the alternation mode experience two separate systems and feel the conflicts and incompatibilities between those systems. Those bicultural persons characterized by the fused style experience a single, highly integrated cultural system emerging from pieces of the prior systems. In a qualitative study, Jean Phinney and Mona Devich-Navarro (1997) also found two similar bicultural styles: (1) alternating types identified with both distinct cultures but recognized conflict between the cultures; and (2) blended types responded positively toward both cultures, and recognized little or no conflict. The following quotation illustrates this from an adolescent with an alternating bicultural style:

> *Knowing things from both cultures, puts me against some things that each culture does. Because I know how things are done in the other culture.* (Amaya, Mexican female, age fourteen)

Over time and with experience, this alternating style is likely to develop into the blended style. The individual resolves conflicts between the two cultural systems and creates a new, integrated whole that underscores bicultural identity and guides personal decision making. This blended type of bicultural identity development is captured in the quotations from Juliana above (p. 166) and Xavier below (p. 179).

Jana Haritatos and Veronica Benet-Martinez (2002) contributed to the literature on the positive and negative processes inherent in biculturalism by describing the construct called *bicultural identity integration*. Bicultural identity integration (BII) was conceived as the extent to which "biculturals perceive their mainstream and ethnic cultural identities as compatible and integrated vs. oppositional and difficult to integrate" (Benet-Martinez et al. 2002, 9). High BII individuals are thought to perceive their multiple cultural identities as complementary; they do not perceive the two cultures to be mutually exclusive, oppositional, or conflicting (Benet-Martinez and Haritatos 2005). Individuals with high BII may perceive themselves as being from a hyphenated culture (such as Mexican-American) or they may perceive themselves as having a new blended culture that incorporates elements from different cultural systems to emerge with an unique integrated system for use in their personal lives. Most important, the dual identities of high-BII individuals are compatible, even complementary (Rotheram-Borus 1990; Padilla 1994; Phinney and Devich-Navarro 1997; Benet-Martinez and Haritatos 2005; Bacallao and Smokowski 2009).

Individuals who have developed high BII usually have spent substantial time in the dominant culture. High-BII individuals are often proficient in the host culture language (i.e., English) and have extensive involvement in and affiliation with the host culture in comparison with those with low BII. Those with higher BII are more open, less neurotic, less anxious, and less depressed than lower BII individuals (Nguyen and Benet-Martinez 2007). High-BII people also tend to have social networks that include a richly interconnected set of host-culture friends (Mok et al. 2007).

Individuals who are low on the BII scale perceive their two cultural systems as being in opposition and difficult to reconcile (Benet-Martinez and Haritatos 2005). Although low-BII individuals perceive cues from and identify with both cultures, they report having greater difficulty incorporating elements from both cultures into a cohesive sense of identity (Gil, Vega, and Dimas 1994; Phinney and Devich-Navarro 1997; Vivero and Jenkins 1999; Bacallao and Smokowski 2009). Low-BII individuals are particularly sensitive to tensions between the two cultural orientations and experience internal conflict from these cultural incompatibilities (Benet-Martinez et al. 2002). Given these conflicts and tensions, low-BII individuals may prefer to identify with one culture, but trying to identify with the two cultures simultaneously causes them to feel dissonance. Low-BII individuals engage in more effortful encoding of cultural information, often accompanied with feelings of anxiety, stress, and depression. In turn, the more systematic and careful processing of cultural cues by low-BII persons may lead to the development of cultural schemas that are complex and difficult to reconcile (Nguyen and Benet-Martinez 2007).

In their research with Chinese American bicultural individuals, Benet-Martinez and colleagues (2002) found that the level of BII moderates cultural code switching. As a result, high-BII individuals were able to navigate cultural situations with fluidity, whereas low-BII individuals exhibited high levels of stress and confusion in similar cultural situations. Interestingly, low-BII individuals often respond to cultural cues in incongruent ways. For example, a high-BII person will process cultural cues and respond in synergy with the culture the cues come from in the situation, that is, he or she will "act Mexican" when Mexican cues are salient. In contrast, when low-BII individuals perceive Mexican cultural cues, rather than responding by "acting Mexican," their response may be to think about how they have become more American. In a socio-cognitive test of this dynamic, Benet-Martinez and colleagues (2002) found that giving American cues to low-BII Hong Kong and Chinese-American bicultural participants prompted responses with externally focused attributions, which is a typically Chinese cognitive style. When primed with Chinese cues, low-BII participants adopted internally focused attributions, which is a typically American style. This response pattern is opposite to the fluid responses high-BII participants made, leaving low-BII individuals to feel stress and dissonance.

Bicultural identity integration appears to consist of two different dimensions (Benet-Martínez and Haritatos 2005). The first component, *cultural distance*, focuses on the extent of overlap or separation perceived between the two cultural systems. The second component, *cultural conflict*, is the extent of harmony or tension perceived between the two cultural systems. Cultural distance is associated with several characteristics, including a closed-minded disposition, low levels of host culture competence, difficulty learning English, and living in a community that is not culturally diverse (Nguyen and Benet-Martinez 2007). Cultural conflict is associated with having a neurotic disposition, having experienced discrimination, and having strained intercultural relations. Low-BII individuals typically perceive their two cultural systems as distant and conflicted, whereas high-BII individuals tend to report that their cultural systems overlap and are harmonious (Benet-Martínez and Haritatos 2005; Nguyen and Benet-

Martinez 2007). One high-BII Peruvian male said the following about his experience becoming bicultural:

> *Living with these two cultures is great, because then I have an advantage almost, because I feel I can get the best of both and just forget about the negative things. Whereas some people just take one or the other. I feel that I'm pretty smart in taking up both.* (Xavier, Peruvian male, age seventeen)

Biculturalism and Family Processes

> *She tells me that we don't understand her. I know this is a difficult age to raise a child, but it's become more difficult here in the United States. She's learning different customs. Customs that belong outside of our home.* (Selena, Colombian mother)

> *I was born in Mexico on August 5, 1990, and three years later my brother was born. Both of us were born in Cuautla, Morelos, where we grew up and went to school. We made a lot of friends; shared a lot of things with our friends and family. Those are beautiful memories. Before we came to the United States, I finished elementary school and took my first communion. We made the trip to the United States where my family and I want to fulfill our dreams so we can return successful to our country. My family wanted to come here to the United States, but I didn't. When we came here, I was sad for having to leave everything we had achieved for so long—my school, my friends, everything that my family had done. Because of the sadness I didn't think about the benefits that I was going to have. But now, I am happy because I have my family. Little by little, I have moved forward. I feel proud to be who I am and to have my family.* (Santiago, sixteen-year-old male from El Salvador)

Research on the family as a unit is limited; however, the available research reinforces the advantage of biculturalism. For example, some studies have shown that bicultural individuals exercise complex parental reasoning about child development (Gutierrez and Sameroff 1990). Compared to low- and high-acculturated families, Alexis Miranda, Diana Estrada, and Miriam Firpo-Jimenez (2000) reported bicultural families displayed significantly lower levels of conflict, and demonstrated more commitment, help, and support among family members. Our research team examined how adolescent and parent acculturation influenced family dynamics in a sample of 402 Latino families living in either North Carolina or Arizona (Smokowski, Rose, and Bacallao 2008). Results from this study suggest that culture-of-origin involvement, which is a construct similar to ethnic identity, and biculturalism are assets with a positive relationship to family cohesion, adaptability, and familism.

Another of our research efforts reported that both adolescent and parent biculturalism were beneficial to adolescent socio-emotional functioning (Smokowski, Buchanan, and Bacallao 2009). We measured culture-of-origin and U.S.-cultural involvement using the Bicultural Involvement Questionnaire (BIQ). The culture-of-origin and U.S.-cultural-involvement subscales from the BIQ each includes twenty items about language, food, media use, and other cultural practices, using a five-point response scale. Responses were averaged to result in two subscales with possible ranges from one to five, with higher scores indicating higher involvement in the culture-of-origin or U.S. culture. Our results showed that, for every one-point increase in an adolescent's involvement in his or her Latino culture, there was a concomitant 13 percent rise on a measure of self-esteem, and a 12 to 13 percent decrease on measures of hopelessness, social problems, and aggressive behavior. In addition, the study showed that the teen children of parents with a strong bicultural perspective were less likely to feel anxiety and faced fewer social problems as compared with adolescents whose parents were not bicultural. Using the same BIQ subscales with a range of one to five completed by parents, for every one-point increase in parental involvement in U.S. culture, the adolescent showed a 15 to 18 percent decrease in measures of social problems, aggression, and anxiety. Parents who were more involved in U.S. culture were in a better position to be proactive in helping their adolescents with developing peer relations, forming friendships, and staying engaged in school. This type of parental support appeared to decrease the chances of social problems arising. In turn, both mental health and social functioning of adolescents benefited from the youths' biculturalism, which maintained ties with their culture-of-origin, and from parents' biculturalism, which was expressed through increased parental involvement in the U.S. culture. The benefits of a parent's bicultural skills are apparent in this quotation:

> *I came here when I was ten years old. It was easiest for my father because he learned English and everybody says they understood him. He helps my sister and I. I guess I don't really need to speak English really well. My dad goes everywhere with us—to Wal-Mart, to summer school. He's making us go to church now. It's not too bad. He says he only wants us to go to an American's church so that we learn English. Oh! And my sister. We do everything together: play, watch novelas, play with the Gameboy. My dad bought me a computer, and I like the computer. A movie of my life would end by showing*

me at work with a computer, I think. Yes. That's what I'd be doing. And I'd be married and hopefully have a baby. And my parents would be living in my trailer. That would be the movie of my life. (Esmeralda, fourteen-year-old Mexican female)

Biculturalism as a family strength has also been emphasized in the intervention research with families conducted by José Szapocznik and his colleagues (Szapocznik et al. 1984; 1986; 1989). These researchers found that interventions that promoted biculturalism were effective in reducing intergenerational and intercultural conflict within troubled family systems. Chapter 7 provides an in-depth discussion of intervention programs designed to promote cultural adaptation, in general, and bicultural development, in particular, in immigrant family systems.

Social Networks and Neighborhood Dynamics in Bicultural Development

I think that failure is like, conformity. To conform yourself with small things, not to achieve what you truly want to, not to struggle . . . you have to try, because if you struggle you can obtain more than if you simply conform and don't do anything: that is a failure. (Sarah, seventeen-year-old Mexican female)

Friendships among Latino adolescents cut across both racial and ethnic lines (Quillian and Campbell 2003). The friendships created by an immigrant adolescent provide a useful reflection of her or his cultural identification. Research has suggested that an immigrant's cultural identification influences with whom he or she interacts, with those who have maintained strong ethnic identification having a greater number of relationships within the same ethnic group (Gudykunst 2001). Similarly, our work with Latino youth showed that adolescents who maintained strong ethnic identification commonly bonded together (e.g., walking together through school hallways, eating lunch together) as a way to cope with acculturation stress and discrimination experiences (see chapter 3). However, youth who were developing bicultural skills often sought out Anglo and African American peers to serve as cultural brokers, and established those friendships without alienating their ethnic group friends (Bacallao and Smokowski 2009). These cultural brokers helped the immigrant adolescents learn English more quickly and modeled mainstream cultural norms and behaviors. Consequently, the immigrant youth developed more sophisticated bicultural

skills and maintained a diverse network of ethnic and cross-ethnic friendships. Our finding was in line with the work of Aurelia Mok and colleagues
(2007), who reported that integrated bicultural identity structures in their
sample of 111 first-generation Chinese Americans were associated with
larger and richly interconnected circles of non-Chinese friends.

However, when taking a wider perspective on immigrants' environments, we find that little attention has been given to neighborhoods as the
context for bicultural development. Some evidence exists showing that
the ethnic composition of the immediate neighborhood plays an important role in influencing how immigrants acculturate (Galster, Metzger, and
Waite 1999; Neto 2001; Myles and Hou 2003). Further, Berry and his colleagues (2006) found that acculturation profiles were significantly related
to neighborhood ethnic composition. The bicultural integration adaptation style was strongly represented in all neighborhoods except those that
were predominantly an individual's own group (i.e., homogeneous ethnic
neighborhoods). In these homogeneous neighborhoods, the ethnic or separated cultural adaptation style was dominant. Neighborhoods with a more
diverse mix of residents (i.e., no one ethnic group constituted a majority)
tended to have a higher proportion of host-culture or assimilated residents
than neighborhoods with homogeneous ethnic residents. Individuals with
the problematic diffused or marginalized cultural adaptation style did not
tend to live in ethnically mixed neighborhoods. Thus, ethnically mixed
communities were home to two groups of teens with divergent cultural adaptation styles: the greatest number of adolescents who exhibited the bicultural cultural adaptation style, and the fewest number of adolescents who
exhibited the diffuse or marginalized style, lived in heterogeneous neighborhoods. Bicultural neighborhoods nurture bicultural adolescents.

Reverse Acculturation: The Latinization of America

Just as bicultural neighborhoods nurture bicultural adolescents, heterogeneous neighborhoods come together to form bicultural or multicultural
cities (such as Miami, Los Angeles, San Francisco, Seattle), ultimately leading to a bicultural or transcultural society. Throughout this book, we have
stressed the dynamic, bidirectional nature of bicultural development. Just as
immigrant families are challenged by the changes required to adjust to the
host society, so too have larger social systems in the United States struggled
to cope with the sweeping influx of immigrant families and growing ethnic
diversity among younger generations. The larger society's process of becoming bicultural has prompted some researchers to consider the concept

of *reverse acculturation*. Although reverse acculturation has garnered much less attention than research on changes made by the immigrant population, immigrants may prompt reconstruction of the collective identity of the dominant society, leading to its gradual transformation (Andreeva and Unger 2008; Berry 2006). Intercultural contact with ethnic minorities and their cultural belief systems, behaviors, and symbols (e.g., cultural primes) may fuel reverse acculturation by prompting the host culture to consider alternative ways of being in the world. With enough exposure and understanding, aspects of the minority culture may become salient enough to become fully integrated into the larger cultural consciousness, causing the host society to become increasingly more bicultural or transcultural.

In 1992, the United States Congress established the Office of Alternative Medicine, which later became known as the National Center for Complementary and Alternative Health. The creation of NCCAH as one of the centers under the National Institutes of Health was prompted by the growing popularity of alternative types of health care, such as Chinese/Korean acupuncture, Latino herbal medicine/traditional healers, Indian Ayurveda-type medicine, Japanese reiki, massage, chiropractic, yoga, spiritual healing/prayer, and homeopathy (Andreeva and Unger 2008; Rosenbaum 2007). Many of these health practices were brought with immigrant families from their cultures-of-origin. Over the past forty years, the popularity of these alternative health practices has been increasing among the general U.S. population (Bausell, Lee, and Berman 2001; Burke et al. 2006). Use of so-called alternative therapies is now common among cancer patients, individuals with chronic conditions such as diabetes or pain disorders, Anglos, females, and those of high socioeconomic status with more education (Andreeva and Unger 2008; Conboy et al. 2005; Kronenberg et al. 2006). Many alternative techniques are so common that they are now taught in medical schools and tested in randomized clinical trials funded by the U.S. government.

Reverse acculturation is also evident in areas outside of complementary and alternative medicine. Mexican and Chinese restaurants are now pervasive throughout the country, even in large, mass market chains such as Mighty Tacos or Chili's. The visibility and size of ethnic communities are driving changes in food supply, tastes, attitudes about food, and food preparation practices (Andreeva and Unger 2008; Satia-Abouta et al. 2002). Ethnic minority group influences in the media are also growing, as demonstrated by the expanding number of Spanish-language channels on cable television; the continuing "crossover" popularity of Latino artists such as Gloria Estefan, Marc Anthony, Los Lobos, Ozomatli, and Ricky Martin; and dance classes integrating Latin styles such as salsa, tango, mambo, rumba, and samba, among others. In the New York City area, the newscast on the Spanish-language Noticias 41 and Noticiero. Univision often have higher ratings than "the big three" network news shows on CBS, NBC, and ABC. Approximately 8.7 percent of Internet users speak Spanish, making it the fourth most common language among the Internet community, trailing only English, Japanese, and German. A recent study of twenty-five metro markets in the United States found that Spanish-language radio programming was the sixth most popular format. It is increasingly difficult to ignore the spread of Spanish in the United States: bank ATMs offer instructions in Spanish, the Yellow Pages in many cities have added a Spanish-language insert, and Spanish is working its way into everyday use.

These prevalent examples of small cultural changes are signs of a broader movement showing that both immigrant families and the larger society are changing, slowly managing the contact, conflict, and adaptation inherent in the process of becoming bicultural. As the research reviewed in this chapter shows, this is a healthy, though challenging, progression in which the best features of both (or multiple) cultural systems can be integrated into a creative new identity.

Conclusions

Studying acculturation is complex and has been driven by competing theoretical frameworks. After several decades of knowledge development, considerable debate remains between proponents of assimilation theory, who find generational differences in large data sets, and alternation theorists, who unpack acculturation with bidimensional scales. It is particularly important to understand these frameworks because they are influential in policy debates and in planning interventions with families and individuals. The burgeoning immigrant population in the United States, especially the Latino population, and the daunting risk factors these groups face make these theories particularly salient. With rapidly growing immigrant populations experiencing high rates of poverty, significant risks for negative health behaviors, and low educational attainment, it is critical to develop appropriate prevention and intervention approaches. To develop these intervention approaches, we must fully understand the theoretical frameworks that underpin work with these groups.

In general, the acculturation research reviewed in chapter 5 indicates that assimilation is an important risk factor for immigrants who, as they acculturate to the host culture, may adopt negative health behaviors and experience mental health problems. The strongest research evidence exists for the links between assimilation and increased alcohol use and youth violence. The association between acculturation and negative health behavior appears to be related to nativity, or place of birth, length of time in the host country, and language facility and use. Highly assimilated, U.S.-born minorities often lack country-of-origin culture-based protective factors that benefit their less assimilated peers. At the same time, these highly assimilated individuals may adopt negative health behaviors as a way to cope with perceived discrimination and social injustice. Research evidence was particularly strong for the immigrant paradox; for example, Latino adults who are first-generation immigrants typically report healthier behaviors despite socioeconomic disadvantages

Equally important, acculturation research also suggests that biculturalism is a beneficial cultural adaptation style that is associated with increases in achievement and socio-cognitive functioning. Bicultural individuals, especially those with high levels of bicultural identity integration, may benefit from having developed wide behavioral repertoires of social skills and mastery of cognitive frame switching that allows them to handle diverse cultural situations.

This detailed look into the developmental process and benefits of bicultural identity leads us to the question, "How can we help to decrease acculturation stress, slow down assimilation, and promote biculturalism?" Knowing that biculturalism has far-ranging benefits is all the more helpful if psychologists, social workers, and social service workers can aid in the development of bicultural skills. In doing so, we might prevent the social problems associated with assimilation (e.g., substance use, youth violence). The next chapter examines how we might use bicultural skills training within prevention programs to help immigrant families maintain their culture-of-origin assets and develop new bicultural capabilities.

7

Entre Dos Mundos/Between Two Worlds

A Bicultural Skills Training Prevention Program to Help Immigrant Families Cope with Acculturation Stress

A growing body of research has suggested that—in the absence of prevention and intervention services—many Latino adolescents and adults are at risk for alcohol and drug use, aggressive behavior, and mental health problems (Rogler, Cortes, and Malgady 1991; Vega et al. 2000; Rounds-Bryant and Staab 2001; Gonzales et al. 2002; Centers for Disease Control and Prevention 2004; Smokowski, David-Ferdon, and Stroupe 2009). Researchers have linked this heightened risk for antisocial behavior and psychopathology to the acculturation stressors many Latinos experience while trying to adapt to life in the United States.

Acculturation stress results from coping with daily difficulties, conflicts, and strains experienced when individuals and families are trying to adjust to a new cultural system. Acculturation stress seems to be heightened by negative experiences such as racial or ethnic discrimination and coping with language barriers. Many authors have hypothesized a link between acculturation stress and negative health behaviors (e.g., Szapocznik and Kurtines 1980; Gil, Vega, and Dimas 1994; Al-Issa and Tousignant 1997; Delgado 1998; Gonzales et al. 2002). Given the growing immigrant population, a clear need exists for effective interventions that address the negative effects of acculturation stress.

Based on our discussions in the previous chapters, assimilation appears to be a consistent, important risk factor for immigrant Latino families. Research has shown that highly assimilated Latinos tend to engage in negative health behaviors, especially alcohol use and aggressive behavior (Bacallao and Smokowski 2005). Prevention interventions are critical to lessen acculturation stress and slow the development of problems related to rapid assimilation. However, it is equally important to support the cultural strengths and assets that families bring with them when they immigrate. To this end, a second body of research shifts the focus from thinking of assimilation as a risk factor to considering an individual's or a family's cultural assets as factors that promote positive outcomes. This growing body of literature has suggested that biculturalism is not only a critical mediator of acculturation processes but also an appropriate target for intervention. These findings prompted us to create a new training program to promote bicultural skills; we called the program Entre Dos Mundos/Between Two Worlds (Bacallao and Smokowski 2005). The name "Entre Dos Mundos/ Between Two Worlds" came from Latino adolescents and parents during our interviews. Families who were at the beginning of the cultural adjustment process consistently told us that they felt like they were trying to balance between two very different worlds. The name "Entre Dos Mundos" aptly captures the distance, effort, and potential conflict that many acculturating individuals and families feel during the initial stage of bicultural development. In our circular model of bicultural identity integration (see figure 1.3), the Entre Dos Mundos intervention is designed for families new to the acculturation process when the culture-of-origin and host-cultural systems are furthest apart and seem incompatible. The Entre Dos Mundos multifamily group intervention was designed to prevent the development of aggression, parent-adolescent conflict, and mental health problems in Latino adolescents by helping participants cope with acculturation stress and by promoting family adaptability through bicultural coping skills. The goal of the Entre Dos Mundos program is to help Latino families adjust to life in the United States and avoid the stress and problems associated with assimilation.

Acculturation-Based Prevention and Intervention Programs

Several programs represent important first steps for acculturation-based prevention and intervention efforts. In general, these programs have both acknowledged the important role that culture plays in intervention and attempted to decrease assimilation stress while increasing bicultural social skills. In this review, we focus attention only on the prevention intervention efforts that incorporate bicultural skills training. Bicultural skills training programs have been used with a broad range of groups, including Native American students (LaFramboise and Rowe 1983; Schinke et al. 1988; Marsiglia, Cross, and Mitchell-Enos 1998); foster parents and children (Mullender 1990); middle-school teenagers (Bilides 1990); African American adults with alcoholism (Beverly 1989); Asian American parents

(Ying 1999); preschool children (Arenas 1978); Latina adolescents (Peeks 1999); and Latino families (Szapocznik et al. 1986; Smokowski and Bacallao 2008, 2009). Our primary concentration is directed toward how the acculturation-based intervention approach has been used with Latino immigrant adolescents and their parents.

Bicultural skills training programs evolved from three strains of empirical research. Originally introduced as a cultural adaptation to social skills training models, bicultural training was regarded by Teresa LaFromboise and Wayne Rowe (1983) as a promising method for teaching assertiveness skills to Native American adults. LaFromboise and Rowe's goals for their bicultural skills training model were (1) to promote communication skills that enhanced self-determination, (2) to teach coping skills that would enable participants to resist the pressure to acculturate, and (3) to aid participants in developing discretionary skills that would help them determine the appropriateness of assertive behavior in Indian and non-Indian cultures (LaFromboise and Rowe 1983). In what was the largest evaluation of the LaFromboise and Rowe model, Steven Schinke and his colleagues (1988) used bicultural training in their work with Native American adolescents at risk for tobacco, alcohol, and substance use. Using an experimental research design, they randomly assigned 137 Native American adolescents from the state of Washington either to a no-intervention comparison condition or to a prevention condition that received ten sessions of bicultural competence skills training. At post-test and at a six-month post-treatment followup, Schinke and colleagues compared participants' performance on measures of knowledge and attitudes related to substance use and reported that adolescents in the bicultural skills training prevention group performed significantly better than their counterparts in the no-intervention control group. Compared with the control group, the bicultural skills training participants had higher ratings on measures of self-control, assertiveness, and making alternative suggestions to substance use pressure. Equally important, participants who received the bicultural prevention intervention reported lower rates of tobacco, alcohol, and marijuana use at posttest and at the six-month followup.

The second strain of bicultural skills training was developed specifically for Puerto Rican children ages five to eight years living in New York City, using Puerto Rican folktales (*cuentos*) as peer models of adaptive behavior (*Cuento* therapy; Costantino, Malgady, and Rogler 1986). These researchers later adapted the model for adolescents, replacing the folktales with biographies of heroic Puerto Ricans (Malgady, Rogler, and Costantino 1990). In this treatment model, the children's mothers attended the sessions and worked with the therapists to present Puerto Rican folktales. Using a randomized experimental design, the researchers assigned 210 high-risk Puerto Rican children, ages five to eight years, to one of four intervention conditions: (1) therapy using an original *cuento* folktale, (2) therapy using an adapted *cuento* folktale, (3) therapy using art/play techniques, and (4) a no-therapy group (Costantino et al. 1986). When compared with children in the two control groups (i.e., art/play therapy and no-therapy group), the children who received the *Cuento* therapy demonstrated less anxiety, higher scores on the Wechsler Intelligence Scale for Children–Revised, and decreased aggression.

In a similar study, Malgady and colleagues (1990) used this therapeutic storytelling approach, substituting biographies of famous Puerto Ricans for the folktales, to create an ethnic modeling therapy. Called "hero/heroine modeling," this prevention intervention was tested by Malgady and his colleagues with ninety Puerto Rican middle-school (i.e., eighth and ninth grades) students who were U.S. born and living in New York City. The goal of the research was to test whether providing ethnic and bicultural role models would help mediate the social and family conflicts these adolescents were experiencing. The researchers randomly assigned the adolescents to either a control group or a culture-based role-modeling intervention. Malgady et al. (1990) reported that, as compared with adolescents in the control group, adolescents who received the treatment intervention had significantly lower scores on measures of anxiety, and higher scores on measures of ethnic identity and self-concept. Program effects varied by participants' grade level, gender, and household composition. This ethnic modeling therapy was particularly effective for high-risk Puerto Rican adolescents from single-parent families.

The third strain of bicultural skills training was developed through the research of Szapocznik and his colleagues (Szapocznik et al. 1984, 1986; Szapocznik et al. 1989). The first model, Bicultural Effectiveness Training (BET; Szapocznik et al. 1984, 1986), was a family intervention modality that focused on reducing intercultural and intergenerational conflict among immigrant parents and their adolescent children who were experiencing conduct problems or social maladjustment. Each of the lessons in the psychoeducational curriculum attempted to create a shared worldview among family members, and to explore how cultural conflicts affect interactions among family members. Therapists worked with the family to reframe problems by placing blame on the acculturation process rather than on any particular family member. In addition, therapists worked to foster intergenerational alliances and increase bicultural coping skills. In a small pilot test with forty-one Cuban American families raising an adolescent with behavior problems, Szapocznik and colleagues (1986) found that BET was equally as effective as brief structural family therapy (BSFT) in improving adolescent problem behaviors and family functioning. At the time of their investigation, theirs was the only study of bicultural skills training programs that measured changes in participants' bicultural skill levels. The scores on measures of biculturalism increased significantly among the participants in the BET group, whereas the BSFT comparison group did not demonstrate an increase in bicultural skills (Szapocznik et al. 1986).

Building from that research, Szapocznik and his colleagues conducted another study in which BET was integrated into a larger intervention package called Family Effectiveness Training (FET; Szapocznik et al. 1989). FET was compared with a no-treatment control condition in a study of seventy-nine Latino (76 percent of whom were Cuban) families with a preadolescent child (i.e., six to eleven years old) with emotional or behavioral problems. The results of the study indicated that families in the FET condition displayed significantly greater improvement than did control families on measures of structural family functioning, child behavior problems, and child self-concept.

Subsequently, the acculturation-based family intervention developed by Szapocznik and his colleagues (1984, 1986; Szapocznik et al. 1989) was adapted by Yu-Wen Ying (1999) for use with Chinese American families (i.e., Strengthening of Intergenerational/Intercultural Ties in Immigrant Chinese American Families). In a pilot test of fifteen immigrant Chinese American parents, statistically significant pre- to post-test changes indicated that parents who received the eight-week parenting program increased their sense of efficacy, sense of coherence, and feeling of responsibility for their child's behavior. The quality of the parent-child relationship also improved from pre- to post-test; however, child self-esteem and parental depression did not change.

J. Douglas Coatsworth, Hilda Pantin, and Jose Szapocznik (2002) presented an evolution of the early BET work as an intervention called Familias Unidas. Like Szapocznik and colleagues' earlier work, Familias Unidas targeted immigrant parents and their adolescent children (twelve- to fourteen-year-olds) living in Dade County, Florida. Whereas the earlier iterations of BET and FET were interventions designed for a target audience of families experiencing problems and undergoing treatment, Familias Unidas was a prevention intervention designed for all immigrant families. Further, Familias Unidas was designed to be delivered in community settings, such as schools. Similar to BET and FET, Familias Unidas was a family-centered intervention that had a primary goal of enhancing parental investment in and involvement with adolescent children. The theory underlying Familias Unidas held that enhancing parental investment and strengthening parental influence across ecological systems (e.g., with school, with the adolescent's friends) would positively influence the adolescent's self-regulation, social competence, academic achievement, and school bonding (Coatsworth, Pantin, and Szapocznik 2002).

Familias Unidas was evaluated in a randomized clinical trial of 167 Latino families with children in sixth and seventh grades (Pantin et al. 2003). Participants were recruited from three middle schools in Miami, Florida. Results from mixed-model analyses indicated that, relative to a no-intervention control group, families in the intervention group reported higher rates of parental investment and decreased conduct problems in adolescent children. The intervention did not affect adolescent academic achievement or school bonding.

Current State of Model Development

Bicultural skills training models have shown promising initial results on a variety of outcome measures. Researchers have reported that the results of bicultural skills training programs were better than no-treatment comparison groups and, in some cases, superior to alternative treatments. These training programs appeared to reduce or mediate some of the risks associated with rapid assimilation (e.g., alcohol and substance use, anxiety, conduct problems). However, without a standard set of outcomes, it is difficult to compare the different intervention models.

Evaluation of these programs remains a challenge because only a few studies have used adequate sample sizes and rigorous methodologies that allow for comparison. Current models have been pilot tested in only a single study, and in several cases, the testing has used small numbers of participants (e.g., sample sizes ranged from seventeen to 210 participants). Evaluation is further complicated because researchers in all three strains of this research changed their intervention models without conducting replication studies (i.e., *Cuento* therapy evolved to Hero/Heroine modeling, BET was integrated into FET). This failure to replicate studies and validate results has kept the progress of model development suspended in the evaluation and advanced development stage (Thomas and Rothman 1994). Whether these earlier models can be generalized to other populations is unknown because none of the tested models has been replicated in diverse field settings. Similarly, no bicultural skills training model has gone through the dissemination stage (Thomas and Rothman 1994) to promote widespread use.

Few studies have measured proximal outcomes that might account for the impact of the intervention. Only the original BET study conducted by Szapocznik and colleagues (1986) measured changes in the participants' bicultural skills. Coatsworth and his colleagues (2002) reported changes in parental investment, which was an important proximal outcome for their Familias Unidas intervention model. Although the other studies provided promising information that bicultural skills training models influenced distal outcomes, the research did not illuminate the mechanisms by which the intervention affected outcomes (i.e., the mechanisms that made the program work).

Bicultural skills training deserves further attention. Current models have shown promising results but require replication and dissemination. Future research in this area would benefit from the use of a standard set of distal outcomes as well as the inclusion of proximal outcomes or pathways that map onto a conceptual model for the program. Inclusion of proximal outcomes, such as parent investment or child self-esteem, would allow researchers to go beyond the question of *whether* the programs work to determine *how* the programs work. These proximal outcomes delineate pathways that are used in exerting the programs' effects. For example, a bicultural skills training program might lower parent-adolescent conflict (e.g., the proximal outcome), which in turn might reduce adolescent aggression. The next generation of bicultural skills training programs needs to be guided by sophisticated conceptual or logic models that articulate hypothesized pathways for program effects. Considering this current state of model development, we move forward to describe a new, experiential model for bicultural skills training.

Entre Dos Mundos/Between Two Worlds Bicultural Skills Training

Theoretical Background

Entre Dos Mundos (Bacallao and Smokowski 2005) is based on knowledge gathered through two streams of research: (1) risk and protective factor research with Latino families living in either North Carolina or Arizona (see Bacallao and Smokowski 2007; Smokowski and Bacallao 2006, 2007), and (2) prior acculturation research (for reviews see Rogler, Cortes, and Malgady 1991; LaFromboise, Coleman, and Gerton 1993; Gonzales et al. 2002). As illustrated in figure 7.1, Entre Dos Mundos attempts to mediate the negative impact of acculturation stress by increasing family adaptability and biculturalism in Latino adolescents and their parents. The theoretical background of the intervention hypothesizes that increasing biculturalism

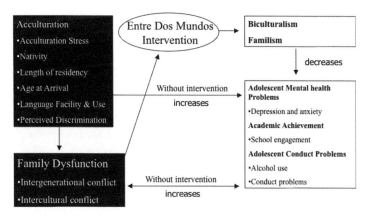

Fig. 7.1. Entre Dos Mundos: conceptual model

and family adaptability in immigrant Latino families will decrease intergenerational cultural conflict between parents and adolescents (Szapocznik et al. 1986). Ultimately, this decrease of intergenerational conflict should lead to decreased levels of adolescent anxiety, depression, and conduct problems.

Entre Dos Mundos Program Design and Description

As we have described previously (Bacallao and Smokowski 2005), Entre Dos Mundos is an eight-week prevention program that uses a multifamily group format in weekly sessions. Bringing groups of adolescents and parents from eight to ten families together to discuss acculturation stressors and challenges provides the opportunity to intervene in problematic parent-adolescent relationship processes. The multifamily group format also builds social support networks among the group members. Each weekly session is devoted to a theme that has been empirically linked to acculturation stress (e.g., handling cultural conflicts in the family, coping with racial discrimination, navigating within U.S. schools). Entre Dos Mundos session themes are posed as questions for families to grapple with during the session and as homework between sessions. The session themes are presented in detail in table 7.1. In the final session, a graduation ceremony is orchestrated to engender a sense of pride and to provide participants a focal point for their new competencies.

In designing a pilot test of Entre Dos Mundos, we chose to include eight lessons in the curriculum design to maximize feasibility and retention in the initial program. However, Entre Dos Mundos can easily be expanded

TABLE 7.1
Entre Dos Mundos Curriculum Themes

Session	Theme Questions
Week 1	How are we as a family changing as we adapt to life in the United States? How do we as a family balance demands from two different cultures (our culture-of-origin and the U.S. host culture)?
Week 2	What worries do adolescents have for their parents? What worries do parents have for their adolescents? How can we help each other decrease some of these worries? How can we comfort one another?
Week 3	When cultural conflict arises, how can we remain united with each other as a family when we have different perspectives?
Week 4	How can we handle discrimination at school and at work? In what ways can family members support each other during or after these experiences?
Week 5	In what ways do adolescents participate in school? In what ways do adolescents wish to participate in school? (Same two questions posed to parents.)
Week 6	How can we strengthen our relationships with non-Latino Americans (peers, teachers, co-workers) outside of our families?
Week 7	What does our future look like in 10 years? (Developing bicultural identities)
Week 8	Review, integration, evaluation, and closure (graduation ceremony and fiesta!)

with additional lessons added for ongoing, established groups. Unlike other bicultural skills training models, the Entre Dos Mundos lessons are designed for use in relatively large multifamily groups that include at least one parent and one adolescent from each of the families attending the weekly sessions. This multifamily format has been used to address a range of mental health problems and has been shown to be more effective than either individual or single-family therapy (McFarlane 2002). Adopting the multifamily group format not only maximizes the potential for promoting positive parent-adolescent communication but also allows multiple family members to practice newly learned skills, and increases the probability of the participating families expanding their social support networks.

Action-Oriented Groups Using Psychodrama Techniques

An integral concept in the Entre Dos Mundos design was that the weekly sessions should be action-oriented groups that fully engage participants of various ages, genders, and levels of acculturation. For example, in the initial testing of Entre Dos Mundos, the action-oriented groups used a variety of psychodrama techniques such as role reversal, doubling, mirroring, empty chair, and enactment of critical scenes from personal and social experiences shared by the participating families. Session content for each theme was experiential, based on psychodramatic strategies for exploring intrapersonal and interpersonal situations, and encouraged practicing behavioral change in a supportive group environment (Oxford and Weiner

2003; Blatner 2005). Structured warm-ups were used to focus the multiple family groups on the week's theme (see table 7.1).

Psychodrama has been used as a therapeutic modality for more than seven decades. It dominated the field of group psychotherapy during the first half of the twentieth century and evolved as a viable alternative to, or complement for, psychoanalytic treatment (Buchanan 1984; Oxford and Weiner 2003; Blatner 2005). Kipper and Ritchie (2003) conducted a meta-analysis of twenty-five experimentally designed studies of psychodramatic techniques such as doubling and role reversal. Their results showed that the large treatment effect size displayed by psychodrama intervention was comparable or superior to other group psychotherapy strategies. Indeed, the overall Cohen's d of .95 compared favorably with many psychosocial and educational interventions that typically fall in the moderate .3 to .6 range. The analytical results showed no difference between the effectiveness of psychodrama techniques used with clinical versus student populations or between psychodrama techniques used in single versus multiple sessions. The most effective psychodrama interventions were doubling and role reversal. Based on this body of evidence, we felt comfortable integrating action methods such as doubling and role reversal in our Entre Dos Mundos prevention program.

Sessions using psychodrama techniques are typically facilitated in three stages: warm-up, action, and sharing. In the warm-up stage, structured activities are used to focus the group on a particular theme. One salient example of a structured warm-up activity central to the Entre Dos Mundos curriculum was a variation on a *spectrogram,* or circular diamond of opposites (Carlson-Sabelli et al. 1992), which focused on acculturation relationships between culture-of-origin and host culture. Depicted in figure 7.2, the circular model of acculturation is the theoretical and experiential backbone of the Entre Dos Mundos prevention program. During each session, a large cutout of this circular model is placed on the floor with "culture-of-origin" on the left side and "dominant culture" on the right. Facilitators can also use masking tape to display the model on the floor. More important, the circular model emphasizes that acculturation is not a linear process and prompts Latino families to think about movement between cultures as a dynamic process. The visual representation of acculturation reinforces the importance of bicultural skills, and this exercise tends to decrease parents' anxieties about losing their children to American assimilation because of linear accommodation to the new culture (Bacallao and Smokowski 2007).

In addition, the developmental focus of this circular model underscores the idea that acculturation interventions should facilitate integration of bicultural identity (Benet-Martinez et al. 2002; Sanchez-Flores 2003).

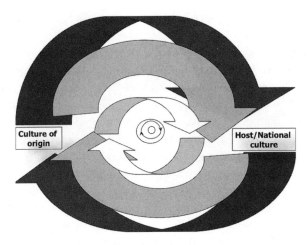

Fig. 7.2. Circular model of bicultural development

Moving between cultures as called for by the situation and context is encouraged because such movement is the manifestation of bicultural skills. An integrated bicultural identity allows participants to move effectively between cultural contexts, and some research supports that such integration increases immigrants' socio-cognitive functioning (Haritatos and Benet-Martinez 2002).

After learning U.S. customs, many Latino youth turn back to culture-of-origin values in a circular cycle (Sanchez-Flores 2003). In other words, bicultural evolution is developmental. Latino adolescents have to navigate the cultural differences between home and school every day. The ease and speed with which Latino youth navigate the circle are indicators of their bicultural development. These stages of development are physically illustrated in the group as parents and adolescents stand on the acculturation circle and speak to each other about their different positions. In subsequent sessions, movement is tracked as a way to process change. Dialogues among adolescents, parents, and group members, who play roles representing the culture-of-origin or host culture, are facilitated using the circular model as the backdrop for the action.

When Entre Dos Mundos has been used with Latino families, activities incorporated into weekly sessions have explored the different poles and pulls in the flow of the circular model. Guided by each session theme, the group facilitator identified psychodramatic scenes that the group members enacted, with the circular model as a container for the experiential action. For example, as Latino adolescents move from their culture-of-origin to host-culture involvement, they commonly experience discrimination from

Anglo or African American peers. The group discussion in session 4 includes a critical example of adolescents' discrimination experiences, such as the difficulty of walking through school hallways while being taunted by peers saying, "Go back to your own country!" Participants first re-create the scene and then explore behavioral options. Doubling, mirroring, role reversal, and other psychodrama techniques are used to encourage catharsis, promote insight, and engender new skills. The circular model is used to identify at what point or stage participants are in the process, and at what point they would like to be, in relation to both their culture-of-origin and the host culture. The circular model is used at the beginning of the session to introduce the session theme, and used again at the end of each session to provide closure and to capture intrasession change. Use of these structured activities and psychodrama techniques characterizes the Entre Dos Mundos action-oriented sessions.

A transcript of session 1 is provided below to illustrate how the groups began. Martica is the director, or main facilitator, and Xiomara is a co-facilitator.

Session 1 Transcript

Martica facilitates a conversation about how families came to the United States, allowing families to get to know each other. Maria, Roberto's wife, says that her older son, also named Roberto, came when he was six years old. So he remembers some things about their native land, and they talk about his grandmother. Maria says that she came with her sons, Roberto and Alex, but Carlos, the youngest son, stayed with his grandparents and came a year later. Martica asks the next family, a mother and her son, Esteban, and the mother says that her kids came just two months after her. She says that at one point they had to go back to Colombia, and she did not see her kids for four and a half months. "I cried the whole time," she says. Martica says it is harder not to see your kids when you are here in this country. Martica says that many families come thinking that they will bring their kids in a few months, but then it ends up taking longer than they expected.

Maria says they were concerned about bringing Carlos because he was young. They might get caught by immigration. They had to walk a lot and cross the river. But then she laughs and says that when they got to the river it was dry, and they only had to walk about fifteen minutes. She says that it was really easy, and after they did it she wished that she had brought him. Martica asks Roberto (the son) if he remembered that day. He says that he remembers crossing over from one side to the other. Xiomara asks her if her husband was with them, and Maria says that he had already been here a year. "Is that a sad story or what?" Roberto (the father) asks. Xiomara says that it is sad in the moment, but now all the family is together, and they've accomplished a lot. "It was a way of getting everyone out and bringing them here," Martica says. She adds that one or two years really isn't very much time and that some families don't see each other for six or eight years. And some get really wet, up to their eyes, Xiomara says, laughing.

The Colombian mother says that she met a Mexican woman six years ago who was not able to bring her children over. "It's really sad," she says, "because the youngest one won't even remember her mother." Roberto (the father) agrees that after six years she won't remember. Maria says it was hard to make the decision to leave her youngest son behind, and when he went with her to where they would catch the bus, he was crying, and she had to turn away from him. She says that she almost wished that they would not be able to pass over just to be able to go back to him. Someone asks her who brought Carlos, and she says his uncle, Roberto's brother, did.

Another mother says that you have to be careful because you can get separated from your kids if you are caught. Roberto agrees, adding that they'll take the parents away and put the kids in a shelter. The mother continues, saying that afterwards you are not able to find your kids because the kids are not capable of saying who they are or who their parents are. Roberto adds that the kids also do not know what town they are from. "There are many lost children," the mother continues. "I knew someone who started a house on the border to collect all the children, and he tried to locate their families in Mexico." "Or here as well," Roberto adds. But the mother says that it is not so easy here because the parents are scared and hiding. At least in Mexico they can locate the family. "But it's really difficult. This is a very, very sad situation that the U.S. government should pay attention to because it's not fair that these kids end up without family. And the same thing happened with a lot of Cubans. It was really terrible." Martica talks about the Peter Pan project, where Cuban families would send their kids to live with families in the United States so that they could escape Communism. Martica says that for Mexicans it is different because the parents come first to this country to work, and then little by little they bring their kids. The parents are able to prepare everything here to bring their kids over, like having an apartment ready. However, the Cubans put them in American families. "And they never saw them again, most of them," a mother says. The group discusses how the different political situation affected immigration issues for Cubans and Mexicans.

Since they've all been talking about their experiences of coming to the United States from their countries, Martica asks how would they change their immigration stories if they could. She asks Maria, "How would things be different now if you had known that it was not so hard to cross the border and that you could have brought Carlos?" Roberto says that they would be a lot better off. He would have taken a plane from Guanajuato to Raleigh with his whole family. It's a lot shorter in a plane, he says, forty hours versus four hours. Martica asks him what he was thinking about during those forty hours. "A lot of things," he says. "There are a lot of things to think about when you are in a car for that long."

Martica uses chairs to set up the seats in a car. She tells the group to pretend that they are driving from their country-of-origin to the United States on their immigration journeys. Each family takes a turn sitting in the car and says out loud what they are thinking as they embark on this long journey. Parents begin to talk about their hopes for a better future and dreams of returning to their homelands after their children get a good education. Adolescents say that they are sad about leaving their cousins and grandparents. They will miss their friends and fear not knowing what the new land will be like.

After each family takes a turn, Martica asks them to think about where they are now on their journeys. She says that the journey does not end when you move to a new place, but continues as you try to adjust to the new culture. She presents the Entre Dos Mundos arch between culture-of-origin and host culture and asks each of them to stand on a place on the line that signifies how close or far they are from each side (e.g., the culture-of-origin pole and the host culture pole). Parents begin telling adolescents where to stand. Martica sees this and stops the group, asking all the adolescents to find their place on the line without discussing this with their parents. Adolescents stand in different places on the line, followed by parents. Parents end up clustered close to the culture-of-origin side of the arch while adolescents display a wider range that goes from the culture-of-origin pole to the midpoint between the two poles. Martica asks each of them to make a statement, saying why they placed themselves on that point on the line. Discussion ensues about differences between parents and adolescent children. Roberto (the father) notes that this difference is what causes difficulties with children at home. Other parents agree. Martica says that is a common reason for stress after immigration and tells the group that they will explore what to do about these parent-adolescent differences in session 3. The session continues with an energetic discussion of how the families are changing because of their move to the United States.

Testing the Entre Dos Mundos Approach

A primary challenge in intervention research is finding ways to isolate the effect of a program and thereby illuminate the mechanisms by which a program creates a desired effect. The randomized experimental trial is the gold standard for testing the efficacy of a new intervention model. In designing an efficacy evaluation of the Entre Dos Mundos program, we had two main concerns.

1. We wanted to test the effect of our psychodramatic action orientation to the program activities. It was important to assess whether the experiential learning activities would be more efficacious for Latino participants than simply letting Latino families discuss the program themes without such structure. Consequently, we wanted to evaluate different formats for delivering the program. The overall objective of the study was to determine which of two implementation formats would show greater sustained benefit in lowering adolescent problems (i.e., decreasing aggressive behavior and mental health problems) in Latino youth at post-test and one year after completing the Entre Dos Mundos program. A fundamental assumption of this research was that prevention program sessions should be active and dynamic. This cornerstone led us to hypothesize that the Entre Dos Mundos session themes delivered in action-oriented skills training (i.e., using psychodrama techniques to enhance bicultural coping skills) would have greater sustained benefit for both adolescent problems and parent-adolescent conflict than the identical themes delivered in unstructured support groups (i.e., traditional discussion format aimed at facilitating parent-adolescent communication and interfamily social networking).

Families in the Entre Dos Mundos support group condition were exposed to the identical session themes listed in table 7.1. However, the support groups did not receive the structured activities for exploring the themes and did not use the circular model of acculturation or psychodrama techniques in any form. Instead, support group facilitators posed the weekly themes as questions for families to discuss. Family members and facilitators shared their experiences and offered interpersonal support. When the participants concurred that the weekly theme had been adequately addressed, the group members were allowed to redirect the discussion to any topic they wanted to discuss.

2. We also wanted to determine whether exposure to the program themes was more critical than the style of delivery, and whether being exposed to more of the themes had a stronger effect than exposure to fewer of the themes. This was a test of program dosage. We hypothesized that commitment to program participation, as indexed by higher attendance rates, would be significantly associated with lower levels of both adolescent problems and parent-adolescent conflict.

An Experimental Trial of Entre Dos Mundos

To distinguish the effect of the Entre Dos Mundos action-oriented groups from the effect of Entre Dos Mundos delivered in a less active form, we designed a study that offered the intervention two formats. One format used the Entre Dos Mundos action-oriented group format as described above with psychodramatic structured activities. The second format offered the identical Entre Dos Mundos topics in a traditional support group format. We used an experimental research design, randomly assigning eighty-one Latino families to the two formats that used identical session themes: fifty-six families attended action-oriented bicultural skills training and twenty-five families attended unstructured support groups.

To be eligible to participate in the Entre Dos Mundos research project, Latino families had to include a foreign-born adolescent between the ages of twelve and eighteen years and have one parent willing to attend program sessions with the adolescent. The classic experimental design was used to test the efficacy of two implementation formats for the prevention program: action-oriented skills training compared to unstructured support groups. Notably, both implementation formats used identical session themes. The program was implemented in agencies, churches, and arts centers serving Latino communities in rural, midsized, and urban settings in North Carolina. Having multiple, diverse settings for the investigation (i.e., rural, urban, and midsized metropolitan sites) added to the external validity or generalizability of the study by making the sample more representative (Campbell and Stanley 1963). Latino families that met eligibility criteria were assigned to these two conditions using a randomized experimental design to evaluate changes from pretest to post-test (eight weeks later) and ultimately to one-year post-program followup. Followup data were collected fourteen months after pretest data collection, which was equivalent to one year after program completion. Data were also collected at three-month and six-month followup interviews. However, the focus of this chapter is on examining proximal outcomes at post-test and distal outcomes at the one-year followup.

An experimental design allows the investigator to observe and measure changes in the dependent variables caused by manipulating the independent variables (i.e., the two Entre Dos Mundos group conditions). We selected an experimental design because it is the most rigorous research design for clinical trials, and guards against nearly all intrinsic and extrinsic threats to internal validity (e.g., history, maturation, instrumentation, and testing; Campbell and Stanley 1963). Further, adherence to an experimental design allows causal inferences to be determined between the antecedent variables and outcome variables (Frankfort-Nachmias and Nachmias 2000). A true experimental design uses random assignment that allows for comparison between two equalized groups. Comparisons were made between the experimental and comparison groups to determine the affect of the Entre Dos Mundos prevention intervention on proximal outcomes at post-test and on four distal outcomes—adolescent oppositional-defiant behavior, anxious depression, parent-adolescent conflict, and total adolescent problems—at one year after program completion.

Intervention Implementation and Fidelity

Entre Dos Mundos program sessions were held in community settings (e.g., churches, arts centers) that were convenient for and familiar to the participants. To reduce attrition and encourage participation, the Entre Dos Mundos research staff provided participants with transportation (i.e., a university van) to program sessions. Each of the sites also provided child care (for younger siblings) and refreshments. All groups were closed; that is, after the random assignment to groups, no new members were allowed to join the groups. Each of the eight program sessions lasted three hours, which began with participants eating a dinner together. Group sessions were videotaped to allow the research team to closely examine implementation fidelity and to guide supervision of group facilitators.

Dr. Martica Bacallao, who is a bicultural, bilingual licensed psychodramatist with clinical experience working with Latino families, facilitated each Entre Dos Mundos action-oriented program session. Bacallao has master's degrees in social work and community counseling, a doctorate in social work, and is certified by the American Board of Examiners in psychodrama, sociometry, and group psychotherapy. Skills in psychodramatic action methods were needed to facilitate the action-oriented groups. Two bicultural, bilingual research staff members with master's degrees in social work and clinical experience working with Latino families facilitated Entre Dos Mundos support group sessions. Group sessions in both intervention conditions were conducted in Spanish. Dr. Paul Smokowski supervised implementation of each of these intervention conditions separately to maintain intervention fidelity and to avoid the possibility of contamination that can occur when staff members provide group supervision.

Table 7.2 presents the sociodemographic characteristics of the families participating in the experimental trial. Of the eighty-one families, fifty-six were randomized to the Entre Dos Mundos action-oriented prevention groups and twenty-five were randomized to the Entre Dos Mundos

TABLE 7.2

Sociodemographic Characteristics by Entre Dos Mundos (EDM) Group

	EDM Action (n = 56) M(SD)	EDM Support Group (n = 25) M(SD)	Total (N = 81) M(SD)
Adolescent's age (years)	14 (1.8)	14 (1.7)	14 (1.8)
Adolescent's gender (% female)	55	52	54
Annual income reported by parent	$19,454 (8,375)	$20,788 (6,839)	$19,857 (7,920)
Time spent living in U.S.—adolescent	3.5 (2.4)	3.8 (2.6)	3.6 (2.5)
Time spent living in U.S.—parent	5.2 (2.7)	5.5 (2.9)	5.3 (2.8)
Country-of-origin (%)			
Mexico	73	89	78
El Salvador	5	7	6
Colombia	10	0	7
Other	12	4	9
Gender of parent (% female)	86	78	83
Parent age	39 (7.0)	40 (7.0)	39 (7.1)
Parent currently working (%)	62	78	.67 (.47)
Parent education (% not high school graduate)	75	72	74
Parent—intervention sessions attended	5.3 (2.7)	5.6 (2.6)	5.4 (2.7)
Adolescent—intervention sessions attended	6.8 (1.9)	6.6 (.2)	6.7 (1.7)

Note: No statistically significant differences were found using chi square and *T*-tests.

support groups. A randomization ratio of 2:1 in favor of the action-oriented condition was implemented to parallel our directional hypotheses that participation in action-oriented programming would be more efficacious than support groups. Participating parents were typically working mothers in their late thirties. Attendance was very good at both the action-oriented prevention program and the support groups. On average, parents attended 5.4 sessions and adolescents attended nearly seven of the eight sessions offered.

ATTRITION

Pretest measures were collected on eighty-one families (fifty-six attended action-oriented groups and twenty-five attended support groups). At the one-year followup, sixty-two families (forty-seven had attended action-oriented groups, fifteen had attended support group) were available and willing to be reassessed. The study attrition rate was 16 percent for families who participated in the action-oriented groups and 40 percent for those who participated in the support groups. These attrition rates are not surprising given that immigrant families are particularly unstable because of employment instability, seasonal employment, risk of deportation, and socioeconomic disadvantage. Indeed, the 84 percent retention rate in the action-oriented groups may be a sign of their satisfaction with participation in the project.

TABLE 7.3
Multivariate Models for Selected Proximal Outcomes at Post-Test

	Family Adaptability		Bicultural Support		Bicultural Identity Integration		Aggression		ADHD		Oppositional Defiant Behavior		Attention Problems	
	Beta	ΔR_2	Beta	ΔR_2	Beta	ΔR_2	Beta	ΔR_2	Beta	ΔR_2	Beta	ΔR_2	Beta	ΔR_2
Pretest score	.72***	.48***	.37**	.11**	.23**	.14**	.62***	.37***	.61***	.42***	.45***	.21***	.64***	.43***
Annual income	-.05	.02	-.05	.02	.26*	.01	-.08	.00	-.13	.00	-.14	.00	-.14	.00
Parent education	-.07	.00	-.13	.01	.09	.01	.15	.01	.17	.02	.10	.00	.16	.02
Time parent has been in U.S.	-.14	.01	-.17	.02	-.10	.00	.06	.00	.18	.01	.08	.00	.18	.02
EDM action-oriented group	-.05	.00	.06	.01	-.23*	.04	.00	.00	.12	.01	-.03	.00	.07	.00
Number of sessions parent attended	.21*	.04*	.28*	.07*	.36**	.12**	-.33**	.10***	-.23*	.05*	-.31**	.09**	-.24*	.06*
Model F	12.76***		3.08*		4.51***		11.74***		10.67***		4.542**		10.910***	
Adjusted R2	.51		.16		.25		.44		.47		.24		.48	

* p < .05, ** p < .01, *** p < .001

To assess attrition bias, we examined sociodemographic indicators and pretest measures for potential differences between families available at followup and those lost to attrition; we found only one statistically significant difference between families with complete data and those with missing data. Families with data missing at followup had attended significantly fewer program sessions. Those with complete data attended an average of six Entre Dos Mundos sessions (standard deviation = 2.2), whereas families lost at followup attended an average of four sessions (standard deviation = 3.1, $t_{(80)}$ = 3.37, p < .001). On all other indicators, the families lost at followup did not differ significantly from families who continued to participate at followup (e.g., adolescents had equivalent levels of problem behaviors; reports of parent-adolescent conflict were equivalent). Consequently, the only bias we detected was that families who were lost to attrition or who declined to be interviewed at followup had shown less commitment to their initial participation in the project. Thus, our results may be more characteristic of Latino immigrant families who are more willing to participate in prevention programming.

RESULTS OF THE EVALUATION

Our findings from *t*-tests and chi-square comparisons revealed no significant sociodemographic differences between the action-oriented and support groups at pretest (see table 7.2). Both format types of Entre Dos Mundos groups were well attended. On average, parents in both study arms attended more than five of the eight sessions offered. Similarly, adolescents had high attendance rates: adolescents in the action-oriented groups attended an average of 6.8 of the eight sessions, and adolescents in the support groups attended an average of 6.6 of the eight sessions.

Shown in table 7.3, multiple regression models confirmed that, at posttest, the number of group sessions attended by parents explained 13 percent of the variance in bicultural identity integration, 7 percent of the variance in bicultural support, and 4 percent of the variance in family adaptability, even when controlling for pretest scores, annual family income, parent education, and time since parent immigration. Each of these proximal outcomes was positively associated with the number of sessions parents attended. Parental attendance also explained variance in three CBCL measures: 10 percent of the variance in adolescent aggression, 9 percent in adolescent oppositional defiant behavior, and approximately 5 percent in attention problems and attention-deficit hyperactivity disorder was explained by parent group attendance. The statistically significant negative regression coefficients in these post-test models indicated substantial reductions in each of these outcomes for parents who came to more group sessions.

TABLE 7.4
High vs. Low Dosage Participants' Means (SD) at Pretest and Post-test—Parent Data

Dependent Variable	Pretest		Post-test		Effect Size
	Low Dosage M (SD)	High Dosage M (SD)	Low Dosage M (SD)	High Dosage M (SD)	
Proximal Outcomes					
Bicultural support	26.47 (6.12)	28.55 (4.47)	22.00 (7.92)	27.29 (4.03)***	.89
Bicultural identity integration	17.16 (3.66)	18.92 (4.18)	17.85 (3.24)	20.05 (3.58)*	.65
Family adaptability	56.95 (6.00)	57.49 (8.63)	53.69 (7.53)	59.13 (7.99)*	.70
Parent-Reported Distal Outcomes					
CBCL—Aggression	5.94 (5.48)	6.38 (5.84)	9.53 (6.42)	5.03 (4.30)**	.84
CBCL—Oppositional defiant behavior	2.50 (2.60)	2.61 (2.35)	3.69 (2.93)	2.16 (1.91)*	.63
CBCL—Attention problems	4.33 (3.60)	4.80 (4.23)	5.33 (3.06)	3.79 (3.36)	.48
CBCL—ADHD	4.00 (2.72)	3.87 (3.05)	4.33 (3.58)	2.95 (2.69)	.44

* $p < .05$, ** $p < .01$, *** $p < .001$

There were two possible explanations for the significant program dosage effects. These effects could be attributed to the prevention program; that is, as a result of the experimental design, with all other factors being equal, we could conclude that higher attendance leads to better proximal and distal outcomes. An alternate explanation is that the attendance effects could be the result of differential attrition; that is, higher-risk families drop out of the program earlier, leaving healthier families with lower outcome scores to persist longer. This alternative hypothesis suggests that the treatment effects were spurious. To explore these rival explanations, we dichotomized the attendance variable into low- and high-dosage groups. Low-dosage parents attended fewer than four of the eight program sessions; they did not participate for even one month of the two-month program. High-dosage parents participated in four or more sessions, completing at least one month of the two-month curriculum.

Table 7.4 shows means and standard deviations for these low- and high-dosage groups. Results of t-tests comparing group differences on pretest and post-test outcome measures showed no significant differences between high- and low-dosage groups at pretest. Specifically, low-dosage participants were not at higher risk at pretest. Indeed, as compared with the high-dosage group, low-dosage participants had lower pretest group means for adolescent aggression, oppositional defiant behavior, and attention problems. This finding stands in opposition to the hypothesis of differential attrition. At post-test comparison with low-dosage parents, parents in the high-dosage group reported significantly higher bicultural support, bicultural identity integration, and family adaptability. The high-dosage group parent-reports of adolescent behavior also indicated significantly lower levels of aggression and oppositional defiant behavior in their adolescents than the parents in low-dosage group. Similarly, parent reports of adolescents' attention problems and attention deficit/hyperactivity problems showed a trend towards significance ($p = .1$) but did not reach the conventional level of statistical significance ($p < .05$).

Relative to low-dosage parents, the high-dosage parent group had a large treatment effect size (.6 to .9) for bicultural support, adolescent aggression, family adaptability, bicultural identity integration, and adolescent oppositional defiant behavior. The effect size for adolescent attention problems and attention deficit/hyperactivity problems was moderate (.4 to .5). Overall, this evidence led us to reject the differential attrition hypothesis and to consider differences in outcomes associated with attendance to be attributable to the Entre Dos Mundos curriculum.

Standardized coefficients from multiple regression models, shown in table 7.5, show the effects of the Entre Dos Mundos program conditions at one year after program completion. When controlling for variation based on pretest scores, length of parent's U.S. residency, family income, parent education, age, and marital status, the dichotomous variable indicating program format (i.e., action-oriented versus support group) was found to be a statistically significant predictor of adolescent aggression, oppositional defiant behavior, problems with anxious-depression, parent-adolescent conflict, and total adolescent problems—all in favor of action-oriented group delivery. On average at the one-year followup, parents who had participated in the action-oriented Entre Dos Mundos skills training groups reported significantly less conflict with their adolescents as compared with

TABLE 7.5
Standardized Regression Coefficients Predicting Distal Outcome Measures at One-Year Followup

	Aggression	Oppositional Defiant Behavior	Anxious-Depressed Behavior	Parent-Adolescent Conflict	Total Problems
Pretest	.663***	.664***	.602***	.539***	.528***
Time parent in United States	.096	.105	.032	.242*	.050
Income	−.138	−.169	−.091	−.198	−.066
Parent education	.126	−.080	−.032	.031	−.031
Parent age	.073	.058	.135	.092	.233
Marital status	.082	.103	.039	.120	.024
EDM intervention (1 = action-oriented, 0 = support groups)	−.230*	−.255*	−.319*	−.276*	−.321*
Attendance (dosage)	−.094	−.089	.040	−.028	−.095
Model F	5.1***	5.5***	3.8**	4.1***	3.3*
Adjusted R^2	.40	.41	.30	.31	.30
R^2 change for intervention	.04*	.06*	.09*	.07*	.08*
Estimated effect size	.4	.5	.7	.6	.6

parents who attended the unstructured support group. Further, parents who had attended the action-oriented group reported significantly fewer mental health problems for their adolescent children than did the parents who attended the support group. The statistically significant negative regression coefficients in these outcome models indicated substantial reductions in each of these outcomes reported by parents who participated in action-oriented Entre Dos Mundos groups.

Participation in action-oriented Entre Dos Mundos groups explained 4 percent of the variance in adolescent aggression, 6 percent of the variance in oppositional defiant behavior, 9 percent in anxious-depressed behavior, 7 percent in parent-adolescent conflict, and 8 percent of total problems— even when controlling for pretest scores, annual family income, parent education, age, marital status, and time since parent immigration. These percentages of variance explained by the intervention condition translate to an estimated program effect size of .5 for aggression and oppositional defiant behavior, .7 for anxious-depressed problems, .6 for parent-adolescent conflict, and .6 for total problems. These effect sizes for adolescent aggression, oppositional defiant behavior, parent-adolescent conflict, and total problems were clearly moderate (.5 and .6), and the program effect for anxious-depression nearly reached the conventionally accepted threshold considered to mark large effects (.7 whereas .8 is considered large).

PROCESS EVALUATION: PARTICIPANT EXIT INTERVIEWS

Process evaluation helps to complement the quantitative outcome evaluation above by chronicling program characteristics that participants find particularly helpful. The transcript below details one exit interview with a group of Entre Dos Mundos action-oriented group participants. Martica is the director, or main facilitator, and Xiomara is a co-facilitator. This exit interview occurred during the last group session (session 8).

The session begins with Martica reminding everyone that their first group meeting began with Xiomara and Karla (the two assistants for the program) calling them all by phone. The theme was "How has our family changed?" Martica walks up to the EDM circular model and asks them how that change was. She reminds them that the second group was about how to manage and communicate about conflict, and she refers to the diagram drawn on the floor for that activity. Martica continues summing up what they talked about in each group session.

"Today we're going to finish the group," Martica says as she takes her seat at the front of the room. "We're going to ask you some questions and then

have a graduation ceremony. What are you going to take from this group and apply to your lives?" Ines replies, "There are a lot of people that feel the way I do. It's not just my situation and my problems, but others have them too. Like they say, 'sharing the load is much easier than carrying it alone.'" She laughs. Martica asks her what she is going to take from this experience and use in her relationship with her daughter. She says that the communication activity helped her a lot because her daughter told her how she felt about their communication. She says that it made her want to work toward better communication with her daughter.

Martica and Xiomara prompt other families to share. Monica says that they learned a lot about respect and communication. Martica asks her if communication only improved within the group or outside as well. Monica says that they are also communicating better outside.

Isabel says that the support has been really helpful, especially in being able to share their experiences with racism. She says that if they always feel alone in the discrimination, they will always have to walk with their heads down. She says that she has learned to talk more with her kids and support them, both as parents and as friends. Carlos adds that improving communication has been really important, especially as their cultures are changing. He thanks everyone for sharing their problems with the group.

Martica asks the group to share their thoughts on how they can improve the group. Xiomara will ask them some questions, and Martica will take notes about what they have to say. "How has it been for you to participate in this group with other families?" Xiomara asks them. Carlos says that at first he thinks that some people felt uncomfortable but that with time, as they got to know each other, they began to trust each other more.

Xiomara asks the adolescents specifically how it was to share their experiences with other adolescents and with their parents. Stephanie says that it was a good experience for her because she has problems with her parents and fights with her dad a lot, and it really relieved her to hear other adolescents with the same problems. "It's not that I'm such a bad daughter," she adds. She says that it also helps to learn from other people that you are not alone in experiencing racism. Xiomara tries to prompt other adolescents to say something since they have all been so quiet this session.

"What helped you most in this group?" Xiomara asks. Ines says that she was most affected by the session when they talked about how to best support their kids and Diana, a Colombian mother, cried. She remembers that they all felt what Diana felt about issues of language and helplessness with their adolescents. She commends Martica and Xiomara for the techniques that they use, standing behind the person and supporting the person through a *difficult moment (e.g., the psychodrama technique called doubling) while at the same time pushing the person to open up and keep talking. Xiomara tells them that they can practice that technique within their own families.*

Diana and David arrive, and Xiomara catches them up on what they are doing in the group. She sums up what Ines has just said. Ines adds that here in this group they were able to share things that they felt like they could not share with other people before. "To take that from your heart is like getting rid of a stone that was on top of you."

Diana says that the group helped her a lot when Ines stood behind her (e.g., doubling) and helped her express in words all that she had confused inside of herself and to clarify her emotions. "Sometimes someone else can see more clearly than you do. When you are in the middle of the conflict, everything is a ruckus and you can't define it. The technique, doubling, is really good, and I've already used it!" She says that she has not used it with David (her older son), but she has with her younger kids, and it has helped her a lot.

Xiomara asks them about something that they have done in the group that they really liked, maybe something small that helped them a lot. Diana says that she really enjoyed seeing the goals of the adolescents, the activity where the adolescents enacted what their futures would look like in ten years. Someone else agrees that this activity was really motivating.

Felipe says that he regrets having missed the session on discrimination, but his wife told him about it. He tells Xiomara and Martica that they should focus more on that subject because, as he puts it, "We are not moving up enough because they are treating us as if we were less. And we are capable. We really need to give our kids an impetus and a lot of trust." He adds that he thinks that the topic of discrimination is important in improving the self-esteem of the adolescents and the parents as well.

Xiomara asks the group if anyone else has anything to say. When they remain silent, she asks them what changes they have seen in their family as a result of participation in this group. Stephanie says that her father values their opinions more now and when there is an argument, they talk about it more in order to arrive at an agreement. Ines says that her daughter, Ana, is talking to her more and sharing more with her. Martica asks Ana if she is talking to her mother now more because of the group. Ana says that she started talking to her mom more after the group because it takes a long time to get home from the group and there is no one else to talk to. Everyone laughs. She adds, "And then I liked how she understood what I said to her, so I decided to talk to her more." Ines says that they would start by talking about the group and then move on to other topics of conversation.

Diana says that David (her son) is nicer to her now. He has always been really quiet with her, but now he is more tolerant as well. Martica asks David why he has changed in this way. "The group has something to do with it, be-cause the opinions of everyone open your mind, and you see how people see things differently. That helped me," he replies.

Xiomara asks the group what they would change if they could change any-thing about the way the group works. "What would it be?" she asks. When no one says anything, she gives an example of what the last group said. Di-ana suggests homework for the parents and adolescents, something more for them to do. Martica says that the homework that she gave was more about things to talk about. Diana said that she would prefer an activity in which the people would have to participate. Felipe agrees that more activity would allow them to share more with each other. Monica adds that more activity gets the adolescents to talk more.

Discussion of Results

This experimental test compared the sustained effects of two alterna-tive delivery methods for the Entre Dos Mundos curriculum; an action-oriented facilitation style characterized by the extensive use of psycho-drama techniques versus a traditional support group format characterized by a passive, discussion-oriented delivery. Interestingly, the pattern of ef-fects suggested that program attendance (or dosage) was critical for foster-ing proximal outcomes at post-test, whereas the program delivery format determined the distal outcomes at one-year followup.

We hypothesized that commitment to program participation, as in-dexed by higher attendance rates, would be significantly associated with proximal outcomes such as lower levels of adolescent problems and parent-adolescent conflict. The multiple regression models for post-test data sup-ported this hypothesis; program dosage was the key for proximal outcomes. Parents who attended higher numbers of Entre Dos Mundos sessions (i.e., received a higher dosage of the multifamily group program) reported sig-nificantly decreased family problems—for both delivery formats—which translated to a moderate-to-large treatment effect size (.6 to .9) for bicul-tural support, adolescent aggression, family adaptability, bicultural identity integration, and adolescent oppositional defiant behavior. The effect size for adolescent attention problems and attention deficit/hyperactivity prob-lems at post-test was moderate (.4 to .5). Consequently, we believe these short term-changes were associated with new learning gained from proc-essing acculturation stress issues (e.g., the weekly themes from the Entre Dos Mundos curriculum) either in action or through group discussion.

This investigation advanced beyond prior studies by measuring program impacts on both proximal and distal outcomes. Given that only the original

BET study (Szapocznik et al. 1986) measured changes in bicultural skills and only Coatsworth, Pantin, and Szapocznik (2002) reported changes in parental investment, few prior studies on bicultural skills training programs illuminated the mechanisms that made the programs work. Consequently, our study is distinguished in its demonstration of program effects on family adaptability, bicultural support, and bicultural identity integration. The Entre Dos Mundos research was the first study since Szapocznik and colleagues (1986) tested BET to show significant changes on variables related to biculturalism based on program participation. Further, our process evaluation illustrated above highlighted participants' perceptions of support from others, seeing other group members' struggles, and psychodramatic doubling to be the most memorable program elements.

The effect sizes that were associated with differences in parents' program dosage were noteworthy. Few prevention programs for adolescent aggression have rendered effect sizes near .8. The large effect we have reported for Entre Dos Mundos may be the result of our program design that included parents and adolescents in the same sessions using a multiple family group format. These multiple family groups provided a context for parents and adolescents to communicate in new ways while discussing challenging acculturation topics. Most of the families reported that they did not discuss acculturation issues at home, which left parents and adolescents to cope with these issues on their own. The Entre Dos Mundos groups allowed family members to come together, provided a forum for discussing acculturation, and enhanced parent-adolescent understanding. This heightened mutual understanding, coupled with support from other participating families and gains in bicultural identity, appeared to be key elements in helping these Latino families adapt to acculturation challenges and decrease problematic behaviors in adolescents.

For long-term learning, skills acquisition, and second-order family system change (i.e., foundational change; Nichols and Schwartz 2005), the one-year followup analyses suggested that program implementation style, specifically adopting an action-oriented delivery approach, was more important than simple attendance. One year after program completion, Entre Dos Mundos sessions that were delivered using action-oriented psychodrama techniques to enhance bicultural coping skills showed sustained benefits on adolescent problems and parent-adolescent conflict compared to support group facilitation of parent-adolescent communication and between-family social networking. As compared with parents who had participated in the unstructured support group, at the one-year followup, parents who had participated in the action-oriented Entre Dos Mundos groups reported significantly lower adolescent aggression, oppositional defiant behavior, anxious depression, and total problems in their adolescent children as well as less parent-adolescent conflict in their families. The percentages of variance explained by Entre Dos Mundos delivery format at one-year followup (.5 for aggression and oppositional defiant behavior, .7 for anxious-depressed problems, .6 for parent-adolescent conflict, and .6 for total problems) showed that post-test effects for aggression and oppositional defiant behavior were sustained at one-year followup for families that attended action-oriented Entre Dos Mundos groups. The moderate post-test effects on attention problems and attention deficit/hyperactivity problems decreased enough at one-year followup to lose their statistical significance; however, beneficial sleeper effects for Entre Dos Mundos action-oriented delivery families were found for decreases in anxious-depressed problems, parent-adolescent conflict, and total adolescent problems at one-year followup that were not significant at post-test. It took additional time beyond the eight-week program to integrate new coping skills in family systems and to create fundamental relationship changes between parents and adolescents.

These positive effects of action-oriented implementation were consistent with earlier evaluations of bicultural skills training packages (Arenas 1978; LaFromboise and Rowe 1983; Costantino, Malgady, and Rogler 1986; Szapocznik et al. 1986; Schinke et al. 1988; Bilides 1990; Malgady, Rogler, and Costantino 1990; Mullender 1990; Marsiglia, Cross, and Mitchell-Enos 1998; Ying 1999; Pantin et al. 2003), further illustrating the utility of bicultural skills training. Equally important, the research on Entre Dos Mundos advanced current knowledge by measuring program impacts one year after program completion. Few prior studies of bicultural skills training programs have evaluated longitudinal data.

In addition, this study contributed to the body of research knowledge supporting the use of psychodramatic methods in prevention and treatment. Although psychodrama is one of the oldest forms of psychotherapy —dating to the 1930s—empirical evidence showing the efficacy of this approach has been limited (Kipper 1978; Buchanan 1984; Kellerman 1987). Two important exceptions to this conclusion are Kipper and Ritchie's (2003) meta-analysis showing large effects for psychodrama techniques such as doubling and role reversal, and the current study that also indicates a large effect size for action methods. We hope that this trial comparing action methods to support groups inspires a new round of research into the utility of psychodrama methods. Adam Blatner (1999), an eminent scholar in psychodrama research, has suggested studying the efficacy of psychodrama by comparing group or family therapy that integrates action methods with interventions that use a similar therapeutic approach but do not incorporate psychodrama. The current study began to fulfill this mandate by empirically demonstrating that action-oriented psychodrama groups proved superior to support groups that used the same topical themes. Further research on psychodrama action methods in prevention and intervention is clearly warranted.

Although this evaluation underscored the promise of action-oriented bicultural skills programs, there were clear limitations. The sample size did not allow us to perform subanalyses on families from different countries-of-origin (e.g., Mexicans versus Colombians). We focused solely on parent reports, which we considered more objective measures of adolescent mental health problems than adolescent reports. Future studies should integrate data from multiple reporters and include larger samples of Latino families. A distinct strength of the evaluation is that conducting the study in metropolitan, small town, and rural communities, rather than in one or two agencies, enhanced generalizability of the findings. However, caution is warranted in generalizing findings beyond Latino immigrant families living in North Carolina, or beyond Latino immigrant families willing to participate in prevention programs. Although our attrition analyses showed no differences in demographic indicators or mental health measures between families with followup data and those lost to attrition, families with followup data had attended significantly more program sessions. Consequently, we must limit our discussion of program effects to Latino immigrant families who are committed to program participation. This limitation is common in prevention science.

Finally, the differences between action-oriented and support groups showed that the Entre Dos Mundos program was more efficacious when implemented using action-oriented psychodrama techniques with structured warm-up activities. However, program effects may be underestimated because participants in the comparison condition (i.e., support group program) received the same weekly themes from the Entre Dos Mundos curriculum. In our next study, we will compare Entre Dos Mundos prevention with either a no-service comparison group or a basic case-management group to provide a suitable contrast between groups focused on acculturation and groups with no acculturation content. It is possible that comparison to no-service control families could produce even stronger program effects.

Conclusion

At post-test, according to parents who received a significant dose of the program, Entre Dos Mundos youth violence prevention was efficacious in lowering adolescent aggression, oppositional defiant behavior, attention problems, and symptoms of attention deficit hyperactivity disorder in acculturating Latino immigrant families. Program participation was also associated with increased family adaptability, bicultural support, and bicultural identity integration. At post-test, the Entre Dos Mundos curriculum was equally efficacious when delivered in action-oriented experiential groups or in unstructured support groups. Having parents commit to attending at least half of the program sessions offered appears to be the critical component related to the enhanced proximal outcomes.

At one-year followup, program delivery format became important for long-term change and skills acquisition. Entre Dos Mundos prevention, when delivered in action-oriented multifamily groups using psychodrama techniques, was efficacious and resulted in parent reports of lower adolescent aggression, oppositional defiant behavior, anxious depression, parent-adolescent conflict, and total problems in acculturating Latino immigrant adolescents. At the one-year followup after program completion, action-oriented experiential groups showed superior effects when compared to support groups focused on the same session themes. Findings were characteristic of Latino immigrant families who participated in more program sessions.

In this evaluation, we showed that bicultural skills and family adaptability were useful targets for prevention programming. Experiential prevention programming, like Entre Dos Mundos, can be used to avoid the negative outcomes associated with the acculturation process. With support and through the development of bicultural skills, Latino families can successfully adapt to their new cultural environments without sacrificing the cultural assets they bring from their homelands.

The recipe for preserving the health and well-being of immigrant families lies in the maintenance of ethnic identity and familism, the development of bicultural identity integration, and the attenuation of parent-adolescent cultural conflict and discrimination experiences. It is our hope that these well-researched cultural assets and risk factors guide a new wave of programs and policies that support immigrant youth as they continue to take an increasingly prominent place in American society. It is clear from the basic and applied research presented in this book that the healthiest goal for immigrant adolescents and their families, and arguably for society as a whole in the United States, is to become bicultural. Biculturalism, in comparison to assimilation, separation/enculturation, or cultural marginality, provides a number of psychological, social, academic, and familial advantages that are noteworthy. The development of bicultural identity integration can be a long and strenuous process, but the resulting bicultural skills represent resilience in the face of acculturation stress and risk factors. Consequently, the process of becoming bicultural is a sign of personal, familial, and national resourcefulness that should be nurtured and celebrated.

References

Achenbach, Thomas M., and Leslie A. Rescorla. 2001. *Manual for ASEBA School-Age Forms and Profiles.* Burlington: University of Vermont, Research Center for Children, Youth, and Families.

Alderete, Ethel, William A. Vega, Bohdan Kolody, and Sergio Aguilar-Gaxiola. 1999. Depressive symptomatology: Prevalence and psychosocial risk factors among Mexican migrant farmworkers in California. *Journal of Community Psychology* 27 (4): 457–71.

Alegría, Margarita, Glorisa Canino, Patrick E. Shrout, Meghan Woo, Naihua Duan, Doryliz Vila, Maria Torres, Chih-nan Chen, and Xiao-Li Meng. 2008. Prevalence of mental illness in immigrant and non-immigrant U.S. Latino groups. *American Journal of Psychiatry* 165 (3): 359–69.

Alegría, Margarita, Meghan Woo, Zhun Cao, Maria Torres, Xiao-li Meng, and Ruth Striegel-Moore. 2007. Prevalence and correlates of eating disorders in Latinos in the United States. *International Journal of Eating Disorders* 40: S15–S21.

Al-Issa, Ihsan, and Michael Tousignant, eds. 1997. *Ethnicity, Immigration, and Psychopathology.* New York: Plenum Press.

Amaro, Hortensia, Rupert Whitaker, Gerald Coffman, and Timothy Heeren. 1990. Acculturation and marijuana and cocaine use: Findings from HHANES, 1982–1984. *American Journal of Public Health* 80: 54–60.

Andreeva, Valentina A., and Jennifer B.Unger. 2008. *Reverse Acculturation and Health Practices: Theory and Evidence.* Unpublished manuscript.

Arenas, Soledad. 1978. Bilingual/bicultural programs for preschool children. *Children Today* 7 (4): 2–6.

Bacallao, Martica L., and Paul R. Smokowski. 2005. *Entre dos mundos* (Between two worlds): Bicultural skills training and Latino immigrant families. *Journal of Primary Prevention* 26 (6): 485–509.

———. 2007. The costs of getting ahead: Mexican family systems after immigration. *Family Relations* 56 (1): 52–66.

———. 2009. *Entre dos mundos* /Between two worlds: Bicultural development in context. *Journal of Primary Prevention* 30 (3–4): 421–52.

Bates, Lisa M., Dolores Acevedo-Garcia, Margarita Alegría, and Nancy Krieger. 2008. Immigration and generational trends in body mass index and obesity in the United States: Results of the National Latino and Asian American Survey, 2002–2003. *American Journal of Public Health* 98 (1): 70–77.

Bausel, R. Barker, Wen-Lin Lee, and Brian M. Berman. 2001. Demographic and health-related correlates of visits to complementary and alternative medical providers. *Medical Care* 39: 190–96.

Benally, Christine J., Marge Werito, Darlene Begay, Todd Jones, and Vangie Yabeny. 2003. *2003 Navajo Middle and High School Youth Risk Behavior Surveillance System Report.* Shiprock, NM: Navajo Area Indian Health Service and Navajo Nation.

Benet-Martínez, Verónica, and Jana Haritatos. 2005. Bicultural Identity Integration (BII): Components and psychosocial antecedents. *Journal of Personality* 73 (4): 1015–50.

Benet-Martínez, Veronica, Fiona Lee, and Janxin Leu. 2006. Biculturalism and cognitive complexity: Expertise in cultural representations. *Journal of Cross-Cultural Psychology* 37 (4): 386–407.

Benet-Martinez, Verónica, Janxin Leu, Fiona Lee, and Michael Morris. 2002. Negotiating biculturalism: Cultural frame switching in biculturals with oppositional versus compatible cultural identities. *Journal of Cross-Cultural Psychology* 33 (5): 492–517.

Berry, John W. 1980. Acculturation as varieties of adaptation. In *Acculturation: Theory, Models, and Some New Findings,* ed. Amado M. Padilla, 9–25. Boulder, CO: Westview Press.

———. 1998. Acculturation stress. In *Readings in Ethnic Psychology,* ed. Pamela Balls Organista, Kevin M. Chun, and Gerardo Marin, 117–22. New York: Routledge.

———. 2001. A psychology of immigration. *Journal of Social Issues* 57 (3): 615–31.

———. 2003. Conceptual approaches to acculturation. In *Acculturation: Advances in Theory, Measurement, and Applied Research,* ed. Kevin M. Chun, Pamela Balls Organista, and Gerardo Marin, 17–37. Washington, DC: American Psychological Association Press.

———. 2006. Stress perspectives on acculturation. In *The Cambridge Handbook of Acculturation Psychology,* ed, David L. Sam and John.W. Berry, 43–57. Cambridge: Cambridge University Press.

Berry, John W., Jean S. Phinney, David L. Sam, and Paul Vedder. 2006. Immigrant youth: Acculturation, identity, and adaptation. *Applied Psychology* 55 (3): 303–32.

Berry, John W., and David L. Sam. 1997. Acculturation and adaptation. In *Handbook of Cross-Cultural Psychology.* Vol. 3, *Social Behavior and Applications,* ed. John W. Berry, Marshall H. Segall, and Ciqdem Kagitcibasi, 2nd edition, 291–326. Boston: Allyn and Bacon.

Beverly, C. 1989. Treatment issues for black, alcoholic clients. *Social-Casework* 70 (6): 370–74.

Bialystok, Ellen. 1999. Cognitive complexity and attentional control in the bilingual mind. *Child Development* 70 (3): 636–44.

Bialystok, Ellen, Fergus I. M. Craik, Raymond Klein, and Mythili Viswanathan. 2004. Bilingualism, aging, and cognitive control: Evidence from the Simon Task. *Psychology and Aging* 19 (2): 290–303.

Bickman, Leonard. 1992. Designing outcome evaluations for children's mental health services: Improving internal validity. *New Directions for Program Evaluation* 54: 57–68.

Bilides, David G. 1990. Race, color, ethnicity, and class: Issues of biculturalism in school-based adolescent counseling groups. *Social Work with Groups* 13 (4): 43–58.

Bird, Hector R., Glorisa Canino, Mark Davies, Cristiane S. Duarte, Vivian Febo, Rafael Ramirez, Christina Hoven, Judith Wicks, George Musa, and Rolf Loeber. 2006. A study of disruptive behavior disorders in Puerto Rican youth: I. Background, design, and survey methods. *Journal of the American Academy of Child and Adolescent Psychiatry* 45 (9): 1032–41.

Bird, Hector R., Mark Davies, Cristiane S. Duarte, Sa Shen, Rolf Loeber, and Glorisa Canino. 2006. A study of disruptive behavior disorders in Puerto Rican youth: II. Baseline prevalence, comorbidity, and correlates in two sites. *Journal of the American Academy of Child and Adolescent Psychiatry* 45 (9): 1042–53.

Blank, Rebecca M. 1997. *It Takes a Nation: A New Agenda for Fighting Poverty.* New York: Sage.

Blatner, Adam. 1999. Psychodramatic methods in psychotherapy. In *Beyond Talk Therapy: Using Movement and Expressive Techniques in Clinical Practice,* ed. Daniel J. Weiner, 125–43. Washington, DC: American Psychological Association.

———. 2005. Psychodrama. In *Current Psychotherapies,* ed. Raymond J. Corsini and Danny Wedding, 7th edition, 405–38. Belmont, CA: Brooks/Cole.

Bourne, Randolph S. 1916. Trans-national America. *Atlantic Monthly* 118: 86–97.

Breslau, Joshua, Sergio, Aguilar-Gaxiola, Guilherme Borges, Ruby Cecilia Castilla Puentes, Kenneth S. Kendler, Maria Elena Medina-Mora, Maxwell Su, and Ronald Kessler. 2007. Mental disorders among English-speaking Mexican immigrants to the US compared to a national sample of Mexicans. *Psychiatry Research* 151 (1–2): 115–22.

Bronfenbrenner, Urie. 1989. Ecological systems theory. In *Annals of Child Development,* Vol. 6, ed. Ross Vasta, 187–251. Greenwich, CT: IAI Press.

Brook, Judith S., Martin Whiteman, Elinor B. Balka, Pe T. Win, and Michal D. Gursen. 1998. African American and Puerto Rican drug use: A longitudinal study. *Journal of* the American Academy of Child and Adolescent Psychiatry 36 (9): 1260–68.

Brown, Benjamin, and William Reed Benedict. 2004. Bullets, blades, and being afraid in Hispanic high schools: An exploratory study of the presence of weapons and fear of weapons-related victimization among high school students in a border town. *Crime & Delinquency* 50: 372–94.

Buchanan, Dale R. 1984. Psychodrama. In *The Psychosocial Therapies: Part II of the Psychiatric Therapies,* ed. T. Byram Karasu, 783–89. Washington, DC: American Psychiatric Association.

Buchanan, Rachel L., and Paul R. Smokowski. 2009. Pathways from acculturation stress to substance use among Latino adolescents: Results from the Latino Acculturation and Health Project. *Substance Use and Misuse* 44 (5): 740–62.

Bui, Hoan N., and Ornum Thongniramol. 2005. Immigration and self-reported delinquency: The interplay of immigration, generations, gender, race, and ethnicity. *Journal of Crime and Justice* 28 (2): 71–80.

Buriel, Raymond, Silverio Calzada, and Richard Vasquez. 1982. The relationship of traditional Mexican American culture to adjustment and delinquency among three generations of Mexican American male adolescents. *Hispanic Journal of Behavioral Sciences* 4 (1): 41–55.

Burke, Adam, Dawn M. Upchurch, Claire Dye, and Laura Chyu. 2006. Acupuncture use in the United States: Findings from the National Health Interview Survey. *Journal of Alternative and Complementary Medicine* 12: 639–48.

Burnam, M. Audrey, Richard L. Hough, Marvin Kamo, Javier I. Escobar, and Cynthia A. Telles. 1987. Acculturation and lifetime prevalence of psychiatric disorders among Mexican Americans in Los Angeles. *Journal of Health and Social Behavior* 28 (1): 89–102.

Cabassa, Leopoldo J. 2003. Measuring acculturation: Where we are and where we need to go. *Hispanic Journal of Behavioral Studies* 25 (2): 127–46.

Caetano, R. 1987. Acculturation and drinking patterns among U.S. Hispanics. *British Journal of Addiction* 82: 789–99.

Campbell, Donald T., and Julian C. Stanley. 1963. *Experimental and Quasi-Experimental Designs for Research.* Boston: Houghton Mifflin.

Carlson-Sabelli, Linnea, Hector Sabelli, M. Patel, and K. Holm. 1992. The union of opposites in sociometry. *Journal of Group Psychotherapy, Psychodrama, and Sociometry* 44 (4): 147–71.

Carringer, Dennis C. 1974. Creative thinking abilities of a Mexican youth: The relationship of bilingualism. *Journal of Cross-Cultural Psychology* 5 (4): 492–504.

Carvajal, Scott C., Carrie E. Hanson, Andrea J. Romero, and Karin K. Coyle. 2002. Behavioural risk factors and protective factors in adolescents: A comparison of Latino and non-Latino whites. *Ethnicity and Health* 7 (3): 181–93.

Carvajal, Scott C., Joanna R. Photiades, Richard I. Evans, and Susan G. Nash. 1997. Relating a social influence model to the role of acculturation in substance use among Latino adolescents. *Journal of Applied Social Psychology* 27 (18): 1617–28.

Castro, Felipe G., Kathryn Coe, Sara Gutierres, and Delia Saenz. 1996. Designing health promotion programs for Latinos. In *Handbook of Diversity Issues in Health Psychology,* ed. Pamela M. Kato and Traci Mann, 319–46. New York: Plenum.

Centers for Disease Control and Prevention. 2002. Youth Risk Behavior Surveillance System (YRBSS): Survey results. Http://www.cdc.gov/HealthyYouth/yrbs/index.htm.

———. 2004. Surveillance summaries, May 21, 2004. *Morbidity and Mortality Weekly Report* 2004: 53. Http://www.cdc.gov/mmwr/PDF/SS/SS5302.pdf.

———. 2007a. Youth online: Comprehensive results. Http://apps.nccd.cdc.gov/yrbss/.

———. 2007b. Youth violence: Facts at a glance. Http://www.cdc.gov/ncipc/dvp/YV_DataSheet.pdf.

———. 2007c. Web-based Injury Statistics Query and Reporting System (WISQARS). National Center for Injury Prevention and Control. Http://www.cdc.gov/injury/wisqars/index.html.

———. 2008. Youth risk behavior surveillance: United States, 2007. *Morbidity and Mortality Weekly Report* 57. Http://www.cdc.gov/healthyyouth/yrbs/pdf/yrbss07_mmwr.pdf.

———. 2009. Youth Risk Behavior

Surveillance System (YRBSS): Survey results. Http://www.cdc.gov/HealthyYouth/yrbs/index.htm.

Chen, Thomas. 2009. Why Asian Americans voted for Obama. Http://www.hcs.harvard.edu/~perspy/2009/02/why-asian-americans-voted-for-obama/.

Christian, Donna, Elizabeth R. Howard, and Michal I. Loeb. 2000. Bilingualism for all: Two-way immersion education in the United States. *Theory into Practice* 39 (4): 258–66.

Chun, Kevin M., Pamela Balls Organista, and Gerardo Marín, eds. 2003. *Acculturation: Advances in Theory, Measurement, and Applied Research*. Washington, DC: American Psychological Association.

Coatsworth, J. Douglas, Mildred Maldonido-Molina, Hilda Pantin, and Jose Szapocznik. 2005. A person-centered and ecological investigation of acculturation strategies in Hispanic immigrant youth. *Journal of Community Psychology* 33 (2): 157–74.

Coatsworth, J. Douglas, Hilda Pantin, and Jose Szapocznik. 2002. *Familias Unidas: A family-centered ecodevelopmental intervention to reduce risk for problem behavior among Hispanic adolescents. Clinical Child and Family Psychology Review* 5 (2): 113–32.

Conboy, Lisa A, Sonal Patel, Ted J. Kaptchuk, Bobbie Gottlieb, David Eisenberg, Delores Acevedo-Garcia. 2005. Sociodemographic determinants of the utilization of specific types of complementary and alternative medicine: An analysis based on a nationally representative survey sample. *Journal of Alternative and Complementary Medicine* 11: 977–94.

Coohey, Carol. 2001. The relationship between familism and child maltreatment in Latino and Anglo families. *Child Maltreatment* 6 (2): 130–42.

Cortes, Dharma E. 1995. Variations in familism in two generations of Puerto Ricans. *Hispanic Journal of Behavioral Sciences* 17 (2): 249–56.

Costantino, Giuseppe, Robert G. Malgady, and Lloyd H. Rogler. 1986. *Cuento* therapy: A culturally sensitive modality for Puerto Rican children. *Journal of Consulting and Clinical Psychology* 54 (5): 639–45.

Crane, D. Russell, So Wa Ngai, Jeffry H. Larson, and McArthur Hafen Jr. 2005. The influence of family functioning and parent-adolescent acculturation on North American Chinese adolescent outcomes. *Family Relations* 54 (3): 400–410.

Crevecoeur, J. Hector St. John de. 1782. Letters from an American Farmer. Http://xroads.virginia.edu/~HYPER/crev/home.html.

Current Population Survey 2002. United States Census Bureau interactive census database. Http://www.census.gov or http://www.census.gov/population/www/socdemo/race.html.

Dahlberg, Linda L., and Etienne G. Krug. 2002. Violence: A global public health problem. In *World Report on Violence and Health*, ed. Etienne G. Krug, Linda L. Dahlberg, James A. Mercy, Anthony B. Zwi, and Rafael Lozano, 1–21. Geneva, Switzerland: World Health Organization.

Dawson, Deborah A. 1998. Beyond black, white, and Hispanic: Race, ethnic origin, and drinking patterns in the United States. *Journal of Substance Abuse* 10 (4): 321–39.

de Anda, Diane. 1984. Bicultural socialization: Factors affecting the minority experience. *Social Work* 29 (2): 101–7.

Decker, Michele R., Anita Raj, and Jay G. Silverman. 2007. Sexual violence against adolescent girls: Influences of immigration and acculturation. *Violence against Women* 13 (5): 498–513.

Dehaene, Stanislas, Emmanuel Dupoux, Jacques Mehler, Laurent Cohen, Eraldo Paulesu, Daniela Perani, Pierre-Francois van de Moortele, Stephanie Lehéricy, and Denis Le Bihan. 1997. Anatomical variability in the cortical representation of first and second language. *NeuroReport* 8 (17): 3809–15.

de Houwer, Annick. 1999. Language acquisition in children raised with two languages from birth: An update. *Revue Parole* 9: 63–88.

de Jong, Ester J. 2002. Effective bilingual education: From theory to academic achievement in a two-way bilingual program. *Bilingual Research Journal* 26 (1): 65–84.

De La Rosa, Mario. 2002. Acculturation and Latino adolescents' substance use: A research agenda for the future. *Substance Use and Misuse* 37 (4): 429–56.

Delgado, Melvin, ed. 1998. *Alcohol Use/Abuse among Latinos: Issues and Examples of*

Culturally Competent Service. New York: Haworth Press.

Department of Homeland Security. 2008. Immigration. Http://www.dhs.gov/ximgtn/.

Dinh, Khanh T., Mark W. Roosa, Jenn-Yun Tein, and Vera A. Lopez. 2002. The relationship between acculturation and problem behavior proneness in a Hispanic youth sample: A longitudinal mediation model. *Journal of Abnormal Child Psychology* 30 (3): 295–309.

Dolby, Nadine. 2000. Changing selves: Multicultural education and the challenge of new identities. *Teachers College Record* 102 (5): 898–912.

Driscoll, Anne K., M. Antonia Biggs, Claire D. Brindis, and Ekua Yankah. 2001. Adolescent Latino reproductive health: A review of the literature. *Hispanic Journal of Behavioral Sciences* 23 (3): 255–326.

Driscoll, Anne K., Stephen T. Russell, and Lisa J. Crockett. 2008. Parenting styles and youth well-being across immigrant generations. *Journal of Family Issues* 29 (2): 185–209.

Dumka, Larry E., Mark W. Roosa, and Kristina M. Jackson. 1997. Risk, conflict, mother's parenting, and children's adjustment in low-income, Mexican immigrant, and Mexican American families. *Journal of Marriage and the Family* 59 (2): 309–23.

Ebin, Vicki J., Carl D. Sneed, Donald E. Morisky, Mary Jane Rotheram-Borus, Ann M. Magnusson, and C. Kevin Malotte. 2001. Acculturation and interrelationships between problem and health-promoting behaviors among Latino adolescents. *Journal of Adolescent Health* 28 (1): 62–72.

Escobar, Javier I. 1998. Immigration and mental health: Why are immigrants better off? *Archives of General Psychiatry* 55 (9): 781–82.

Escobar, Javier, Audrey Burnam, Marvin Karno, Alan Forsythe, John Landsverk, and Jacqueline M. Golding. 1986. Use of the Mini-Mental State Examination (MMSE) in a community population of mixed ethnicity: Cultural and linguistic artifacts. *Journal of Nervous and Mental Disease* 174 (10): 607–14.

Escobar, Javier, Constanza Nervi, and Michael Gara. 2000. Immigration and mental health: Mexican Americans in the United States. *Harvard Review of Psychiatry* 8 (2): 64–72.

Feliciano, Cynthia. 2001. The benefits of biculturalism: Exposure to immigrant culture and dropping out of school among Asian and Latino youths. *Social Science Quarterly* 82 (4): 865–79.

Flannery, William P., Steven P. Reise, and Jiajuan Yu. 2001. An empirical comparison of acculturation models. *Personality and Social Psychology Bulletin* 27 (8): 1035–45.

Flores-Gonzales, Nilda. 2002. *School Kids/Street Kids: Identity Development in Latino Students.* New York: Teachers College Press.

Ford, Kathleen, and Anne E. Norris 1993. Urban Hispanic adolescents and young adults: Relationship of acculturation to sexual behavior. *Journal of Sex Research* 30 (4): 316–23.

Frankfort-Nachmias, Chava, and David Nachmias. 2000. *Research Methods in the Social Sciences,* 6th edition. New York: Worth.

Freedenthal, Stacey, and Arlene Rubin Stiffman. 2004. Suicidal behavior in urban American Indian adolescents: A comparison with reservation youth in a southwestern state. *Suicide and Life Threatening Behavior* 34 (2): 160–71.

Fridrich, Angela H., and Daniel J. Flannery. 1995. The effects of ethnicity and acculturation on early adolescent delinquency. *Journal of Child and Family Studies* 4 (1): 69–87.

Fuligni, Andrew J. 1998. Authority, autonomy, and parent-adolescent conflict and cohesion: A study of adolescents from Mexican, Chinese, Filipino, and European backgrounds. *Developmental Psychology* 34 (4): 782–92.

Fuligni, Andrew J., Tiffany Yip, and Vivian Tseng. 2002. The impact of family obligation on the daily activities and psychological well-being of Chinese American adolescents. *Child Development* 73 (1): 302–14.

Galster, George C., Kurt Metzger, and Ruth Waite. 1999. Neighborhood opportunity and immigrants' socioeconomic advancement. *Journal of Housing Research* 10 (1): 95–127.

Gandara, Patricia, Julie Maxwell-Jolly, Eugene Garcia, Jolynn Asoto, Kris Gutierrez, Tom Stritikus, and Julia Curry. 2000. *The Initial Impact of Proposition 227 on the Instruction of English Learners.* Santa Barbara: University of California Linguistic Minority Research Institute.

García Coll, Cynthia, and Katherine Magnuson. 2001. The psychological experience of immigration: A developmental perspective. In *Interdisciplinary Perspectives on the New Immigration.* Volume 4, *The New Immigrant and the American Family,* ed. Marcelo M. Suarez-Orozco, Carola Suarez-Orozco, and Desiree Qin-Hilliard, 69–110. New York: Routledge.

Genesee, Fred. 1989. Early bilingual development: One language or two? *Journal of Child Language* 16 (1): 161–79.

Gil, Andres G., and William A. Vega. 1996. Two different worlds: Acculturation stress and adaptation among Cuban and Nicaraguan families. *Journal of Social and Personal Relationships* 13 (3): 435–56.

Gil, Andres G., William A. Vega, and Juanita M. Dimas. 1994. Acculturative stress and personal adjustment among Hispanic adolescent boys. *Journal of Community Psychology* 22 (1): 43–54.

Gil, Andres G., Eric F. Wagner, and William A. Vega. 2000. Acculturation, familism, and alcohol use among Latino adolescent males: Longitudinal relations. *Journal of Community Psychology* 28 (4): 443–58.

Gilbert, M. Jean. 1987. Alcohol consumption patterns in immigrant and later-generation Mexican American women. *Hispanic Journal of Behavioral Sciences* 9: 299–313.

Glover, Saundra H., Andres J. Pumariega, Charles E. Holzer, Brian K. Wise, and Moises Rodriguez. 1999. Anxiety symptomatology in Mexican-American adolescents. *Journal of Child and Family Studies* 8 (1): 47–57.

Go, Charles G., and Thao N. Le. 2005. Gender differences in Cambodian delinquency: The role of ethnic identity, parental discipline, and peer delinquency. *Crime and Delinquency* 51 (2): 220–37.

Gomez, Maria J., and Ruth E. Fassinger. 1994. An initial model of Latina achievement: Acculturation, biculturalism, and achieving styles. *Journal of Counseling Psychology* 41 (2): 205–15.

Gonzales, Nancy A., Julianna Deardorff, Diana Formoso, Alicia Barr, and Manuel Barrera Jr. 2006. Family mediators of the relation between acculturation and adolescent mental health. *Family Relations* 55 (3): 318–30.

Gonzales, Nancy, George P. Knight, Dina Birman, and Amalia A. Sirolli. 2004. Acculturation and enculturation among Latino youth. In *Investing in Children, Youth, Families, and Communities: Strengths-Based Research and Policy,* ed. Kenneth I. Maton, Cynthia J. Schellenbach, Bonnie J. Leadbeater, and Andrea L. Solarz, 285–302. Washington, DC: American Psychological Association.

Gonzales, Nancy A., George P. Knight, Antonio A. Morgan-Lopez, Delia Saenz, and Amalia Sirolli. 2002. Acculturation and the mental health of Latino youths: An integration and critique of the literature. In *Latino Children and Families in the United States,* ed. Josefina M. Contreras, Kathryn A. Kerns, and Angela M. Neal-Barnett, 45–76. Westport, CT: Praeger.

Graves, Theodore D. 1967. Acculturation, access, and alcohol in a tri-ethnic community. *American Anthropologist* 69 (3): 306–21.

Grunbaum, Jo Anne, Richard Lowry, Laura Kann, and Beth Patemen. 2000. Prevalence of health risk behaviors among Asian American/Pacific Islander high school students. *Journal of Adolescent Health* 27 (5): 322–30.

Gudykunst, William B. 2001. *Asian American Ethnicity and Communication.* Thousand Oaks, CA: Sage.

Guendelman, Sylvia, and Barbara Abrams. 1994. Dietary, alcohol, and tobacco intake among Mexican-American women of childbearing age: Results from HANES data. *American Journal of Health Promotion* 8 (5): 363–72.

Gutierrez, Jeannie, and Arnold Sameroff. 1990. Determinants of complexity in Mexican-American and Anglo-American mothers' conceptions of child development. *Child Development* 61 (2): 384–94.

Hahne, Anja, and Angela D. Friederici. 2001. Processing a second language: Late learners' comprehension mechanisms as revealed by event-related brain potential. *Bilingualism: Language and Cognition* 4 (2): 123–41.

Hakuta, Kenji, Yuko Goto Butler, and Daria

Witt. 2000. *How Long Does It Take Learners to Obtain English Proficiency? (Policy Report, 2000–2001)*. Santa Barbara: University of California Linguistic Minority Research Institute.

Halpern, Carolyn Tucker, Selene G. Oslak, Mary L. Young, Sandra L. Martin, and Lawrence L. Kupper. 2001. Partner violence among adolescents in opposite-sex romantic relationships: Findings from the National Longitudinal Study of Adolescent Health. *American Journal of Public Health* 91 (10): 1679–85.

Haritatos, Jana, and Veronica Benet-Martinez. 2002. Bicultural identities: The interface of cultural, personality, and socio-cognitive processes. *Journal of Research in Personality* 36 (6): 598–606.

Harker, Kathryn. 2001. Immigrant generation, assimilation, and adolescent psychological well-being. *Social Forces* 79 (3): 969–1004.

Harris, Kathleen M. 1999. The health status and risk behavior of adolescents in immigrant families. In *Children of Immigrants: Health, Adjustment, and Public Assistance*, ed. Donald J. Hernandez, 286–347. Washington, DC: National Academy Press.

Hebel, Sara. 2008. Obama, Helped by Youth Vote, Wins Presidency and Makes History. *Chronicle of Higher Education,* November 5, 2008. Http://chronicle.com/article/Obama -Helped-by-Youth-Vote/1303,

Henning-Stout, Mary. 1996. *Que podemos hacer?* Roles for school psychologists with Mexican and Latino migrant children. *School Psychology Review* 25 (2): 152–66.

Hernandez, Arturo E., Elizabeth A. Bates, and Luis X. Avila. 1994. On-line sentence interpretation in Spanish-English bilinguals: What does it mean to be "in between"? *Applied Psycholinguistics* 15 (4): 417–46.

Hernandez, Arturo E., Antigona Martinez, and Kathryn Kohnert. 2000. In search of the language switch: An fMRI study of picture naming in Spanish-English bilinguals. *Brain and Language* 73 (3): 421–31.

Hernandez, Miguel, and Monica McGoldrick. 1999. Migration and the family life cycle. In *The Expanded Family Life Cycle: Individual, Family, and Social Perspectives,* ed. Betty Carter and Monica McGoldrick, 3rd edition, 169–84. Needham Heights, MA: Allyn and Bacon.

Hirschman, Charles. 1994. Problems and prospects of studying immigrant adaptation from the 1990 population census: From generational comparisons to the process of "becoming American." *International Migration Review* 28 (4): 690–711.

Holowka, Siobhan, Francoise Brosseau-Lapré, and Laura Ann Petitto. 2002. Semantic and conceptual knowledge underlying bilingual babies' first signs and words. *Language Learning* 52 (2): 205–62.

Hong, Ying-yi, Michael W. Morris, Chi-vue Chiu, and Veronica Benet-Martinez. 2000. Multicultural minds: A dynamic constructivist approach to culture and cognition. *American Psychologist* 55 (7): 709–20.

Hovey, Joseph D. 1998. Acculturative stress, depression, and suicidal ideation among Mexican-American adolescents: Implications for the development of suicide prevention programs in schools. *Psychological Reports* 83 (1): 249–50.

Hovey, Joseph D., and Cheryl A. King. 1996. Acculturative stress, depression, and suicidal ideation among immigrant and second-generation Latino adolescents. *Journal of the American Academy of Child and Adolescent Psychiatry* 35 (9): 1183–92.

Howard-Pitney, Beth, Teresa D. LaFromboise, Mike Basil, Benedette September, and Mike Johnson. 1992. Psychological and social indicators of suicidal ideation and suicide attempts in Zuni adolescents. *Journal of Consulting and Clinical Psychology* 60 (3): 473–76.

Hunt Linda M., Suzanne Schneider, and Brendon Comer. 2004. Should "acculturation" be a variable in health research? A critical review of research on U.S. Hispanics. *Social Science and Medicine* 59 (5): 973–86.

Indian Health Service. 2007. Indian Health Service fact sheets: Indian population. Http://info.ihs.gov/Files/IndianPopTrends -Jan2007.doc.

Jamieson, Amie, Andrea Curry, and Gladys Martinez. 2001. School enrollment in the United States–Social and economic characteristics of students: October 1999. U.S. Census Bureau. Http://www.census.gov/ prod/2001pubs/p20-533.pdf.

Kallen, Horace M. 1915. Democracy versus the Melting Pot: A Study of American Nationality. *The Nation,* February 25, 1915.

Kao, Grace. 1999. Psychological well-being and educational achievement among immigrant youth. In *Children of Immigrants: Health, Adjustment, and Public Assistance*, ed. Donald J. Hernandez, 410–77. Washington, DC: National Academy Press.

Katragadda, Chandrika P., and Romeria Tidwell. 1998. Rural Hispanic adolescents at risk for depressive symptoms. *Journal of Applied Social Psychology* 28 (20): 1916–30.

Kaufman, Phillip, Xianglei Chen, Susan P. Choy, Katharine Peter, Sally A. Ruddy, Amanda K. Miller, Jill K. Fleury, and Kathryn A. Chandler. 2001. *Indicators of School Crime and Safety: 2001*. Washington, DC: U.S. Department of Education and U.S. Department of Justice.

Kellerman, Peter Felix. 1987. Outcome research in classical psychodrama. *Small Group Research* 18 (4): 459–69.

Kim, Karl H. S., Norman R. Relkin, Kyoung-Min Lee, and Joy Hirsch. 1997. Distinct cortical areas associated with native and second languages. *Nature* 388 (6638): 171–74.

Kipper, David A. 1978. Trends in the research on the effectiveness of psychodrama. *Group Psychotherapy, Psychodrama, and Sociometry* 31: 5–18.

Kipper, David A., and T. D. Ritchie. 2003. The effectiveness of psychodramatic techniques: A meta-analysis. *Group Dynamics: Theory, Research, and Practice* 7: 13–25.

Knight, George P., Lynn M. Virdin, and Mark Roosa. 1994. Socialization and family correlates of mental health outcomes among Hispanic and Anglo-American families. *Child Development* 65 (1): 212–24.

Kovelman, Ioulia, Stephanie A. Baker, and Laura-Ann Petito. 2008. Bilingual and monolingual brains compared: A functional magnetic resonance imaging investigation of syntactic processing and a possible "neural signature" of bilingualism. *Journal of Cognitive Neuroscience* 20 (1): 153–69.

Kronenberg, Fredi, Linda F. Cushman, Christine M. Wade, Debra Kalmuss, and Maria T. Chao. 2006. Race/ethnicity and women's use of complementary and alternative medicine in the United States: Results of a national survey. *American Journal of Public Health* 96: 1236–42.

LaFromboise, Teresa D., Hardin L. Coleman, and Jennifer Gerton. 1993. Psychological impact of biculturalism: Evidence and theory. *Psychological Bulletin* 114 (3): 395–412.

LaFromboise, Teresa D., and Wayne Rowe. 1983. Skills training for bicultural competence: Rationale and application. *Journal of Counseling Psychology* 30 (4): 589–95.

Lang, John G., Ricardo F. Munoz, Guillermo Bernal, and James L. Sorensen. 1982. Quality of life and psychological well-being in a bicultural Latino community. *Hispanic Journal of Behavioral Sciences* 4 (4): 433–50.

Lau, Anna S., Nadine M. Jernewall, Nolan Zane, and Hector F. Meyers. 2002. Correlates of suicidal behaviors among Asian American outpatient youths. *Cultural Diversity and Ethnic Minority Psychology* 8 (3): 199–213.

Lau, Anna S., Kristen M. McCabe, May Yeh, Ann F. Garland, Patricia A. Wood, and Richard L. Hough. 2005. The acculturation gap-distress hypothesis among high-risk Mexican American families. *Journal of Family Psychology* 19 (3): 367–75.

Le, Thao N., and Gary D. Stockdale. 2005. Individualism, collectivism, and delinquency in Asian American adolescents. *Journal of Clinical Child and Adolescent Psychology* 34 (4): 681–91.

———. 2008. Acculturative dissonance, ethnic identity, and youth violence. *Cultural Diversity and Ethnic Minority Psychology* 14 (1): 1–9.

Le, Thao N., and Judy Wallen. 2007. Risks of nonfamilial violent physical and emotional victimization in four Asian ethnic groups. *Journal of Immigrant and Minority Health* 11 (3): 174–87.

Malgady, Robert G., Lloyd H. Rogler, and Giuseppe Costantino. 1990. Culturally sensitive psychotherapy for Puerto Rican children and adolescents: A program of treatment outcome research. *Journal of Consulting and Clinical Psychology* 58 (6): 704–12.

Marian, Viorica, Yeveniy Shildkrot, Henrike K. Blumenfeld, Margarita Kaushanskaya, Yasmeen Faroqi-Shah, and Joy Hirsch. 2007. Cortical activation during word processing in late bilinguals: Similarities and differences as revealed by functional magnetic resonance imaging. *Journal of*

Clinical and Experimental Neuropsychology 29 (3): 247–65.

Marian, V., Michael Spivey, and Joy Hirsch. 2003. Shared and separate systems in bilingual language processing: Converging evidence from eye tracking and brain imaging. *Brain and Language* 86 (1): 70–82.

Marino Weisman, Evelyn. 2001. Bicultural identity and language attitudes: Perspectives of four Latina teachers. *Urban Education* 36 (2): 203–15.

Marks, Gary, Melissa Garcia, and Julia M. Solis. 1990. Health risk behaviors of Hispanics in the United States: Findings from the HHANES, 1982–1984. *American Journal of Public Health* 80: 20–26.

Marsiglia, Flavio F., Suzanne Cross, and Violet Mitchell-Enos. 1998. Culturally grounded group work with adolescent American Indian students. *Social Work with Groups* 21 (1–2): 89–102.

Martin, Joyce A., Brady E. Hamilton, Paul D. Sutton, Stephanie J. Ventura, Fay Menacker, and Sharon Kirmeyer. 2006. Births: Final data for 2004. *National Vital Statistics Reports* 55 (1). Hyattsville, MD: National Center for Health Statistics.

Martinez, Charles R. Jr. 2006. Effects of differential family acculturation on Latino adolescent substance use. *Family Relations* 55 (3): 306–17.

Martinez, Ruben O., and Richard L. Dukes. 1997. The effects of ethnic identity, ethnicity, and gender on adolescent well-being. *Journal of Youth and Adolescence* 26 (5): 503–16.

McFarlane, William R. 2002. *Multifamily Groups in the Treatment of Severe Psychiatric Disorders.* New York: Guilford Press.

McQueen, Amy, J. Greg Getz, and James H. Bray. 2003. Acculturation, substance use, and deviant behavior: Examining detachment and family conflict as mediators. *Child Development* 74 (6): 1737–50.

Mechelli Andrea, Jenny T. Crinion, Uta Noppeney, John O'Doherty, John Ashburner, Richard S. Frackowiak, and Cathy J. Price. 2004. Neurolinguistics: Structural plasticity in the bilingual brain. *Nature* 431 (7010): 757.

Miranda, Alexis O., Diane Estrada, and Miriam Firpo-Jimenez. 2000. Differences in family cohesion, adaptability, and environment among Latino families in dissimilar stages of acculturation. *Family Journal* 8 (4): 341–50.

Miranda, Alexis O., and Debra L. Umhoefer. 1998. Depression and social interest differences between Latinos in dissimilar acculturation stages. *Journal of Mental Health Counseling* 20 (2): 159–71.

Mok, Aurelia, Michael W. Morris, Verónica Benet-Martínez, and Zahide Karakitapoglu-Aygun. 2007. Embracing American culture: Structures of social identity and social networks among first-generation biculturals. *Journal of Cross-Cultural Psychology* 38 (5): 629–35.

Mora, Jill Kerper. 2002. Caught in a policy web: The impact of education reform on Latino education. *Journal of Latinos and Education* 1 (1): 29–44.

Mullender, Audrey. 1990. The Ebony project: Bicultural group work with transracial foster parents. *Social Work with Groups* 13 (4): 23–41.

Myles, John, and Feng Hou. 2003. Neighbourhood attainment and residential segregation among Toronto's visible minorities. Http://www.statcan.ca/english/research/ 11F0019MIE/11F0019MIE2003206.pdf,

Neff, James A. 1986. Alcohol consumption and psychological distress among U.S. Anglos, Hispanics and blacks. *Alcohol and Alcoholism* 21 (1): 111–19.

Neter, John, Michael H. Kutner, Christopher J. Nachtsheim, and William Wasserman. 1996. *Applied Linear Regression Models,* 3rd edition. Chicago: Irwin.

Neto, Felix. 2001. Satisfaction with life among adolescents from immigrant families in Portugal. *Journal of Youth and Adolescence* 30 (1): 53–67.

Ng, Bernardo. 1996. Characteristics of sixty-one Mexican American adolescents who attempted suicide. *Hispanic Journal of Behavioral Sciences* 18 (1): 3–12.

Ngo, Hieu M., and Thao N. Le. 2007. Stressful life events, culture, and violence. *Journal of Immigrant Health* 9 (2): 75–84.

Nguyen, Angela-MinhTu D., and Verónica Benet-Martínez. 2007. Biculturalism unpacked: Components, individual differences, measurement, and outcomes. *Social and Personality Psychology Compass* 1 (1): 101–14.

Nichols, Michael, and Richard C. Schwartz. 2005. *Family Therapy: Concepts and Methods*, 7th edition. Needham Heights, MA: Allyn and Bacon.

Novins, Douglas K., Janette Beals, Robert E. Roberts, and Spero E. Manson. 1999. Factors associated with suicidal ideation among American Indian adolescents: Does culture matter? *Suicide and Life Threatening Behavior* 29 (4): 332–46.

Obama, Barack. 1995/ 2004. *Dreams from My Father: A Story of Race and Inheritance.* New York: Three Rivers Press.

Olson, David H. 1992. *Family Inventories Manual*. Minneapolis, MN: Life Innovations.

Olvera, Rene L. 2001. Suicidal ideation in Hispanic and mixed-ancestry adolescents. *Suicide and Life-Threatening Behavior* 31: 416–27.

Organista, Pamela Balls, Kurt C. Organista, and Karen Kurasaki. 2003. The relationship between acculturation and ethnic minority mental health. In *Acculturation: Advances in Theory, Measurement, and Applied Research*, ed. Kevin M. Chun, Pamela Balls Organista, and Gerardo Marin, 139–62. Washington, DC: American Psychological Association.

Ortega, Alexander N., Glorisa Canino, and Margarita Algeria. 2008. Lifetime and twelve-month intermittent explosive disorder in Latinos. *American Journal of Orthopsychiatry* 78 (1): 133–39.

Oxford, Linda K., Daniel J. Weiner. 2003. Rescripting family dramas using psychodramatic methods. In *Action Therapy with Families and Groups: Using Creative Arts Improvisation in Clinical Practice*, ed. Daniel J. Weiner and Linda K. Oxford, 45–74. Washington, DC: American Psychological Association.

Padilla, Amado M. 1994. Bicultural development: A theoretical and empirical examination. In *Theoretical and Conceptual Issues in Hispanic Mental Health*, ed. Robert G. Malgady and Orlando Rodriguez, 20–51. Melbourne, FL: Krieger Publishing.

Padilla, Amado M., and William Perez. 2003. Acculturation, social identity, and social cognition: A new perspective. *Hispanic Journal of Behavioral Sciences* 25: 35–55.

Pantin, Hilda, J. Douglas Coatsworth, Daniel J. Feaster, Frederick Newman, Ervin

Briones, Guillermo Prado, Seth Schwartz, and Jose Szapocznik. 2003. *Familias unidas*: The efficacy of an intervention to increase parental investment in Hispanic immigrant families. *Prevention Science* 4 (3): 189–201.

Parra-Cardona, José, Laurie A. Bulock, David R. Imig, Francisco A. Villarruel, and Steven J. Gold. 2006. "*Trabajando duro todos los dias*": Learning from the experiences of Mexican-origin migrant families. *Family Relations* 55 (3): 361–75.

Pasch, Lauri A., Julianna Deardorff, Jeanne M. Tschann, Elena Flores, Carlos Penilla, and Philip Pantoja. 2006. Acculturation, parent-adolescent conflict, and adolescent adjustment in Mexican American families. *Family Process* 45 (1): 75–86.

Passel, Jeffrey S., and D'Vera Cohn. 2008. *U.S. Population Projections, 2005–2050.*Washington, DC: Pew Research Center.

Pearson, Barbara Zurer, Sylvia C. Fernandez, and D. Kimbrough Oller. 1993. Lexical development in bilingual infants and toddlers: Comparison to monolingual norms. *Language Learning: A Journal of Applied Linguistics* 43 (1): 93–120.

Pedhazur, Elazar J., and Liora Pedhazur Schmelkin. 1991. *Measurement, Design, and Analysis: An Integrated Approach*. Hillsdale, NJ: Lawrence Erlbaum.

Peeks, Anna L. 1999. Conducting a social skills group with Latina adolescents. *Journal of Child and Adolescent Group Therapy* 9 (3): 139–56.

Perry, Steven W. 2004. *American Indians and Crime*. Washington, DC: U.S. Department of Justice, Bureau of Justice Statistics. Http://www.ojp.usdoj.gov/bjs/pub/pdf/aic02.pdf.

Petitto, Laura Ann, Marina A. Katerelos, Bronna G. Levy, Kristine Gauna, Karine Tetreault, and Vittoria Ferraro. 2001. Bilingual signed and spoken language acquisition from birth: Implications for the mechanisms underlying early bilingual language acquisition. *Journal of Child Language* 28 (2): 453–96.

Petitto, Laura Ann, and Ioulia Kovelman I. 2003. The bilingual paradox: How signing-speaking bilingual children help us to resolve it and teach us about the brain's mechanisms underlying all language acquisition. *Learning Languages* 8 (3): 5–19.

Phinney, Jean S. 1989. Stages of ethnic identity development in minority group adolescents. *Journal of Early Adolescence* 9 (1–2): 34–49.

———. 1996. When we talk about American ethnic groups what do we mean? *American Psychologist* 51 (9): 918–27.

Phinney, Jean S., Cindy Lou Cantu, and Dawn Kurtz. 1997. Ethnic and American identity as predictors of self-esteem among African-American, Latino, and white adolescents. *Journal of Youth and Adolescence* 26 (2): 165–85.

Phinney, Jean S., and Veronica Chavira. 1995. Parental ethnic socialization and adolescent coping with problems related to ethnicity. *Journal of Research on Adolescence* 5 (1): 31–53.

Phinney, Jean S., and Mona Devich-Navarro. 1997. Variations in bicultural identification among African American and Mexican American adolescents. *Journal of Research on Adolescence* 7 (1): 3–32.

Phinney, Jean S., and Anthony D. Ong. 2007. Conceptualization and measurement of ethnic identity: Current status and future directions. *Journal of Counseling Psychology* 54 (3): 271–81.

Phinney, Jean S., Anthony Ong, and Tanya Madden. 2000. Cultural values and intergenerational value discrepancies in immigrant and nonimmigrant families. *Child Development* 71 (2): 528–39.

Portes, Alejandro, and Ruben G. Rumbaut. 2001. *Legacies: The Story of the Immigrant Second Generation*. Berkeley: University of California Press.

Price, Cathy J., David W. Green, and Roswitha von Studnitz. 1999. A functional imaging study of translation and language switching. *Brain* 122 (12): 2221–35.

Pumariega, Andres J., Jeffrey W. Swanson, Charles E. Holzer, and Arthur O. Linskey. 1992. Cultural context and substance abuse in Hispanic adolescents. *Journal of Child and Family Studies* 1 (1): 75–92.

Quaresima, Valentina, Marco Ferrari, Marco C. P. van der Sluijs, Jan Menssen, and Willy N. J. M. Colier. 2002. Lateral frontal cortex oxygenation changes during translation and language switching revealed by noninvasive near-infrared multipoint measurements. *Brain Research Bulletin* 59 (3): 235–43.

Quillian, Lincoln, and Mary E. Campbell. 2003. Beyond black and white: The present and future of multiracial friendship segregation. *American Sociological Review* 68 (4): 540–66.

Ramirez, Roberto R., and G. Patricia de la Cruz. 2003. The Hispanic population in the United States: March 2002. Http://www .census.gov/prod/2003pubs/p20-545.pdf.

Ramirez-Esparza, Nairán, Samuel D. Gosling, Verónica Benet-Martínez, Jeffrey Potter, and James W. Pennebaker. 2006. Do bilinguals have two personalities? A special case of cultural frame-switching. *Journal of Research in Personality* 40 (2): 99–120.

Rashid, Hakim M. 1984. Promoting biculturalism in young African American children. *Young Children* 39 (2): 13–23.

Rasmussen, Katherine M., Charles Negy, Ralph Carlson, and JoAnn M. Burns. 1997. Suicide ideation and acculturation among low socioeconomic status Mexican American adolescents. *Journal of Early Adolescence* 17 (4): 390–407.

Redfield, Robert, Ralph Linton, and Melville J. Herskovits. 1936. Memorandum for the study of acculturation. *American Anthropologist* 38: 149–52.

Rivera-Sinclair, Elsa A. 1997. Acculturation/biculturalism and its relationship to adjustment in Cuban-Americans. *International Journal of Intercultural Relations* 21 (3): 379–91.

Robin, Arthur L., and Sharon L. Foster. 1989. *Negotiating Parent-Adolescent Conflict: A Behavioral-Family Systems Approach*. New York: Guilford.

Robledo, Maria M., and Josie D. Cortez. 2002. Successful bilingual education programs: Development and the dissemination of criteria to identify promising and exemplary practices in bilingual education at the national level. *Bilingual Research Journal* 26 (1): 1–21.

Rodriguez-Fornells, Antoni, Michael Rotte, Hans-Jochen Heinze, Tömme Nösselt, and Thomas F. Münte. 2002. Brain potential and functional MRI evidence for how to handle two languages with one brain. *Nature* 415 (6875): 1026–29.

Rodriguez-Fornells, Antoni, Arie van der Lugt, Michael Rotte, Belinda Britti, Hans-Jochen Heinze, and Thomas F. Münte.

2005. Second language interferes with word production in fluent bilinguals: Brain potential and functional imaging evidence. *Journal of Cognitive Neuroscience* 17 (3): 422–33.

Roer-Strier, Dorit. 1997. In the mind of the beholder: Evaluation of coping styles of immigrant parents. *International Migration* 35 (2): 271–88.

Rogler, Lloyd H., and Rosemary S. Cooney. 1984. *Puerto Rican Families in New York City: Intergenerational Processes.* Maplewood, NJ: Waterfront.

Rogler, Lloyd H., Dharma E. Cortes, and Robert G. Malgady. 1991. Acculturation and mental health status among Hispanics: Convergence and new directions for research. *American Psychologist* 46 (6): 585–97.

Romero, Andrea J., and Robert E. Roberts. 2003. Stress within a bicultural context for adolescents of Mexican descent. *Cultural Diversity and Ethnic Minority Psychology* 9 (2): 171–84.

Rosenbaum, Cathy Creger. 2007. The history of complementary and alternative medicine in the U.S. *Annals of Pharmacotherapy* 41: 1256–60.

Rotheram-Borus, M. J. 1990. Adolescents' reference-group choices, self-esteem, and adjustment. *Journal of Personality and Social Psychology* 59: 1075–81.

Rounds-Bryant, Jennifer L., and Jennifer Staab. 2001. Patient characteristics and treatment outcomes for African American, Hispanic, and white adolescents in DATOS-A. *Journal of Adolescent Research* 16 (6): 624–41.

Rumbaut, Ruben G. 1995. The new Californians: Comparative research findings on the educational progress of immigrant children. In *California's Immigrant Children: Theory, Research, and Implications for Educational Policy*, ed. Ruben G. Rumbaut and Wayne A. Cornelius, 17–69. San Diego: University of California, San Diego, Center for U.S.-Mexican Studies.

Rumberger, Russell W., and Katharine A. Larson. 1998. Towards explaining differences in educational achievement among Mexican American language minority students. *Sociology of Education* 71 (1): 68–92.

Rush, A. John, and Task Force for the Handbook of Psychiatric Measures. 2000. *Handbook of Psychiatric Measures.* Washington, DC: American Psychiatric Association.

Samaniego, Roxanna Y., and Nancy A. Gonzales. 1999. Multiple mediators of the effects of acculturation status on delinquency for Mexican American adolescents. *American Journal of Community Psychology* 27 (2): 189–210.

Sanchez-Flores, Hector. 2003. Teen pregnancy prevention for Latino youth. Presentation at North Carolina Teen Pregnancy Prevention Conference, November 9, in Chapel Hill, NC.

Sanderson, Maureen, Ann L. Coker, Robert E. Roberts, Susan R. Tortolero, and Belinda M. Reininger. 2004. Acculturation, ethnic identity, and dating violence among Latino ninth-grade students. *Preventive Medicine* 39 (2): 373–83.

Satia-Abouta, Jessie, Ruth E. Patterson, Amrion L. Neuhouser, and John Elder. 2002. Dietary acculturation: Applications to nutrition research and dietetics. *Journal of the American Dietetic Association* 102: 1105–17.

Schinke, Steven P., Mario A. Orlandi, Gilbert J. Botvin, Lewayne D. Gilchrist, Joseph E. Trimble, and Von S. Locklear. 1988. Preventing substance abuse among American-Indian adolescents: A bicultural competence skills approach. *Journal of Counseling Psychology* 35 (1): 87–90.

Schwartz, Seth J., Byron L. Zamboanga, and Lorna Hernandez Jarvis. 2007. Ethnic identity and acculturation in Hispanic early adolescents: Mediated relationships to academic grades, prosocial behaviors, and externalizing symptoms. *Cultural Diversity and Ethnic Minority Psychology* 13 (4): 364–73.

Shaughnessy, Lana, Cheryl Branum, and Sherry Everett-Jones. 2001. *Youth Risk Behavior Survey of High School Students Attending Bureau-Funded Schools.* U.S. Dept. of Interior, Bureau of Indian Affairs, Office of Indian Education Programs.

Shrake, Eunai K., and Siyon Rhee. 2004. Ethnic identity as a predictor of problem behaviors among Korean American adolescents. *Adolescence* 39 (155): 601–22.

Silverman, Jay G., Michelle R. Decker, and Anita Raj. 2007. Immigration-based disparities in adolescent girls' vulnerability to dating violence. *Maternal and Child Health Journal* 11 (1): 37–43.

Smith, Emily P., and Nancy G. Guerra. 2006. Introduction. In *Preventing Youth Violence in a Multicultural Society*, ed. Nancy G. Guerra and Emily P. Smith, 3–14. Washington, DC: American Psychological Association.

Smokowski, Paul R., and Martica L. Bacallao. 2006. Acculturation and aggression in Latino adolescents: A structural model focusing on cultural risk factors and assets. *Journal of Abnormal Child Psychology* 34 (5): 657–71.

———. 2007. Acculturation, internalizing mental health symptoms, and self-esteem: Cultural experiences of Latino adolescents in North Carolina. *Child Psychiatry and Human Development* 37 (3): 273–92.

———. 2008. *Entre dos mundos*/between two worlds: Youth violence prevention for acculturating Latino families. *Research on Social Work Practice* 19 (2): 165–78.

———. 2009. *Entre dos mundos*/between two worlds youth violence prevention: Comparing psychodramatic and support group delivery formats. *Small Group Research* 40 (1): 3–27.

Smokowski, Paul R., Martica Bacallao, and Rachel L. Buchanan. Forthcoming. Mediation pathways from acculturation stressors to adolescent internalizing problems: An ecological structural model for Latino youth. *Journal of Community Psychology*.

Smokowski, Paul R., Martica Bacallao, and Roderick Rose. 2010. Influence of risk factors and cultural assets on Latino adolescents' trajectories of self-esteem and internalizing symptoms. *Child Psychiatry and Human Development* 41 (2): 133–55.

Smokowski, Paul R., Rachel L. Buchanan, and Martica L. Bacallao. 2009. Acculturation and adjustment in Latino adolescents: How cultural risk factors and assets influence multiple domains of adolescent mental health. *Journal of Primary Prevention* 30 (3–4): 371–94.

———. Forthcoming. Acculturation stress and aggressive behavior in Latino adolescents: Examining mediation pathways in the Latino Acculturation and Health Project. *International Journal of Child Health and Human Development*.

Smokowski, Paul R., Corinne David-Ferdon, and Nancy Stroupe. 2009. Acculturation, youth violence, and suicidal behavior in minority adolescents: A review of the empirical literature. *Journal of Primary Prevention* 30 (3–4): 215–64.

Smokowski, Paul R., Roderick A. Rose, and Martica Bacallao. 2008. Acculturation and Latino family processes: How parent-adolescent acculturation gaps influence family dynamics. *Family Relations* 57 (3): 295–308.

———. 2009. Acculturation and aggression in Latino adolescents: Modeling longitudinal trajectories from the Latino Acculturation and Health Project. *Child Psychiatry and Human Development* 40 (4): 589–608.

Sommers, Ira, Jeffrey Fagan, and Deborah Baskin. 1993. Sociocultural influences on the explanation of delinquency for Puerto Rican youths. *Hispanic Journal of Behavioral Sciences* 15 (1): 36–62.

Stanton-Salazar, Ricardo D., and Sanford M. Dornbusch. 1995. Social capital and the reproduction of inequality: Information networks among Mexican-origin high school students. *Sociology of Education* 68 (2): 116–35.

Suarez-Orozco, Carola, and Marcelo M. Suarez-Orozco. 2001. *Children of Immigrants*. Cambridge, MA: Harvard University Press.

Sundquist, Jan, and Marilyn A. Winkleby. 1999. Cardiovascular risk factors in Mexican American adults: A transcultural analysis of NHANES III, 1988–1994. *American Journal of Public Health* 89 (5): 723–30.

Swanson, Jeffrey W., Arthur O. Linskey, Ruben Quintero-Salinas, Andres Pumariega, and Charles E. Holzer. 1992. A binational school survey of depressive symptoms, drug use, and suicidal ideation. *Journal of the American Academy of Child and Adolescent Psychiatry* 31 (4): 669–78.

Szapocznik, Jose, and William Kurtines. 1980. Acculturation, biculturalism, and adjustment among Cuban Americans. In *Acculturation: Theory, Models, and Some New Findings*, ed. Amado M. Padilla, 139–59. Boulder, CO: Praeger.

Szapocznik, Jose, David Santisteban, William Kurtines, Angel Perez-Vidal, and Olga Hervis.1984. Bicultural Effectiveness Training: A treatment intervention for enhancing intercultural adjustment in Cuban American families. *Hispanic Journal of Behavioral Sciences* 6 (4): 317–44.

———. 1986. Bicultural Effectiveness Training (BET): An experimental test of an intervention modality for families experiencing intergenerational/intercultural conflict. *Hispanic Journal of Behavioral Sciences* 8 (4): 303–30.

Szapocznik, Jose, David Santisteban, Arturo Rio, Angel Perez-Vidal, Daniel Santisteban, and William M. Kurtines. 1989. Family Effectiveness Training: An intervention to prevent drug abuse and problem behaviors in Hispanic adolescents. *Hispanic Journal of Behavioral Sciences* 11 (1): 4–27.

Szapocznik, Jose, and Robert A. Williams. 2000. Brief strategic family therapy: Twenty-five years of interplay among theory, research, and practice in adolescent behavior problems and drug abuse. *Clinical Child and Family Psychology Review* 3 (2): 117–34.

Tabachnick, Barbara G., and Linda S. Fidell. 2001. *Using Multivariate Statistics*, 4th edition. Boston: Allyn and Bacon.

Takeuchi, David T., Nolan Zane, Seunghye Hong, David H. Chae, Fang Gong, Gilbert C. Gee, Emily Walton, Stanley Sue, and Margarita Alegría. 2007. Immigration-related factors and mental disorders among Asian Americans. *American Journal of Public Health* 97 (1): 84–90.

Taylor, Dorothy L., Frank A. Biafora, George J. Warheit, and Andres G. Gil. 1997. Family factors, theft, vandalism, and major deviance among a multiracial/multiethnic sample of adolescent girls. *Journal of Social Distress and the Homeless* 6 (1): 71–97.

Thomas, Edwin J., and Jack Rothman. 1994. An integrative perspective on intervention research. In *Intervention Research: Design and Development for Human Service,* ed. Jack Rothman and Edwin J. Thomas, 3–24. New York: Haworth Press.

Toppleberg, Claudio O., Laura Medrano, Liana Pena Morgens, and Alfonso Nieto-Castanon. 2002. Bilingual children referred for psychiatric services: Associations of language disorders, language skills, and psychopathology. *Journal of the American Academy of Child and Adolescent Psychiatry* 41 (6): 712–22.

Torres-Matrullo, Christine M. 1976. Acculturation and psychopathology among Puerto Rican women in mainland United States. *American Journal of Orthopsychiatry* 46 (4): 710–19.

Trimble, Joseph E. 2003. Introduction: Social change and acculturation. In *Acculturation: Advances in Theory, Measurement, and Applied Research,* ed. Kevin M. Chun, Pamela Balls Organista, and Gerardo Marin. Washington, DC: American Psychological Association.

Trueba, Enrique T., and Peter McLaren. 2000. Critical ethnography for the study of immigrants. In *Immigrant Voices: In Search of Educational Equity,* eds. Enrique T. Trueba and Lilia I. Bartolome, 37–74. Lanham, MD: Rowman and Littlefield.

Trueba, Henry T. 2002. Multiple ethnic, racial, and cultural identities in action: From marginality to a new cultural capital in modern society. *Journal of Latinos and Education* 1 (1): 7–28.

U.S. Census Bureau. 2001a. *United States Census Bureau Interactive Census Database.* Http://factfinder.census.gov/home/saff/main.html?_lang=en.

———. 2001b. *The Hispanic Population in the United States.* United States Census Bureau. Http://www.census.gov/population/www/socdemo/hispanic/hispanic_pop_presentation.html

———. 2002. Current Population Survey. Http://www.census.gov/population/www/socdemo/race.html.

———. 2007a. *Minority Population Tops 100 Million.* Http://www.census.gov/Press-Release/www/releases/archives/population/010048.html.

———. 2007b. *The Hispanic Population in the United States: 2004 Detailed Tables.* Http://www.census.gov/population/www/socdemo/hispanic/cps2004.html.

———. 2007c. *The American Community: Hispanics 2004.* Http://www.census.gov/Press-Release/www/releases/archives/american_community_survey_acs/009634.html.

———. 2007d. *The American Community:*

Asians 2004. Http://www.census.gov/prod/2007pubs/acs-05.pdf.

———. 2007e. *The American Community: Pacific Islanders 2004.* Http://www.census.gov/prod/2007pubs/acs-06.pdf.

———. 2007f. *The American Community: American Indians and Alaska Natives 2004.* Http://www.census.gov/prod/2007pubs/acs-07.pdf.

———. 2007g. *Census 2000 Summary File 1: 2000 Census of Population and Housing.* Http://www.census.gov/prod/cen2000/doc/sf1.pdf.

———. 2009. *United States Census Bureau Interactive Census Database.* Http://factfinder.census.gov/home/saff/main.html?_lang=en.

U.S. Department of Health and Human Services. 2001. *Mental Health: Culture, Race, and Ethnicity. Supplement to Mental Health: Report of the Surgeon General.* Rockville, MD: U.S. Department of Health and Human Services, Substance Abuse and Mental Health Services Administration, Center for Mental Health Services.

U.S. Department of Homeland Security, Office of Immigration Statistics. 2008. *Yearbook of Immigration Statistics: 2007, Table 3; Persons Obtaining Legal Permanent Resident Status by Region and Country of Birth, Fiscal Years 1998 to 2008.* Http://www.dhs.gov/ximgtn/statistics/publications/LPR07.shtm.

U.S. Department of the Interior. 2007. Indian entities recognized and eligible to receive services from the United States Bureau of Indian Affairs, Notice. *Federal Register* 72 (55): 647–52.

Vega, William A., Ethel Alderete, Bohdan Kolody, and Sergio Aguilar-Gaxiola. 2000. Adulthood sequela of adolescent heavy drinking among Mexican Americans. *Hispanic Journal of Behavioral Sciences* 22 (2): 254–66.

Vega, William A., Glorisa Canino, Zhun Cao, and Margarita Alegría. 2009. Prevalence and correlates of dual diagnoses in U.S. Latinos. *Drug and Alcohol Dependence* 100 (1–2): 32–38.

Vega, William A., and Andres G. Gil. 1998. *Drug Use and Ethnicity in Early Adolescence.* New York: Plenum Press.

Vega, William A., Andres G. Gil, George J. Warheit, Rick S. Zimmerman, and Eleni

Apospori. 1993. Acculturation and delinquent behavior among Cuban American adolescents: Toward an empirical model. *American Journal of Community Psychology* 21 (1): 113–25.

Vega, William A., Bohdan Kolody, Sergio Aguilar-Gaxiola, Ethel Alderete, Ralph Catalano, and Jorge Caraveo-Anduaga. 1998. Lifetime prevalence of *DSM-III-R* psychiatric disorders among urban and rural Mexican Americans in California. *Archives of General Psychiatry* 55 (9): 771–78.

Vega, William A., Rick S. Zimmerman, Elizabeth L. Khoury, Andres G. Gil, and George J. Warheit. 1995. Cultural conflicts and problem behaviors of Latino adolescents in home and school environments. *Journal of Community Psychology* 23 (2): 167–79.

Vihman, Marilyn May. 1985. Language differentiation by the bilingual infant. *Journal of Child Language* 12 (3): 297–324.

Vivero, Veronica N., and Sharon R. Jenkins. 1999. Existential hazards of the multicultural individual: Defining and understanding cultural homelessness. *Cultural Diversity and Ethnic Minority Psychology* 5 (1): 6–26.

Volterra, Virginia, and Traute Taeschner. 1978. The acquisition and development of language by bilingual children. *Journal of Child Language* 5 (3): 311–26.

Wall, Julie A., Thomas G. Power, and Consuelo Arbona. 1993. Susceptibility to antisocial peer pressure and its relation to acculturation in Mexican American adolescents. *Journal of Adolescent Research* 8 (4): 403–18.

Wartenburger, Isabell, Hauke R. Heekeren, Jubin Abutalebi, Stefano F. Cappa, Arno Villringer, and Daniela Perani. 2003. Early setting of grammatical processing in the bilingual brain. *Neuron* 37 (1): 159–70.

Weber-Fox, Christine, and Helen J. Neville. 1996. Maturational constraints on functional specializations for language processing: ERP and behavioral evidence in bilingual speakers. *Journal of Cognitive Neuroscience* 8 (3): 231–56.

———. 2001. Sensitive periods differentiate processing of open- and closed-class words: An ERP study of bilinguals. *Journal of Speech, Language, and Hearing Research* 44 (6): 1338–53.

Welte, John W., and Grace M. Barnes. 1995. Alcohol and other drug use among Hispanics in New York State. *Alcoholism: Clinical and Experimental Research* 19 (4): 1061–66.

"We Shall Remain." 2009. *An American Experience Production*. Public Broadcasting Service. Http://www.pbs.org/wgbh/amex/weshallremain/.

Willgerodt, Mayumi A., and Elaine Adams Thompson. 2006. Ethnic and generational influences on emotional distress and risk behaviors among Chinese and Filipino American adolescents. *Research in Nursing and Health* 29 (4): 311–24.

Winkleby Marilyn A, Helena C. Kraemer, David K. Ahn, Ann N. Varady. 1998. Ethnic and socioeconomic differences in cardiovascular disease risk factors: Findings for women from the Third National Health and Nutrition Examination Survey, 1988–1994. *Journal of the American Medical Association* 280 (4): 356–62.

Winsler, Adam, Rafael M. Díaz, Linda Espinosa, and James Rodriguez. 1999. When learning a second language does not mean losing the first: Bilingual language development in low-income, Spanish-speaking children attending bilingual preschool. *Child Development* 70 (2): 349–62.

Yamada, Ann-Marie, and Theodore M. Singelis. 1999. Biculturalism and self-construal. *International Journal of Intercultural Relations* 23 (5): 697–709.

Ying, Yu-Wen. 1999. Strengthening intergenerational/intercultural ties in migrant families: A new intervention for parents. *Journal of Community Psychology* 27 (1): 89–96.

Yoder, Kevin A., Les B. Whitbeck, Dan R. Hoyt, and Teresa LaFromboise. 2006. Suicidal ideation among American Indian youths. *Archives of Suicide Research* 10 (2): 177–90.

Yu, Stella M., Zhihuan J. Huang, Renee H. Schwalberg, Mary Overpeck, and Michael D. Kogan. 2003. Acculturation and the health and well-being of U.S. immigrant adolescents. *Journal of Adolescent Health* 33 (6): 479–88.

Yuen, Noelle Y. C., Linda B. Nahulu, Earl S. Hishinuma, and Robin H. Miyamoto. 2000. Cultural identification and attempted suicide in Native Hawaiian adolescents. *Journal of the American Academy of Child and Adolescent Psychiatry* 39 (3): 360–67.

Zambrana, Ruth E., Kathleen Ell, Claudia Dorrington, and Laura Wachsman. 1994. The relationship between psychosocial status of immigrant Latino mothers and use of emergency pediatric services. *Health & Social Work* 19 (2): 93–102.

Zapata, Jesse T., and David S. Katims. 1994. Antecedents of substance abuse among Mexican-American school-age children. *Journal of Drug Education* 24 (3): 233–51.

Zayas, Luis H., and Josephine Palleja. 1988. Puerto Rican familism: Considerations for family therapy. *Family Relations* 37: 260–64.

Index

Acculturation, 1, 2, 10, 12, 13, 21, 22, 23, 24, 25, 26, 30, 56, 61, 62, 106, 108, 121, 123, 131; adolescent sexual behavior and, 156–157; American Indian/Alaskan Native youth, 153; Asian/Pacific Islander youth, 146, 150–151; bicultural identity integration and, 25; birth outcomes, 156; birth rates, 156; churches and, 73, 96–98; circular model of, 25–26; conflicts, 13, 119, 143–145, 155, 156, 163; criteria and theoretical frameworks, 14; dating violence 102; discrimination (*see* discrimination); health behaviors and constructs of, 24; health in adolescents and, 133–157; health in adults and, 157–160; internalizing anxiety and depression problems and, 154–156; maladjustment and, 131; mental health, 43–47, 80, 83–87, 129–163, 165–168, 186 (*see also* assimilation, discrimination; Latino immigrant families in the U.S., acculturation gaps); peer networks and, 120–127; phases of (contact, conflict, adaptation), 13–14; pilgrims and, 12–13; prevention and intervention programs, 187–192; reverse, 182–184; self-directed violence and, 134, 141–142, 151–154; sexual behavior, 156–157; stress, 25–26, 31, 69, 175; substance use and, 133–134, 145; theories and major research findings, 102, 132–133; youth violence and, 134–150

Acculturation/assimilation stress, 10, 15, 26, 31, 43, 50, 57, 58, 69, 70, 80, 83, 84, 102, 112, 135, 151, 155, 156, 162, 163, 186, 216; alcohol/substance use and, 159; coping with acculturation stress with negative behaviors, 161; definition of, 133; internalizing problems and, 157

Acculturation discrepancy theory, 43–44; scores and measuring, 46; in the family, 49

Acculturation Rating Scale for Mexican Americans, 152

Acculturative dissonance, definition of, 150
Achievement gap, 74, 76
Adaptation styles, 14
Aggressive behavior, 50, 55, 134, 143, 145; parent adolescent conflict and, 144
Alcohol and substance use, 157; immigrant paradox and, 158–159
Alternation, 21–22, 23, 24, 101, 102; cultural pluralism/multiculturalism and, 22; model of, 24; original definition of acculturation and, 24; theory of, 21–22, 24, 101–102, 108, 111, 131, 165
American Indians, 6, 8, 11, 18–19, 23, 153
Americanization, 19, 47, 48, 64, 66, 114, 131; American influences and, 102. *See also* assimilation
Anti-miscengenation laws, 20
Asian/Pacific Islanders, 5, 6, 8, 11, 15, 20, 21, 23, 24; dating violence victimization and, 151; immigrant paradox and, 159; self-directed violence and, 152; youth, 146–150
Assimilation, 1, 12, 13, 14, 15, 16–20, 21, 22, 23, 24, 27, 28, 44, 54, 56, 57, 58, 59, 61, 73, 79, 92, 93, 95, 101, 103, 104, 109, 112, 127, 129, 130–133, 135, 146, 150, 152, 165, 175, 185, 216; adolescent sexual behavior and, 156; adult alcohol consumption and, 159; aggressive behavior and, 134–135, 145; anti-miscegenation laws, 19–20; assimilation theory and, 21, 23, 24, 61, 62, 131, 160, 162, 184; behavior adaptation hypothesis and, 16, 161; definition of, 12, 17; European immigration, 18–21, 175; explanations of high assimilation as a risk factor, 160–162; explanations of low assimilation as a risk factor, 162–163; health promoting behaviors and, 143; history of, 18–20; immigrant families and, 62; Immigration and Nationality Act of 1965 and, 20; interracial marriage and, 19–21; Japanese Americans after World War II and, 20;

About the Authors

Paul Smokowski is Professor at the School of Social Work, University of North Carolina–Chapel Hill, Director, Latino Acculturation and Health Project, and Co-Director, Parent Teen Biculturalism Project.

Martica Bacallao is Assistant Professor in the Department of Social Work, University of North Carolina–Greensboro, and Co-Director, Parent Teen Biculturalism Project.